THE ELDER EDDA
AND
ANCIENT SCANDINAVIAN
DRAMA

Fig. 1. Plate from a helmet found at Vendel in Uppland.

Fig. 2. Bronze plate from Torslunda,
Öland, Sweden.

Fig. 3. Bronze plate from Torslunda,
Öland, Sweden.

THE ELDER EDDA

AND

ANCIENT SCANDINAVIAN DRAMA

BY

BERTHA S. PHILLPOTTS, O.B.E., Litt.D.

Formerly Pfeiffer Student of Girton College, Cambridge
Late Lady Carlisle Research Fellow, Somerville College, Oxford
Principal of Westfield College (University of London)
Author of *Kindred and Clan*

CAMBRIDGE
AT THE UNIVERSITY PRESS
1920

CAMBRIDGE UNIVERSITY PRESS
Cambridge, New York, Melbourne, Madrid, Cape Town,
Singapore, São Paulo, Delhi, Tokyo, Mexico City

Cambridge University Press
The Edinburgh Building, Cambridge CB2 8RU, UK

Published in the United States of America by Cambridge University Press, New York

www.cambridge.org
Information on this title: www.cambridge.org/9781107694842

First published 1920
First paperback edition 2011

A catalogue record for this publication is available from the British Library

ISBN 978-1-107-69484-2 Paperback

TO

SOMERVILLE COLLEGE, OXFORD

ἠ μεγάλα χάρις
δώρῳ σὺν ὀλίγῳ.

PREFACE

THIS book was begun in the spring of 1914, and only two chapters were unwritten in March 1916. In adding these two chapters in 1920 I have endeavoured to bring the rest of the book up to date, but the occupations of the intervening years left little time to keep abreast of the advances of scholarship, and the endeavour has not been wholly successful. My task has not been lightened by the loss of a note-book and some pages of the MS. through causes connected with the war, and I am conscious that there is much to apologise for. But it seemed better to publish the book as it is, with all its imperfections, than to wait for the uncertain hour when I could attempt an elaborate revision and expansion. My aim is simply to place before scholars a theory of the dramatic origin of the older Eddic poems. I shall be satisfied if I have made clear the grounds which have forced me to formulate the theory: should there be any truth in it, others, better fitted than I, will work it out in all its many bearings on history, religion and literature.

The dedication intimates that this book is my gift to Somerville College. In a more fundamental sense it is the gift of Somerville College to me. It is the product of my tenure of the Lady Carlisle Research Fellowship, and the central idea of the book occurred to me while I was trying to present a rational picture of early Scandinavian literature to the College Literary and Philosophical Society. The idea struck root in favourable soil. Miss Pope, Tutor in Modern Languages at Somerville, was working at a theory of the genesis of the Old French epic: Professor Gilbert Murray, Vice-President of the College, was always ready to stimulate and illumine discussion on the relation of epic and drama: Miss Spens of Lady Margaret Hall was writing her book on Shakespeare's indebtedness to folk-drama. Moreover I think that the air of Oxford was friendly to the growth of a theory like mine, and gave me courage to act on the belief that a clear understanding of the form of primitive Scandinavian literature was an essential preliminary to an understanding of primitive Scandinavian history. It was only after I had written the first part of the book—an attempt to solve a literary problem on purely literary lines—that I was able to realise the significance of the heroic poems of the Edda as a source for Scandinavian history and religion from the sixth century onwards.

Since the theories put forward have a direct bearing on the problem of Greek tragedy, and may also be of interest to mediaevalists, I have assumed that some of my readers may be unacquainted with Old Norse, and have accordingly given my quotations in English, adding the original in the notes wherever there is any doubt as to the reading. I had originally planned to give translations of the more important poems in an appendix, but joyfully abandoned the project on finding that there is some hope that the poet and scholar who has made Greek tragedy live in English dress may do a similar service to the heroic poems of the Edda. In the meantime readers may be referred to the translations in Vigfússon and Powell's *Corpus Poeticum Boreale*, on which those in the present work are usually based. It is however a disadvantage to the general reader that the Editors of the *Corpus* made a new combination of the episodes in the Helgi Lays, so that it is not easy to trace each separate poem as it is given in the MS. For this it is necessary to refer to one of the two chief German translations, Gering's or Genzmer's. Both are scholarly. The mythical poems have been translated into English by Miss Bray, in *The Elder or Poetic Edda*, published by the Viking Society.

References in the text are to Sophus Bugge's *Norrœn Fornkvœði*, to Holder's edition of Saxo, and to Finnur Jónsson's critical edition of Snorri's Edda.

My treatment of Icelandic proper names is explained in the Preface to my previous book *Kindred and Clan*. I have not sacrificed to consistency so far as to de-anglicise the names Sigurd,

Gudrun and Odin. For my treatment of Saxo's names I can, I fear, adduce no principle, and I can only hope that the multitude of Saxo's own inconsistencies may excuse mine.

I am greatly indebted to Professor Chadwick for very kindly reading a rough draft of this book in 1915, and for various suggestions and criticisms made at that time.

My thanks are also due to Professor Montelius both as author, and as President of the Swedish Royal Academy of Letters, for permission to reproduce the three illustrations in the frontispiece, two from his *Civilisation of Sweden in Heathen Times*, and one from Stolpe and Arne, *Graffältet vid Vendel*, published by the Academy.

Finally I desire to express my obligation to the Syndics of the Cambridge University Press, for publishing the book with an almost pre-war celerity.

B. S. P.

WESTFIELD COLLEGE
(UNIVERSITY OF LONDON).
June 2, 1920.

CONTENTS

CHAPTER I

THE EDDIC PROBLEM

"I DID the worst to him I loved the most," says Gudrun in Laxdale Saga, when her son presses her to tell him which of her lovers in long past days had been nearest to her heart.

Of all the generations of story-tellers who breathed life into the character of the Laxdale Gudrun, there was probably not one who could wholly dismiss from his mind the personality of a heroine more famous still, the Brynhild of the Edda poems. This must be our justification for using the tragic figure of Gudrun merely to point a contrast. Brynhild compasses Sigurd's death, as Gudrun compasses Kjartan's, and both are driven to the deed by like motives.

Jealousy works on them both, and fierce resentment, but, if we read the old stories aright, they are both swayed by a deeper motive. Neither Brynhild nor Gudrun can endure the consciousness of loving another man better than her own husband, and each breaks the tangled web of Fate in the same way. Lest they should succumb to dishonour, the man who threatens their inmost peace must die. It is a situation of great dramatic interest, and both Edda-poet and Saga-man do justice to its psychological subtleties. But in how different a way they handle the subject! Although those who told the story of Gudrun have been so obviously stirred by the Brynhild poets, yet the conventions of their art have restrained them from all but the faintest approximation to the poets' manner of presentment. Laxdale Saga adheres to the Saga tradition in spite of all temptation, and deals out speech to its characters with a sparing hand. And their brief utterances are used as much to veil their thoughts as to reveal. "Notable doings to-day" says Gudrun to her husband: "I have spun twelve ells of yarn, and thou hast killed Kjartan." A pallor, which Bolli comments on, and those half-dozen words

whispered to her son in her old age—that is all the self-reve-
lation that the stern Saga tradition allows her, and we may well
doubt whether she would have been granted even so much but
for her epic prototype.

How different is the tradition of the Edda! Brynhild may
express her very soul in words, if the poet's skill can but reach
so far. When the news of Sigurd's death has been brought to
her, she answers the reproaches of Gunnarr by a long account of
the past, and openly dwells on her intention to die with Sigurd.
But she has not done yet: she bids Gunnarr sit down while she
tells him, at some length, of all the woes yet to befall his
doomed house. Then for six more strophes she issues directions
as to the double funeral. Nor does her tongue weary even after
death: as she drives to Hel the objurgations of a giantess rouse
her to another exposition of the events which drove her to act as
she did. And she is not peculiar in this readiness to give expression to her thoughts. Her rival, the Eddic Gudrun, the
Kriemhild of the *Nibelungenlied*, is even more eloquent, and
other characters are well dowered with the gift of self-expression.
It is evident that there is a great gulf fixed between the conventions of Edda and Saga.

In the early literature of the North any diversity of form is
all the more worthy of attention, since the early literature of
other Teutonic countries shows such faint variations from a
common type. The latter knows only one way of telling a story,
as distinguished from the mere record of fact. It is a fine way,
and has given us poems like *Beowulf* and the fragments of the
Hildebrandslied. But in Northern literature we have the unique
opportunity of seeing what is essentially the same story shaped
by master hands into forms which are poles asunder in spirit and
style. And the distinction is as clearly marked between the two
types of literature, Edda-poem and Saga, as in the definite case
we have been discussing. So all-important to the poet's mind is
the direct speech of his characters that many of the Eddic poems
consist of nothing but speech; most of the mythological poems
are in this pure speech-form, and so are the two older lays recounting the fates of the two Helgis, Helgi Hjörvarðsson and
Helgi Hundingsbane. The speech-poem is also found among the

poems on the Volsung or Nibelungen cycle, though here it is not so prominent. The *Prophecy of Grípir* is a dialogue between Sigurd and his mother's brother; *Reginsmál* is a series of speeches by various personages; *Fáfnismál* depicts, in dialogue form, Sigurd's slaying of the dragon and his detection of Reginn's treachery; *Sigrdrífumál*, the third part of this Sigurd trilogy, is a conversation between Sigurd and a valkyrie. The *Hel-Ride of Brynhild* is a dialogue, the *Second Lay of Gudrun* a monologue. In other poems of this cycle the narrative verses are usually few in number, and confine themselves to the briefest indication of the circumstances. Yet the poems are not mere lyrical outbursts: rather it seems as if the poet were unable or unwilling to depict events as they happen, and could only weave them into his verse through the mouth of one of his characters, as retrospective narrative or prophetic vision.

It is one of the more baffling literary phenomena of the North that a story received from the South in epic or ballad form[1] should thus lose its outline under the hands of Northern poets. For the wholly native Northern literature, the prose Saga, shows all the architectonic sense, all the restraint, all the spaciousness, all the due marshalling of subordinate matter, which distinguish the epic. Why then do the Northern poets shatter the mould in which they must have received the Nibelungen story? For there is no trace of a German or English treatment of the subject in speech-form. Both German and English poets use plenty of direct speech, but they show no tendency to shirk narrative, and they evince a real delight in describing battle-scenes and other moving incidents. This delight is shared by Northern skald[2] and Northern Saga-man, but it is most strangely absent in the Edda. The *Lay of Helgi Hjörvarðsson* leaves it to a scrap of prose to say: "*There was a great fight and Helgi received a mortal wound there.*" So in *Fáfnismál* only a prose "aside" tells us that "*Sigurd hewed the head off Reginn.*"

---

[1] Ranisch, *Völsungasaga* (1891), p. ix, thinks that the Nibelungen story came to the North in the form of dialogic poems like *Reginsmál*. For this there is no evidence other than the Northern tendency to treat the subject in speech-form—a tendency which, as we shall see, is even more marked in poems on native subjects.

[2] The skalds are the Court-poets.

This exclusion of narrative verse in poems which are so full of incident is a very strange feature[1], and has been explained in various ways. Müllenhoff put forward a suggestion connecting the older dialogue poems (those on mythological subjects) with festival games, but his suggestion has so far proved sterile, and has recently been criticised as affording no explanation of the chief peculiarity of these poems, the presentment of action in direct speech.

Certain scholars have maintained that the dialogue form interspersed with explanatory fragments of prose is an early form not only of Teutonic but even of Aryan literature, and instance as a cognate example verse dialogues among the hymns of the Rig-Veda, in which the connecting links of narrative, it is supposed, were supplied in prose, now lost. But it has been objected[2] with great force that even granting the original existence of prose narratives in the hymns, these would still be constructed on a totally different principle from that adopted in the poems of the Edda. In the latter the narrative is not given in the prose "asides," but is mirrored in the speeches of the protagonists[3]; and the prose only serves to make plain what is not sufficiently clearly indicated in the dialogue, as for instance in *Fáfnismál*: "*Reginn had gone away while Sigurd was slaying Fáfnir, and came back as Sigurd was wiping the blood from his sword. Reginn said—*" and then follows the verse. Or in the mythological poem *Skírnismál*: "*Then Skírnir rode home. Frey was standing without and greeted him and asked tidings.*" In other places the prose only serves to link up two fragments, or to add some fact known to the collector; and in some cases it stands for forgotten verses. Thus it cannot always be considered

---

[1] The lyrical monologues in Anglo-Saxon offer no exact parallel, for they are lyrical laments, not poems of incident.

[2] Heusler, *ZfdA*. XLVI. (1902), p. 215.

[3] Broadly speaking, there is a marked difference between the older and the later poems as regards the way in which this is achieved. The older mythological poems, the two early Helgi lays and the Sigurd trilogy all reflect the action in the dialogue as it occurs: we are supposed to imagine the action taking place as the characters speak. In the poems on the Nibelungen cycle this feature disappears, but much of the narrative is still left to the characters, who recount their past and foretell the future.

an integral part of the poem, and the view which would trace a historical connection between these speech-poems and the Sam-vada hymns has been vigorously attacked by such scholars as Heusler and Sijmons.

The controversy, however, has not been without unfortunate results, for these scholars have contented themselves with demonstrating the non-essential character of the prose statements, and have accepted or merely amplified the current explanations put forward to account for the dialogue verse itself. Moreover they have tended to regard the secondary nature of the prose statements as implying the secondary nature of the pure speech-poem, so that those who take the pure speech-poem seriously are thrown into the arms of what we may call the Rig-Veda school. Yet there is nothing impossible in the assumption that though the prose statements may be late, yet the speech-poems themselves may represent a primitive form.

In the eyes of Heusler and Sijmons, however, and of a large majority of scholars, the speech-form is only a secondary phenomenon, due to a variety of causes of a more or less accidental character. So far as the heroic poems are concerned, the tendency to omit narrative is apparently ascribed to what Professor Ker calls "the Norse intolerance of tame expression, and of everything unimpassioned and unemphatic[1]." The passion, the emphasis, are clear enough in many of the heroic poems. Even so there is something bewildering in learning that the poet so eagerly shuns tame expression that he depicts his fights and his slayings either in conversation or in singularly matter-of-fact prose. We can fancy an unregenerate critic objecting that if emphasis and compression were so dear to the authors of these poems, they would surely cut a good deal of the talk and come to the business. But even if we grant that their desire for passionate lyrical expression might explain their preference for direct speech in the heroic poems, we have not accounted for the monologues and dialogues of the first part of the Edda—the mythological poems. We must beware of explaining the earlier by the later, and there is no doubt that the mythological poems are, as a

---

[1] Professor Ker uses these words not of Eddic but of skaldic poems.

whole, earlier than the heroic poems in their present form. It is not lyricism which has forced these mythological poems into the mould of direct speech, for hardly one is lyrical. As a whole they are neither lyrical, nor emphatic, nor passionate in their language; and so far as these qualities appear, they are more noticeable in the semi-narrative poems than in the dialogues and monologues. It may be said that some of them fall naturally into speech-form, because their intention is didactic, and that others take the same form because they belong to a type—that of the "flyting" or interchange of abuse—in which dialogue must necessarily play the main part. We may be allowed to observe in passing that didactic poems do not invariably assume a purely monologic or dialogic character, and that some trouble has been taken by the Edda poets to put into pure speech-form the framework of incident which is present in all of them. In other literatures even the "flyting" type of verse usually has at least a narrative opening: in the Edda the preliminaries and the sequel of the dispute are usually given at some length in dialogue. Be this as it may, we must note that we are now furnished with three explanations of the Eddic tendency towards the pure speech-poem. (1) In the heroic poems it is because of the Norse intolerance of everything tame and unimpassioned. In the mythological poems it is (2) because didactic verse is apt to fall into that form, and (3) because dialogue must necessarily form the main part of a "flyting." We still need a fourth explanation for the pure speech-form of *Skírnismál*, which is full of incident, and for three or four mythological fragments which must belong to the same type of poem as *Skírnismál*. So far as this fourth explanation is vouchsafed to us, it takes the form that as so many poems were (for more or less accidental reasons) already in dialogue, it was natural to choose that form even for an incident-poem such as *Skírnismál*, and presumably for the three or four other mythological incident-poems represented by the fragments[1]. Our guides insist on the greater age of the semi-narrative incident-

---

[1] The strophe which represents Gná flying on an errand for Frigg (No. 4), the strophe from a Balder poem (No. 5), that from a Heimdall poem (No. 3), and the two strophes (Nos. 6 & 7), probably from one poem, giving episodes from the life of Thor.

poem (there are three of them in the mythological part) but for some reason these models did not deter the authors of at least four more incident-poems from adapting the dialogue-form to their uses. We cannot judge of the fragments, but *Skírnismál* is composed with a skill which shows that the poem cannot possibly be the first to use dialogue to depict incident.

This fourth explanation must presumably also serve for at least two of the older poems in the second part of the Edda: *Reginsmál* and *Fáfnismál*. Both cumber their path with mythological irrelevances, and neither can be said to show a tendency towards lyricism or passion or an over-emphatic style. Yet both use dialogue to mirror a series of events which would be more easily told in narrative form.

It is certainly difficult to accept the antiquity of the speech-poem-plus-prose merely or mainly on the ground of its supposed resemblance to a type of literature postulated but not proved for a remote period in India. On the other hand, if we accept the doctrine that the speech-poem is late and secondary, we are hard put to it to account for its prevalence in the Edda, unless we frankly declare what many scholars imply, that its use for unsuitable purposes was simply due to the wrongheadedness, or the original sin, of the Edda poets.

But this wrongheadedness influences the Edda poets even further than most scholars are willing to admit. We have not only to account for the obstinate use of the pure speech-poem, but for a much more disconcerting feature—the persistent tendency to represent events indirectly, through the speech of the characters, in poems which do contain narrative verses; and this although the events would be very much more telling if narrated directly by the poet. This characteristic is quite peculiar to the Eddic poems, and it deserves our consideration.

Firstly we must note the fact that there is a marked difference between the older and later speech-poems as regards presentation of the action. The older, mainly mythological speech-poems, the greater part of the two older Helgi lays[1], and the Sigurd

---

[1] The *First Lay of Helgi Hundingsbane* is a late *réchauffé* of parts of the *Second Lay*. The references to the "Helgi lays" in this book are to the *Lay of Helgi Hjörvarðsson* and the *Second Lay of Helgi Hundingsbane*.

trilogy[1] reflect the action as it occurs. They hardly ever allow a character to narrate past events, to say "I did this," but always show him in the act of performance. Still less do they permit their characters to say "You did, or will do, this." The action takes place as the characters speak. In the later speech-poems there is no present action to represent, for the poets depict a situation, not as an incident, or a series of incidents. Yet not only in the later speech-poems, but also in the narrative lays, the characters acquaint us with the course of events by means of retrospective monologues or prophetic utterances. It cannot be said that the poets take this means of telling the story solely for the opportunity it gives for psychological insight into the character of the hero or heroine, for their mouthpiece is quite free to tell the story by saying "You did this[2]" (as in Hamðir's speech to his mother) or "You will do this," as in the *Prophecy of Grípir*, the *Fragmentary Sigurd Lay*, and the *Short Sigurd Lay*[3]. Moreover the character of the mouthpiece is sometimes of no importance, and the story is told by making the mouthpiece say "They did this," as in the *Lament of Oddrún*.

If this device for acquainting us with the story were confined to the pure speech-poem, it would be legitimate, if wearisome. But it is not confined to the pure speech-poem. None of the extant Nibelung lays tells the whole story with due proportion of narrative and speech, though it might have been done in a poem no longer than the Greenlandic Atli poem. Of these Nibelung lays only the Atli lays and the *Lay of Hamðir* transfer their scene, and then only once[4], so that the attempt to tell the whole

---

[1] *Reginsmál, Fáfnismál* and *Sigrdrífumál*. In the MS. these are treated as one poem, and follow one another without a break.

[2] The most curious instance of this is in the *Lay of Helgi Hjörvarðsson*, in which Helgi tells his brother Hedinn of the latter's meeting with the trollwoman, which he had not even witnessed (str. 35).

[3] The dictum of Heusler: Die Lieder der Lücke im Cod. reg. der Edda (*Germ. Abh. Herm. Paul dargebracht*, 1902), p. 84: "Diese Dichtart zieht es vor, die Fakta in den lyrisch gefärbten, seelenvolleren Ich-Bericht zu kleiden," does not quite take account of this point.

[4] The scene of the *Fragmentary Sigurd Lay* can hardly be said to include the slaying of Sigurd, as although one strophe refers to this, it is in almost a parenthetic manner.

story in the ordinary way would be manifestly impossible to them. But they are nearly all determined to tell us the whole story, and the means they adopt is to select a single situation of such a nature that it will justify one or more of their characters in telling the story, usually as a retrospective lament or as prophecy. As the heroes cannot fitly indulge in lamentation this rôle falls to the women. The three *Lays of Gudrun*, the *Lament of Oddrún*, the *Egging of Gudrun* are all of this type. Of the *Short Lay of Sigurd* Heusler observes that it is strange how Brynhild's retrospect teaches us more of occurrences which are yet within the framework of the poem than the narrative itself in str. 3. He regards this as characteristic of late poems, but we may note that in the early *Fragmentary Lay of Sigurd* we learn more of the manner of Sigurd's death from Högni's speech than from the narrative in str. 5:

Sigurd fell south of the Rhine.

It is important to consider this characteristic structure of the Eddic Nibelungen lays in connection with the stylistic peculiarities of the earlier speech-poems—that is to say the bulk of the mythological poems and the Sigurd trilogy, which are certainly earlier than the Nibelungen lays as a whole.

We have here a literature which contains a large number of poems in dialogue depicting events as they happen, through the speeches of the characters. The authors of these poems can link one episode to another by giving us a series of scenes so arranged that we hardly notice how the story is made to progress: the technique does not obtrude itself. At a later period we find the successors of these poets using narrative verse, and dealing with long connected stories about foreign heroes. Evidently they have become acquainted with the tales in narrative form. But they are quite unable to make the story progress comfortably from one episode to another[1], and still choose to depict events mainly through the mouths of their characters, though in order to achieve this they are forced to shape the story as retrospect or prophecy. Is not this tantamount to saying that the direct

---

[1] Ten Brink says of Teutonic epic as a whole that it spends such a deal of movement without getting from the spot. The narrative poets of the Edda have simply renounced all hope of ever getting from the spot.

speech-poem has imposed its limitations on the technique of the narrative poem?

In a well-arranged archaeological museum one may observe how the earliest copper and bronze axes still slavishly follow the shape of their flint prototype, in spite of the greater possibilities of the new material, by which the maker is as yet unable to profit. The hesitations and the awkwardnesses in the Eddic narrative technique are surely best explained on the assumption that the Eddic poets have not yet mastered the possibilities of the ordinary epic style of narrative and speech combined, but are still hampered by traditions bidding them depict events as well as emotions through the direct speech of their characters.

In the realm of archaeology it has sometimes happened that some pattern different from the normal, traced on a vessel or ornament, has revealed secrets of the transmission of artistic influences and has thus been the means of discovering historical facts in an antiquity far beyond the ken of documents. The methods of archaeology may be fruitful in other spheres, and for the literary historian, especially, it should surely be an axiom that the more primitive a literature, the more important it is to note any diversity in form which may betray a diversity of origin. The Eddic monologues and dialogues as a means of depicting incident stand alone in early Teutonic literature. The tendency seems therefore a promising starting-point for research, and the obligation on Eddic students to neglect no possible line of enquiry is all the greater since it seems that the philological method can no longer be expected to throw much more light on the subject. The new science of early Teutonic and Scandinavian metre, the analysis of the vocabulary of the Edda poems and their syntactical peculiarities, the enquiries into similarities of expression or idea in different poems, all these tools which the philologists have forged, and with which they have cleared the ground of so many misconceptions of the past, will not alone suffice to rear a new structure on the ruins of the old theories.

The difficulties presented by the Eddic collection are somewhat different in kind from those which beset the student of other early literatures. There is surely no parallel to the difficulty

of locating, within a thousand miles or so, any given Eddic poem.
No other extant poems are variously referred by experts to
such widely distant regions as the further coast of Greenland,
Iceland, the southern parts of Norway, or the British Isles. We
cannot wonder that uncertainty on such a vital point has led
philologists to concentrate their attention on the provenance of
the poems, to the partial exclusion of the anomalies of form
which we have just been discussing. Yet the form of a literature is an even more fundamental matter than its provenance.

The attempts to localize the poems by differentiating between
the literary and religious outlook of the Norwegians and Icelanders may be said to have already yielded too many and too
contradictory results to be satisfactory. The study of the vocabulary of the poems has now been pursued far enough to discover
that the oldest words and phrases or forms do not, alas! invariably and exclusively occur in the oldest poems. The detection of wilful archaisms in the Runic inscription on the Swedish
Rök stone, a literary monument with so many affinities with
certain of the Edda poems, may well cause scholars to hesitate.
But wilful archaisms are not the chief trouble. The question
is complicated by the fact that most of the poems have been
preserved by oral tradition for two or three centuries, so that
the hope of dating them more precisely by word-forms and
the like is almost as vain as a similar attempt in respect of
any given ballad text. And if these tests fail there seems little
reason to hope that the syntax-test and the metre-test will
lead us very much further. If oral tradition has confused the
vocabularies and verbal forms of several generations, will it
not also have blurred the sharp chronological outlines of metre
and syntax?

Then there is the attempt to establish the relative chronology
of the poems by attributing cases of similarity of expression or
even of metre to direct imitation. This is perhaps the only point
in which Eddic scholars can be charged with undue precipitancy.
We have indications of such a vastly greater body of poetry than
has come down to us that the Edda must be considered a mere
sample of the whole. But in that case, turns of phrase or tricks

of metre, which in one poem we may regard as highly reminiscent of another extant poem, may in point of fact belong either to a third poem, lost to us but known to the authors of the other two, or to a common tradition, possibly a local one, of which we have no other hint.

Yet in vain do we search the best and newest commentaries for suggestions of any other methods of approaching the problem. The experts seem to rely on philology and philology alone. It is perhaps a sign of Scandinavian dissatisfaction with this position that we find more and more articles in the new Scandinavian folk-lore periodicals bringing folk-lore and archaeology to bear on such questions as Ragnarök in *Völuspá*, and Frey's quest for a bride in *Skírnismál*. Students of primitive literatures cannot help feeling a certain anxiety as to the fruitfulness of the purely critical philological method applied to the Edda. They remember the barrenness of its dominion over Homer: they see the advances made in that subject by the invasion of all kinds of audacious theories from the regions of anthropology. They observe the new vitality infusing the researches into the origin of the French epic since Bédier's re-statement of the question from a wholly new standpoint. If by focussing attention upon some neglected aspect of the Eddic poems, while availing ourselves to the full of the results of philological research, we are driven to formulate a new theory for the origin of the poems, we are furthering the advance of knowledge, whether the theory is ultimately proved right or no.

The following pages are therefore devoted to a study of the form and structure of the poems, with special reference to their dialogic and monologic tendency. We shall bear in mind that this tendency is most noticeable in the mythological group (which is as a whole admittedly older than the bulk of the heroic group) and that even in poems which do contain narrative verse the possibilities of narrative are only very partially and fumblingly realized: that is to say that the narrative poets are to a greater or less extent hampered by the conventions of dialogic or monologic verse. On the one hand we have the awkward jumble of narrative and retrospective monologue in such a poem as the *Short Sigurd Lay*. On the other we are confronted with the triumphant technique of *Skírnismál*, which depicts a series of events in dialogue with an economy of means and vividness of touch which could hardly be bettered.

Let us just glance at the structure of this poem. The story is simple: Frey is pining for love of the giantess Gerð, and his squire Skírnir is induced to seek her and woo her on his master's behalf. Finally he succeeds in breaking down her opposition, and she agrees to meet Frey. Skírnir returns to Frey and reports the success of his errand.

The first scene shows the goddess Skaði asking Skírnir to find out why Frey is so ill at ease. Skírnir's answer, expressing unwillingness to question Frey, increases the impression that the god's condition is very serious. However Frey confides at once in Skírnir, and persuades him to undertake the mission. The device used by the poet to show Skírnir's departure and at the same time indicate the perils he is about to encounter is extraordinarily vivid.

Skírnir said to the horse:

> Dark 'tis without,   'tis time for us to fare
>   over the reeking fells
>   over the goblin folk[1];
> Together we'll win through   or together he shall take us,
>   that mighty giant.

We see the dangers of the journey from the point of view of those who undertake it.

The arrival, and the perils still to meet, the high wall and the dogs in the gateway, are shown by the dialogue:

> Say thou, shepherd   who sittest on the cairn
>   and keepest watch all ways:
> how may I win a word   with the young maiden
>   for the hounds of Gymir?

The shepherd said:

> Art thou doomed   or already dead
>   .   .   .   .   .   [2]
> for ever thou'lt fail   to win a word
>   with Gymir's goodly maid.

---

[1] I translate *þurs* as goblin to distinguish it from *jötunn*—giant.

[2] A line missing.

Skírnir replies that a man can only die once, and his daring leap over the barrier is cleverly indicated by Gerð's words to yet another supernumerary personage, the maid :

> What is that din of dins   which comes to my ears
>   now, in our halls?
> The earth trembles   and all Gymir's dwellings
>   quiver at the sound.

The maid said [evidently at the door] :

> Here's a man without   has leapt from his steed,
>   he lets his beast crop the grass.

Without a single line of narrative the poet has given us a series of scenes full of life and action, and done it so deftly that we are not conscious of any effort. But he will not repeat his effects : Skírnir's return is dealt with in a line of prose : *Then Skírnir rode home. Frey was standing without and greeted him and asked tidings.*

The general attitude of scholars towards *Skírnismál* seems to have been that it is so unlike other Eddic poems that it is best not to devote too much attention to it. But is it really so unlike other Eddic poems ?

The description of the scene in the direct speech of the characters is a characteristic feature of most of the older poems in direct speech. We will deal more fully with this point later, but in the meantime we may note the charming strophe of fare-well addressed by Frigg to Odin in *Vafthrúðnismál*, and the subsequent speech of Odin showing that he has arrived at his destination :

> Hail to thee, Vafthrúðnir!   Now am I come into thy hall
>   to look upon thyself.

In *Lokasenna* the introductory verses between Loki and the serving-man Eldir show us that we are outside Ægir's hall and that the gods are carousing within. Loki's entrance is indicated by the words :

> Thirsty I've come,   I, Lopt, to this hall
>   from far afield.

The fragmentary verse on Thor's visit to Geirröð describes the rising river by somewhat the same means as Skírnir describes the scenes he is about to pass through. Skírnir addresses his horse : Thor, fording the river Vimur, addresses it, saying :

Wax not, Vimur,   since I needs must ford thee
  to reach the giants' dwellings;
Know thou, if thou wax,   that my god's might
  will wax as high as heaven.

In dialogue, then, the Eddic poets are capable of linking one episode to another by giving us a well-arranged and deftly indicated series of scenes, while in narrative they are quite unable to progress comfortably from one episode to another, and in fact seldom attempt to do so.

Where else in literature do we find similar technique for indicating the scene, or more especially the change of scene between one episode and another, in the speeches of the characters? Surely nowhere but in primitive drama, which is unassisted by modern methods of scene-changing. The same innocent arts as in the Edda are used, though more naïvely, in the mediaeval miracle or mystery plays. A character embarks for Turkey: "the wynd is good" says the skipper and immediately adds: "Yond there is the land of Torke." The devices of the miracle play are a little more ingenuous, a little less developed than those of *Skírnismál*.

A suspicion that *Skírnismál* is extraordinarily difficult to explain as a development of the epic style, and might be much more easily understood by assuming a dramatic tradition, has recently haunted Scandinavian scholars, though it has scarcely been put into words. After describing the gold plates, found in Norway, representing a ritual wedding, Professor Magnus Olsen observes: "At the point where the poet of *Skírnismál* breaks off, with Frey's outburst of longing for the meeting at Barri, the artist has set to work, and given us the scene which the Edda poet only hints at....Has *Skírnismál* direct connection with a cult, like the plates, and did it give a similar representation of the scene[1]?" Professor Montelius says of the old heathen feasts in Sweden: "On these occasions certain ritual games were probably enacted— there was the play of the god who pined away for love, but ultimately won the beloved goddess, of the god who sought and was ultimately reunited with his mate, the fight of the Lord of the May with the Winter-Lord, and so on[2]."

---

[1] Fra gammelnorsk myte og kultus, in *Maal og Minne*, 1909, p. 32.

[2] *Svenska Folkets Historia*, Bd. I. p. 266.

These are the only hints that Eddic scholars have considered the possibility of a dramatic origin for *Skírnismál*. A theory that the Edda poems are survivals of mysteries or religious dramas was however suggested by the Oriental scholar von Schroeder in his *Mysterium und Mimus der Rig-Veda*, published in 1908, and was adopted by Winternitz in a review of von Schroeder's book which appeared in the *Vienna Oriental Journal* in the following year. I have not been able to find any discussion of these speculations in the periodicals devoted to Northern subjects. Indeed the suggestions of von Schroeder and Winternitz were not likely to appeal to Eddic scholars. Beyond the argument that the Edda poems struck them as closely akin to the dialogic hymns of the Rig-Veda (and the dramatic nature of these is combated by most experts on the subject), they could only adduce the fact, already discounted by Eddic authorities, that songs on Eddic subjects are used for dancing in the Faroes. Northern scholars are confronted with a much more complex problem than could be solved by such generalities. The Eddic collection is a jumble of styles and forms and periods. It is not even the product of a homogeneous society. It contains, not only speech-poems of very varying types, but also a number of poems that are not pure dialogue, as well as lengthy sequences of strophes which contain no direct speech at all. For many of these the idea of drama cannot be entertained for a moment. All this, however, should not blind us to the fact that the structure of *Skírnismál* and of some other poems is in a high degree dramatic, that it is in a metre only used for direct speech, and that though there is nothing else quite like *Skírnismál* extant in the Eddic collection, it cannot possibly be an isolated effort of a single poet to tell a story in this fashion, but must go back to a long tradition in which events are depicted in dialogue, with a well-developed technique for indicating change of scene.

But before any light can be shed on the subject of a dramatic origin for any of the Eddic poems it will be necessary to come to some conclusions as to the form and provenance of the various groups of poems and as to the relations of the groups to each other. If we are to achieve this we must first consider the general attitude of scholars to the thirty or forty poems or fragments of poems which go under the name of the Elder Edda, and, as yet another preliminary, we must attempt to place them in their proper setting with regard to other contemporary verse in the North. Finally we must regard them in perspective as part of the poetic achievement of the early Teutonic races in general. Only then will it be possible to attempt a new grouping of the poems by researches into their form and structure.

CHAPTER II

THE EDDA POEMS

THE greater part of the poems of the Elder Edda are preserved only in the fine Icelandic Codex Regius, now in the Royal Library of Copenhagen. This manuscript has suffered violence, a sheet of eight leaves having been removed from it before its discovery in the seventeenth century; and we can only be thankful that the general drift of the lost poems is known to us through the agency of *Volsunga Saga*, whose author set down their contents in his prose tale some time in the latter half of the thirteenth century. Other Icelandic manuscripts harbour a few Edda poems, notably A.M. 748 of the Arna-Magnaean collection in the University Library of Copenhagen. This was perhaps originally a collection as full as Codex Regius, but it is now a mere fragment. Both it and Codex Regius are derived directly or indirectly from one written original, now lost. Both are good manuscripts, but the text they preserve for us is terribly mangled. Evidently the poems were corrupt and fragmentary even when first committed to writing. As Professor Ker says, they "seem to have lost their vogue and freshness before they came to be written down. They were imperfectly remembered and reported; the text of them is broken and confused, and the gaps are made up with prose explanations[1]." Codex Regius is from the second half of the thirteenth century, A.M. 748 from the early part of the fourteenth. In the thirteenth century two other collections must have been extant, from which Snorri and the author of *Volsunga Saga* respectively drew their information and citations.

The name Edda, or Saemund's Edda, was given to the collection on the discovery of Codex Regius by seventeenth century scholars, and it is still a matter of dispute whether it was given erroneously, by analogy with Snorri's prose "Edda" (a mythological primer for the use of poets) or whether there really existed a tradition

---

[1] *Epic and Romance*, Eversley edition, 1908, p. 93.

connecting the collection with Oddi in the south of Iceland, the home of Saemund the Learned, to whom it was attributed at the time of its discovery[1].

The mythological poems form the first part of the collection. Some of these deal with the adventures of various Scandinavian gods, others with divine lore. The second part is mainly composed of poems dealing with various phases of the Nibelungen story and with other stories, both German and native Norwegian, which were arbitrarily connected with the Nibelungen cycle in the North. Each part has thus a certain unity of subject-matter, but the poems of the first part vary enormously in style and treatment. The heroic poems of the second part all show a similarity of aim, which we may define as the attainment of tragic pathos, expressed to a great degree in the speeches of the characters. There is tragic imagination in the *Fragmentary Sigurd Lay*, in the three *Lays of Gudrun*, in the *Lament of Oddrún*, in the *Hel-Ride of Brynhild*, in the *Lay of Atli*, and in the Greenlandic Atli poem. And the poems dealing with the story of Svanhild, the *Egging of Gudrun* and the *Lay of Hamðir* do not fall behind the others. In fact the poems of the Nibelungen and Ermanaric cycles show high imaginative quality and a dignified, even lofty, style. But there is one very curious exception ; the trilogy dealing with Sigurd's upbringing, his slaying of the dragon, and his meeting with the valkyrie. The first of these three poems, *Reginsmál*, which contains the scene with the pike and the gods, gives a glimpse into a far more primitive and unsophisticated world than that in which the rest of the great Nibelungen tragedy is enacted. The literary affinities of the advice given by Hnikarr (Odin) to the young Sigurd are more with the mythological poems than with anything else in this second part. The fight with the dragon (*Fáfnismál*), surely an occasion for spirited verse (we have only to recall how *Beowulf* treats the same theme), culminates in mythological instruction imparted by the dying dragon, while the physical circumstances

---

[1] Whether the collection originally went by this name or not, the usage of several centuries has surely justified its use. Homer is Homer on no surer grounds. I do not therefore speak of "the so-called Edda" but simply of the Edda, and refer to the later work of the same name as Snorri's Edda.

are only sketchily indicated, or even left to be stated in a prose
" aside." Not until the last part of the bird colloquy—in a different
metre, and probably an interpolation—are we reminded of the
Sigurd of the high destiny, the Sigurd of the Nibelungen story.
Even in the third part, *Sigrdrífumál*, where Sigurd delivers
a valkyrie, the romance of the theme is but faintly felt. The
valkyrie's advice is singularly impersonal, and those scholars who
desire to give it point by making it square with Sigurd's future
have to assume interpolations on a very large scale[1].

It is perhaps worthy of note that the two Helgi Lays, to
which we owe some of the most beautiful passages in the Edda,
also contain scenes which certainly fall below the heroic level in
dignity and even in decorousness. We doubt whether the poets
of the Nibelungen lays would have introduced us to a hero
grinding corn in the garb of a bondmaid, like Helgi in the *Second
Lay of Helgi Hundingsbane*, or indulging in coarse flytings, as
the warriors of the Helgi lays do. On the other hand, nowhere
does the tragic imagination of the Nibelung poets rise so high
as in the *Second Lay*, a poem celebrating a native hero.

We will quote a few passages from this, the most beautiful of
all the poems. Sigrún seeks out Helgi on the battlefield where
her father and brother lie slain : he had fought against them at
her appeal to rescue her from an unwelcome suitor.

Helgi said: All has not gone well for thee, thou warrior-maid—and yet
in part surely this was the work of the Norns. There fell this morning at
Frekasteinn Bragi and Högni, and I was their slayer. They lie dead, the
most of thy kin. This slaughter was no work of thine, but thou wast fated to
be a cause of strife among the mighty. (*Sigrún wept.*) Take comfort, Sigrún.
A battle-maiden hast thou been to me, and kings must bow to Fate.

Sigrún said: Fain were I that some should live who now are dead, and
yet I would clasp thee in my arms.

Dag, Sigrún's brother, kills Helgi, and comes to tell his sister:

Dag said: Loth am I, sister, and slow to tell thee this thing : I was sore
constrained, and unwilling did I cause thee grief. There fell this morning at
Fetterwood the noblest prince in the world, Helgi, who had set his foot upon
the necks of princes.

Sigrún utters a terrible curse on her brother. Later in the

---

[1] Cp. F. Jónsson, *Litt. Hist.* I. p. 281 ; Symons (Sijmons), *ZfdPh.* XXIV. (1892),
p. 18.

poem her handmaid comes in and tells her that Helgi is returned from the dead ; " the grave-mound is agape, Helgi is come with gory wounds, and would have thee salve the smart."

Sigrún appears to hand Helgi a goblet, for he says :

I yet shall drain a draught of precious wine, though I have lost both love and lands. For me let none chant mournful dirges, though wounds show on my breast. For now is a maiden housed in the grave-chamber, a royal lady, with me a ghost.

Sigrún prepared a bed in the grave-chamber, and said:

Lo I have heaped thee a bed, Helgi, a very painless bed, thou son of the Ylfings. I would fain sleep in thine arms, my prince, as I would if thou wert yet quick.

Helgi said : Now I swear that men at Sevafell shall marvel at nought hereafter, neither soon nor late ; since thou wouldst rest in the arms of the dead, thou radiant daughter of royal Högni. But it is time for me to ride the reddening ways, to urge my pale steed on the paths of the air: I must be west of the bridge of Vindhelm before the cock on Valhöll awakes the warrior host.

There is tragic imagination, too, in the *Lay of Völund*, the only poem in this second part that is not somehow or other connected with the Nibelungen lays. Like them, however, its subject-matter is borrowed, perhaps from England. The main theme of the poem is the capture of Völund, *anglice* Wayland the Smith, here called the King of the elves, and his terrible vengeance on King Niðuð; but this is preceded by a confused and fragmentary account of Völund's love for a swan maiden who deserts him. Its style differs from that of the other poems of the second part, and various scholars have seen in it Anglo-Saxon and Celtic affinities.

In the mythological poems we seem to be transported to a different world altogether. It is true that in *Völuspá*, the Prophecy of the Sibyl concerning the course of the world and its final destruction, there is a sense of tragic doom akin to the spirit of heroic poetry. And akin to heroic poetry is the short poem *Balder's Dreams*, also called the *Lay of Vegtam*, in which Odin communes with a dead sibyl over the fate of Balder. In *Grímnismál* too, in spite of what strikes us as Odin's didactic loquacity, we are made to feel the tragic catastrophe at the close, when the god, unrecognized and tortured, reveals himself in his full might, and the doomed king falls on his own sword before him. But these are the only exceptions. Most of the mythological poems seem to our modern taste to be either heavily didactic or else trivial or even flippant.

The various poems incorporated under the title of *Hávamál*, the "Sayings of the High One," are definitely didactic, as also the monologue *Grímnismál*[1] and the dialogues *Vafthrúðnismál*, *Alvíssmál*, *Svipdagsmál*, and *Hyndluljóð*, the *Lay of Hyndla*. The last-named is didactic in a different sphere: it gives the genealogies of certain South Norwegian Kings.

To the second class belong *Hárbarðsljóð* (the Flyting of Hárbarð) and *Lokasenna* (the Taunting of Loki), both dialogues, and also the *Lay of Thrym* and the *Lay of Hymir*. *Hárbarðsljóð* is an exchange of taunts and abuse between Thor and a ferryman "Hoarbeard," usually taken to be Odin in disguise. In *Lokasenna* Loki twits all the gods and goddesses present at a feast with infidelity to their mates or other disreputable conduct, and is answered by abuse. The *Lay of Thrym* recounts in rollicking ballad-like style how Thor dressed up as Freyja to win back his hammer, which the giant Thrym had stolen. The *Lay of Hymir* narrates another of Thor's exploits from much the same point of view, though in more sophisticated form.

Rígsthula, or *Ríg's Lay*, and *Skírnismál* cannot be classified under either head. *Ríg's Lay* is a curious account of the origin of the three classes of men, thralls, yeomen and jarls. It contains several words of Celtic origin and is usually thought to have been composed in one of the Scandinavian colonies round the coast of Great Britain. It is fragmentary, and the extant part is remarkable for containing no direct speech save the apostrophe of a bird to the hero. *Skírnismál*, on the other hand, is, as we have seen, all direct speech. In a skilfully handled dialogue it shows us the god Frey, sick of desire for the giant's daughter Gerð, despatching his messenger Skírnir to plead with her for her love. Skírnir's perilous journey is indicated, and then follows his colloquy

---

[1] I leave *mál* untranslated because of the ambiguity of its meaning. It is usually translated "sayings," but this translation is a misleading title for such an incident poem as *Skírnismál*. It must be remembered that *mál* has the secondary significance of "transactions," "affair," "business," especially in cases where public speaking is involved, and it may well be that the word is used in the titles of poems in this secondary meaning. I use "Lay" only for poems in the *fornyrðislag* metre.

with Gerð, whose reluctance he overcomes by the cumulative horror of his threats. He returns and reports his success to Frey, who answers by bewailing the nine nights which still separate him from his heart's desire. There is more action in *Skírnismál* than in any other of the extant mythological dialogue-poems, but it should be noted that none of these is a mere colloquy : in each a dramatic situation develops, and in three of them (*Grímnismál, Vafthrúðnismál* and *Alvíssmál*) the life of the god's interlocutor is clearly forfeit : that is to say, the dénouement of each of these poems is a death or slaying. Moreover four fragments, one from a poem on Balder's death, one from a poem on Frigg's search for her mate, another from a poem on Thor's visit to the giant Geirröð and yet another on Heimdall and Loki's adventures, all in direct speech, show that *Skírnismál* cannot have been the only mythological poem to deal with lively incident in dialogue form.

For us many of the mythological poems are marred as literature by their rather childlike absorption in mythological detail, while others seem merely to reflect the rude animal spirits of a barbaric society. Even the poems which are neither didactic nor flippant—for instance *Skírnismál*, and, if we may judge from fragments, the poem introducing Gná and that on Thor's visit to Geirröð, owe their charm to a certain primitive naïveté of which there is no trace in the mass of the heroic poems, though both it and the absorption in mythological detail re-appear in the Sigurd trilogy. This naïveté characterizes the general outlook of almost all the mythological poems with the exception of *Völuspá*. Their authors seem to consider that they have explained the universe when they have mapped it out, named the rivers which divide Hel from Jötunheim, and peopled it with beings whose function it is to draw the sun-chariot, make the wind, and so forth. When, as in *Vafthrúðnismál*, they set out to give a general view of the world, and of the final fate of the gods and of mankind, they do it with a certain competence and dignity, but questions as to the ultimate why and wherefore never trouble them. They tell us what Odin's warriors in Valhöll eat and drink, what is the name of the battlefield where the gods meet their enemies at the crack of doom, and the names of the pair of human beings who survive to repopulate the earth, and with such things they are satisfied. There is no trace of moral judgment in the poems, and very little expression of emotion.

The attitude of the authors of the heroic poems is very different. Not only is the emotional content of these poems immeasurably greater, but they reveal an intense intellectual preoccupation with the fundamental mysteries of life—failure and death, and above all with the causes which drive men and women into evil acts. The contrast with the mythological poem is very curious here. All that the audience of the latter required was a certain liveliness of incident and the ultimate success of the god's undertaking. Frey wins his Gerð, Thor retrieves his hammer, the gods get the cauldron to brew their ale, and no doubt Gná in the lost poem accomplishes her errand for Frigg as successfully as Skírnir performed his for Frey. The Balder poem, of which but a strophe remains[1], must have been an exception, for the grief of the gods is movingly depicted in Snorri's account, founded on the lost poem. But even in this poem the funeral scene, if we are to trust Snorri, must have been as near comedy as tragedy. Among the themes of the heroic poetry, on the other hand, there is not one that is not tragic. The only approximation to the attitude of the mythological poems is found in the Sigurd trilogy, and in certain scenes in the Helgi lays. The *Lay of Völund* reveals the aims of the heroic poetry in an especially interesting fashion, for it purposely rejects the natural triumphant ending. Völund, who has been the hero throughout, has accomplished his revenge, slain the king's sons and seduced their sister Böðvild. Thereupon he flies away, taunting his victims, but by a sudden shift of sympathy the poem is made to end on the tragic note of Böðvild's shame and despair.

A moral conflict underlies all the heroic stories. In the *Lay of Helgi Hjörvarðsson* Helgi is induced in the exaltation of a banquet to swear he will wed his brother's bride: is he to keep

---

[1] The reply of the giantess Thökk to Odin's request that all the world should weep Balder out of Hel:

Thökk will weep　　　with dry eyes
　　the obsequies of Balder
What son of man　　　avails me aught
　　Let Hel keep what she holds !

his oath, sworn in solemn ritual, or shall he suffer the crushing degradation of a broken vow? In the story of Helgi Hundingsbane Sigrún decides to cleave to her lover, Helgi, though he has slain her father and brother. Every character in the Nibelungen story is the battleground of conflicting passions and duties, but the motives which sway them are too well known to need discussion here.

What was the cause of this great difference in outlook between the heroic poems on the one hand, penetrated with the sense of the mystery and dignity of human life, and the mythological poems on the other? It cannot have been merely the difference in subject, for in *Völuspá* we see mythological themes handled with a high dignity, while among the heroic poems the Sigurd trilogy treats its hero's adventures with more than a touch of the naïve, non-moral simplicity of the mythological poems. We must almost assume a traditional difference of public. If the heroic poems were in the North, as their counterparts were elsewhere, the product of an intellectually emancipated community with a high sense of the dignity of human life—in a word, of an aristocracy, then the origin of the mythological poems must be sought in a wider, less enlightened society, which had not yet begun to question the primitive traditional conceptions bequeathed to it by the past.

Before passing on to other types of Northern literature, it will be well for us to examine the metrical composition of the Edda poems.

All the poetry of the North is strophic, and dependent on alliteration. In the Edda three metres are employed, which in thirteenth-century Iceland go by the names *fornyrðislag*[1], *ljóðaháttr*, and *málaháttr*. The first was used long before any of our Eddic poems were extant in their present form, in the verses occasionally found in Runic inscriptions; and this no doubt accounts for the name, which may be rendered "old-lore metre." It seems that it is the counterpart of the early German and English epic measure. The strophe has four long lines[2], each divided into

---

[1] It seems possible that an earlier name for this metre was *kviðuháttr*. Six or seven of the poems in it are called *kviða* in the MSS. *Kviða*, meaning "What is uttered," is usually translated "Lay."

[2] Scandinavian editions usually print each long line as a pair of short lines, so that the strophe appears as eight-lined.

two parts by a caesura. Each half-line has two stresses, and each pair of half-lines is connected by alliteration[1]. Normally there are two unstressed syllables in each half-line, but a certain amount of latitude was allowed in this respect. The opening strophe from *Völuspá* will serve as an example of the metre:

Hljóðs bið'k allar helgar kindir
meiri ok minni mǫgu Heimdallar
vilt' at ek, Valfǫðr vel framtelja
forn spjǫll fira þaus fremst um man.

Some of the Edda poems in *fornyrðislag* are partly or even mainly narrative, but others contain nothing but direct speech.

Ljóðaháttr signifies "the measure of the *ljóð* or song." The original meaning of *ljóð* seems to have been "spell," or, in the plural, "magic song[2]," and something of the supernatural undoubtedly clung to the word[3]. We will translate *ljóðaháttr* as "chant-metre." It is only used for direct speech. The strophe consists of four lines, divided into two syntactically independent half-strophes, each composed of one long line with a caesura[4], the two parts connected by alliteration, and followed by one three-stressed line, containing two alliterative beats within itself. The number of unstressed syllables is perhaps not so rigidly restricted as in the old-lore metre, and indeed a great deal of latitude is characteristic of this metre[5]. A fairly normal strophe is the following from *Skírnismál*:

Ørinde mín viljak ǫll[6] vita
áðr ek ríða heim heðan
nær þú á þingi munt enom þroska
nenna Njarðar syni.

---

[1] The first half-line of each pair often shows the alliterating initial letter in both stresses.

[2] It is used in the plural in the titles of poems: *Hyndluljóð*, etc.

[3] Since the poem *Hyndluljóð* is not in *ljóðaháttr*, and *Hárbarðsljóð* shows only a few scattered verses in the metre, it has been suggested that *ljóðaháttr* was not the original name for chant-metre. We shall have something to say later of *Hyndluljóð* and *Hárbarðsljóð*, but in the meantime we must observe that the *ljóð* or magic charms of Odin in *Hávamál* are in this metre, and also the spell-song of Skírnir in *Skírnismál*. This seems almost conclusive evidence that *ljóðaháttr* was the traditional name of the metre.

[4] These long lines, divided by a caesura, are printed in Scandinavian editions as a pair of short lines, so that the strophe appears as six-lined.

[5] So A. Heusler, Der Ljódaháttr, *Acta Germanica*, I. (1889–90). But cp. Gering, *Die Rhythmik des Ljóðaháttr*, Halle, 1902.

[6] All vowels and semi-vowels alliterate together.

A variation of chant-metre is the *galdra-lag* or "incantation-metre," in which one of the three-stressed lines, usually the last, is repeated with slight variation.

Málaháttr, "the metre of speeches," occurs in uncontaminated form only in one Edda-poem, the Greenlandic *Atlamál*. It is closely allied to *fornyrðislag*, but has an additional unstressed syllable to each half-line. Two other *málaháttr* poems, *Hamðismál* and the *Atli Lay*, appear to have been worked over by a poet composing in *fornyrðislag*—the old-lore metre, or else to be the result of the fusion, in each case, of two ancient poems, one in speech-metre and one in old-lore metre. These two, like *Atlamál*, are only partly dialogue, so that the name "speech-metre" seems hardly to apply.

Of these three metres employed in the Edda, we find that one is entirely reserved for direct speech, while the name of another points to some such traditional restriction. There is moreover a distinct tendency to exclude narrative verses even in poems composed in the third metre. Several of these prefer, like the poems in chant-metre, to have recourse to prose "asides," where dialogue, however skilfully handled, does not make the scene sufficiently clear. It only remains to add that there appear to have been fashions in metre which led to the recasting of metrical form or to the composition of parallel poems in a different metre. To judge from the number of interpolations or passages from parallel poems in old-lore metre, inserted in poems of chant-metre or speech-metre type, the old-lore metre must have enjoyed great popularity at a time when chant-metre and speech-metre[1] were no longer fashionable.

We may now remember that the Edda poems are not the sole literary achievement of the Viking Age, and we must attempt to place them in their proper setting.

---

[1] Most scholars (but not all) now follow Ranisch (*Zur Kritik der Metrik in Hamðismál*) in regarding the speech-metre forms of the *Atli Lay* and *Hamðismál* as earlier than the old-lore verses in the poems.

CHAPTER III

THE EDDA POEMS IN RELATION TO OTHER
EARLY SCANDINAVIAN VERSE

I

IN South Norway there is a Runic inscription of the sixth century which is sometimes referred to as the earliest example of Northern verse. It has alliteration throughout, and the last four words can be arranged to form one line in old-lore metre:

> (Ek Wiwaz after Woðuriðe)
> witaða-halaiban   worahto runoz
> (I Wiwaz in memory of Woðuriðaz)
> (my) lord, (?)   wrought the runes.

Alliteration without regular metrical form is very common, not only on Runic stones but in Old Northern laws and formulas, and unintentional verse is by this means very readily achieved. This one possible couplet does not therefore justify us in assuming the existence of regular verse in old-lore metre in the sixth century, especially as there are no other clear cases of such verse until about the beginning of the ninth century. Most famous among such later Runic verses is the inscription on the Swedish Rök stone, from the beginning of the tenth century:

> Reið Þjóðrekr   hinn þormóði
> stillir Flotna   strondu Hreiðmarar;
> sitr nú gorr   á gota sínum
> skjaldi of fatlaðr   skati Mæringa[1].

"Theodoric the bold, the leader of the Flutnir[2], ruled (or rode?) over the shore of the East-Gothic sea....Now the prince of the Maerings sits on his steed, armed, his shield on its strap."

This strophe on the long-dead Theodoric the Ostrogoth is inserted in the midst of prose retailing the great deeds performed

---

[1] The forms are normalized into Old Icelandic. The rendering is Brate's.
[2] So Schück—others read "of ships' crews."

by heroes of a later day. The clause immediately following, though not in metrical form, may perhaps be quoted here, as showing poetical phraseology :

> Let us say, twelfthly, where the steed of Gunn sees fodder on the battle-field, whereon lie twenty kings.

Gunn is a valkyrie-name, the valkyrie's steed is thought of as a wolf: a wolf's fodder is of course corpses. So we have here a Swedish example of that use of "kennings" or complicated periphrastic expressions beloved of the Norwegian Court-poets.

The aim of all Runic verse appears to be the praise or the commemoration of the newly-dead—for even the Rök strophe must be taken as redounding in some way to the glory of that Vémóð to whom the stone was set up. It is essentially "occasional" verse, always composed for a definite purpose or occasion, and it is aristocratic in so far as Runic inscriptions only commemorate persons of high social standing.

II

In all these characteristics Runic verse is closely akin to skaldic verse. Skaldic verse, too, is eulogistic in aim, though it naturally concerns itself oftenest with the living. If the Rök inscription is, as it seems, genealogic, we may compare it with the earliest and most famous of the skaldic genealogical lays, *Ynglingatal,* a poem of the ninth century, tracing the descent of Harald Fairhair from the Yngling dynasty of Upsala. In this, as in the Rök inscription, there is but a moderate use of the favourite skaldic device of kennings. We may instance the strophe on a king's death by fire:

> And that which stalks abroad with smoke (fire) trampled at Raening on Ingjald (while yet) living, when the house-thief (fire) trod fiery-footed on the kinsman of gods.

These kennings do not differ very greatly from those common in Anglo-Saxon verse, and it is only in the eulogies of living princes that the kenning acquires a complexity which almost obliterates the poetic quality of the verse, and which finally caused skaldic lays to approximate to versified conundrums.

Professor Schück[1] has adduced some grounds for suspecting

---

[1] H. Schück, Studier i Ynglingatal, *Ups. Univ. Årskr.* 1905–10. Cp. *Bidrag till tolkning af Rökindskr.*, Upsala, 1908, by the same author.

that *Ynglingatal* is founded on older Swedish verse. In any case
the verse on the Swedish Rök stone suffices to show that Sweden
possessed something very like the genealogical skaldic verse of
Norway.

The development of the skaldic encomia on living persons, so
far as we are able to trace it, is extremely interesting. The earliest
skaldic verse of this type is eulogistic only in so far as the poet
praises his patron for the gift of a shield: the bulk of the poem
describes the scenes from mythology or heroic legend which adorn
the gift. The two chief encomia of the ninth century, Bragi's
Ragnarsdrápa and Thjóðólf's *Haustlöng*, are of this type[1]. Another curious form is that in which Thórbjörn hornklofi has clothed
his *Hrafnsmál*. First he speaks in his own person, and then reproduces, in direct speech, the dialogue between a raven and a
valkyrie, which he declares he overheard. This pair speak in high
terms of the king, and end by praising his generosity to his skalds.
The poem dates apparently from the close of the ninth century. In
the tenth century these encomia take the form of direct narration
by the skald.

In language and metre the distinction between skaldic and
Eddic verse is a little difficult to draw. Much, but not all, skaldic
verse is composed in a very much more complicated metre than
any in the Edda, and makes use of internal rhyme as well as of
alliteration. It can be broadly laid down that the skaldic poems
are more complex and artificial, and the style is very much more
involved, than is the case in Eddic poems. Further, whereas the
latter all contain a very large proportion of direct speech by the
characters, in the skaldic verse it is usually the poet himself who
speaks, in strictly narrative, style. But these distinctions break
down in the case of the early dirges, which are dialogic and extremely simple in language, and also in the case of *Hrafnsmál*,
which is dialogic, though not simple in language. A more
definitely distinguishing characteristic is the "occasional" nature
of skaldic verse. It is always composed for a definite purpose or
on a definite occasion. The circumstances of the composition of
skaldic and Eddic verse must have been very different. We do

---

[1] It is interesting to note that the verse of the Swedish Rök inscription, quoted above,
suggests that it is a description of a carving or pictorial representation of some kind.

not know who were the authors of the Eddic poems. They are not merely anonymous in the sense that we cannot point to any poem and state its author: their anonymity is of that more profound type which wraps in obscurity not only the individual but the whole class. We know absolutely nothing of the creators of the Eddic forms. Of the skalds, on the other hand, we know more than of any other class of persons who haunted the courts of kings and earls in the hey-day of Scandinavian power.

There is another and more vital difference between the two forms of poetry. We might almost term it an antagonism, so profound is the gulf which separates the literary ideals pursued by the two types of poet. The Eddic verse ignores externals, and gains its effects by its skill in the dramatic presentation of states of mind. The skaldic verse aims at a series of pictorial images. One is psychological, the other descriptive. The Eddic poem keeps the dramatic situation well in view, and works up to a climax of dramatic tension. The skaldic poet aims at arresting attention by the vividness and variety of his images; he is indifferent to continuity of idea, and for this reason his poems suffer little from the fragmentary condition in which they have come down to us. For this reason, too, they can be quoted without doing them an injustice, whereas the Eddic poem makes its effect as a whole. We take a couple of verses from the earliest skaldic poem we possess, Bragi's shield-song, describing the scene of the vengeance wreaked on the drunken Jörmunrekk by Sörli and Hamðir, and their death by stoning, since weapons could not harm them:

As from an evil dream did Jörmunrekk awake, with the blood-stained host eddying in battle around him: there was tumult in the house of the king when Erp's swart brothers wreaked vengeance for their grief.

The benches swam in battle-dew (blood): (the king's) hands and feet were seen lopped and gory on the floor: he fell headlong, and the (spilt liquor from the) beakers was mingled with his blood. *This is painted on the shield.* Round the place where he lies are clustered the tall warriors. Straightway, as with but one will, all set to batter Hamðir and Sörli with the unyielding globes of Earth (stones).

A fine scene from mythology is that where Thjóðólf in his shield-song describes Thor's descent from the sky to fight the giant Hrungnir:

The whole vault of holy heaven blazed before the path of Ull's kinsman (Thor): but down below the earth was whipped with hail, when the goats drew the chariot-god to the tryst with Hrungnir: the sky was all but rent.

Balder's brother (Thor) spared not there the ravening enemy of mankind (the giant): the cliffs quaked, and the mountains brast asunder: the vault of heaven was all aflame. I have heard that the guardian of the ships' road (sea: Hrungnir) rushed mightily forward, when he espied his slayer ready for the fray.

More typical of the ordinary theme of the Court-poets is the description of Harald Fairhair's many fights, elicited from the raven by the "white-necked, bright-locked" valkyrie, in Thórbjörn hornklofi's *Hrafnsmál*. She asks:

What ails you, ye ravens? Whence are ye come with gory beak at the dawn of day? Gobbets of flesh cleave to your talons; the stench of corpses issues from your beaks: I trow ye spent the night where ye knew corpses lay.

The dusky-feathered one stirred, the eagle's foster-brother dried his beak, and made answer: We have been with Harald, Halfdan's son, the young Yngling, since we came from the egg. I thought thou wouldest know the king who dwells at Kvinna[1], the lord of the Northmen, who holds sway over deep-keeled ships, with red-stained timbers and ruddy shields, tarred oars and foam-flecked awnings. The gallant prince will celebrate Yule out at sea, if he may have his way. From his youth up he has loathed the glowing hearth, and to loll indoors in the warm bower, on pillows filled with down. One might hear how at Hafrsfjörd the king of a famous line battled with Kjötvi the Wealthy: vessels were come from the east eager for the fray, with gaping figure-heads and carven stems.

Of the skalds the raven is made to say:

By their garments and their golden rings ye shall see that they are friends of the king: red cloaks they have, bordered with fur, and with fair stripes; their swords are silver-wrought; woven mail-coats they have and gilded baldrics: their helms are adorned with figures, their arms with rings which Harald has given them.

It is a characteristic of early skaldic verse that its inspiration is so often sought in "pictures"—scenes on shields and the like. In later times we are told once or twice that a skaldic poet was asked to improvise a verse describing a scene on tapestry. We cannot believe that he felt himself at all hampered by his subject, for the skald loves to dwell on bright colour and the outward semblance of things. His greatest effort at psychological analysis leads him little further than to say that men—or much more often wolves—"were glad," or "eager for battle."

---

[1] So the MS. But cp. *Maal og Minne*, 1913, pp. 67 ff.

This particular phraseology, curiously enough, is avoided by the Edda poems, which prefer to describe states of mind by the actions of the person affected. Völund's sullen brooding is indicated by the lines which show him sitting for ever sleepless, engaged at his forge. When Jörmunrekk hears of the coming of Svanhild's avengers he laughs, pulls his beard, tosses his hair, and quaffs from his cup. Freyja bursts her necklace in her rage[1]. The skaldic poems have nothing to show like this. The earlier skalds have plenty of vivid imagination, but it has been put to the work of finding telling pictorial phrases—"the flame of the sea" for gold, "the woof of spears" for battle, and so on. It is not that they cannot indicate grief or joy or excitement, but they do so in another manner. The lament on the loss of his sons, by Egill Skallagrímsson, shows the skald's grief embodying itself in a series of visual images:

Down there the sea roars, close by the doorways of the dwelling where my son is housed (his grave-mound).

My race nears its end, it is like the storm-stripped rowan in the forest[2]. There is no joy in him who bears the body of his beloved kinsman from out the dwelling-place.

Yet will I first speak of my mother's and my father's death: from the house of speech (my mouth) I will bear forth that hewn tree of song (matter for song) leafy with words.

Grievous to me was the gap which the surges battered in the wall of my father's kinsmen. Well I wot that the breach which the sea made when it snatched my son will ever remain yawning and void.

Sorely hath Rán (the sea goddess) stripped me; I have no dear friends: the sea has snapped asunder the bond of my kin, that stout thread which I had woven myself.

Know that if I could urge my suit[3] at the sword's point, it would go ill with him who brews ale for the gods (Aegir, the sea-god): could I but slay him I would enter the lists against the billows.

We have only to compare this poem with the earlier Eddic poetry quoted above to see to what different uses the two types of poets put their high imaginative powers.

---

[1] Cp. A. Hoffmann, *Das bildl. Ausdrück im Beowulf und in der Edda*. Engl. Stud. VI. pp. 177 f.

[2] In Iceland, where this poem was composed, the rowan might easily be the tallest tree in the "forest."

[3] The poet is thinking of the slaying-suit he would institute if his son had been slain by a mortal foe.

3

The older Edda poems disregard outward things in the strangest way. In especial, they are almost bafflingly restrained about their fights and their slayings. A dragon-fight is represented in dialogue, with no word of the dragon's awful appearance, of the fury of the fight, of the flowing of blood, of the mighty strokes dealt by the slayer. The few attempts at describing stirring scenes are obviously skaldic devices: "There was a din in the court-yard, crowded with horses, the *weapon-song* of champions." "Frodi's peace was broken between the foes, *Odin's greedy hounds* (wolves) ravined over the island." More often the battle is merely indicated in a prose "aside," as in the *Lay of Helgi Hjörvarðsson*: *There was a great fight, and Helgi received a mortal wound there.* The event, as such, hardly seems to concern these Eddic poets at all. Character and "situation," in the dramatic sense, are the whole interest of the heroic poetry of the Edda. "The eye," says Professor Heusler, "is not the organ with which these poets regard the world[1]." Such a cleavage between two contemporary forms of literature, both of which are usually called epic, must be almost unique, and can only be explained on the hypothesis that the origins of the two forms lay very far apart.

III

Here we must leave the firm ground of skaldic poetry, with its fixed chronology and famous authors, for another group of anonymous verses. These are the dialogue poems which are found scattered up and down the late legendary sagas called *Fornaldar Sögur*, dating from the thirteenth and fourteenth centuries, and dealing with heroes belonging to the very earliest dawn of Scandinavian history. The slight traditions attaching to the names of these ancient champions have been expanded by the judicious use of stock incidents into tales of a considerable length, and these tales incorporate our dialogue poems. The earliest of the poems is usually dated as from about 1100, and is thus only

---

[1] *ZfdA.* XLVI. (1902), p. 220. Cp. Wackernagel, Die epische Poesie, in *Schweiz. Museum f. hist. Wiss.* I. p. 363: "Die Edda is fast nur Wechselrede, in der sogar die äusseren Thatsachen kaum angedeutet werden."

contemporary with the latest of the Edda poems; but their source of inspiration is so evidently the Eddic collection that it is worth while to consider them here. They are intentionally archaic, and evidently base themselves on the oldest models. They are distinguished from true Eddic verse by a certain self-consciousness, an artificial simplicity, and a definiteness of ideal and aim which are quite foreign to the older poems. It is curious, and a little pathetic, to find that these Christians writers should turn so whole-heartedly to the past for their inspiration, and glorify not only the adventurous spirit of the long past Viking Age, but also the heathen ideas which infused it. Tragic love, the central theme of the older heroic poetry, plays but a small part in these later poems. Most of them consciously exalt what they took to be ancient Viking qualities—extreme valour, as much superior to the sense of supernatural awe as to physical fear; and miraculous success in arms. The mists of centuries have so magnified the prowess of their heroes that if these suffer defeat it can only be because Odin is hostile to them, or the Fates wrath, or their guardian spirits remiss, or through the agency of a magic weapon. The poems are not without literary qualities, but they do not attain to the dramatic interest of the older dialogue poems, partly because they lack the art of furthering and depicting the action through the speeches of their characters. We miss the skilfully indicated movement of *Skírnismál*, of *Fáfnismál* or of the *Second Lay of Helgi Hundingsbane*. The protagonists simply stand there and talk, discussing their chances of victory, the grief of their lady-love, or enlarging on their prowess and their birth, and on their opponents' shortcomings in these directions. The pathos is less restrained and more drawn out than in the Edda. Thus Hjalmar is made to say:

> Carry back my helmet and my mail-coat to the King's hall, such is my wish, the heart of the King's daughter will be moved when she sees the buckler of my breast hewn through. Draw the red ring off my arm, and bear it to the young Ingibjörg. It will be a lasting sorrow of heart to her that I shall never come to Upsala again.

By far the finest of these secondary poems deals not with fighting but with a more romantic theme: the quest of the sword Tyrfing, which the maid Hervör goes to fetch from her dead father, that she may avenge him. Professor Ker truly says of it that "the poem of the *Waking of Angantýr* is so filled with mystery and terror that it is hard to find in it anything else," but in Hervör's forcibly expressed contempt for supernatural terrors we may trace the same apotheosis of Viking courage which marks other poems of this type. They are all pure speech-poems[1].

The secondary status of the whole group has often been contested in the past, but their recent publication under the title of *Eddica Minora* seems to mark a growing consensus of opinion as to their true place.

IV

There is no such agreement among scholars as to the real nature of the Northern poems translated into Latin by the Dane Saxo Grammaticus, who wrote his *History of the Kings of Denmark* in the first years of the thirteenth century.

Most scholars regard the most famous of these, *Bjarkamál*, as a real Eddic poem. Like all the poems translated by Saxo[2], it is in speech form. The speeches are supposed to be made during a desperate fight, and if it is fair to judge, not by Saxo's diffuse Latin, but by Olrik's greatly curtailed re-rendering of the poem[3], they were somewhat lengthy and general in tone for such an occasion, and the poem rather suggests an imitation of the Eddic style.

A poem of this name was recited, we are told, at the battle of Stiklastað in 1030, and a few verses in the vernacular are still extant, but owing to the number of "kennings" (periphrastic expressions) they contain they are frequently suspected of skaldic origin[4]. A skaldic version would certainly seem more

---

[1] Heusler, *ZfdA.* XLVI. (1902), p. 204, regards the narrative verses in the Hervör poem as interpolations, so also Heusler and Ranisch, *Eddica Minora* (1903), p. xvii. Boer, however (*Aarb. f. n. O.* 1911, p. 11), regards them as genuine.

[2] Except one strophe of skaldic type.

[3] Cp. Olrik, *Danmarks Heltedigtning*, pp. 44 ff. In *Danske Oldkvad i Sakses Historie*, Copenhagen, 1898, Prof. Olrik gave a spirited version in Danish of the Ingjald and Hagbard poems.

[4] These may however be from a later redaction: so Heusler and Ranisch, *Eddica Minora*, p. xxv.

suitable for recitation before a battle than the poem preserved to us by Saxo.

Another poem preserved to us in Saxo's translation, the *Egging of Ingjald*, is a monologue by the old warrior Starkad, who enters Ingjald's hall, rebukes him for his effeminate life, and bids him avenge himself on the sons of his father's slayer, who are present. The monologue continues while the speaker sees Ingjald take his advice and kill the sons of Sverting, and there is no denying that the effect is somewhat artificial. The third great poem in Saxo is far more truly dramatic. It represents Hagbard in disguise, approaching Signe: this is followed by a love scene between the two, and this again by the taunts of Signe's mother, and Hagbard's answer, as he is led to the gallows on his detection. The poem ends with his rejoicing at the fidelity of his love, who sets fire to her bower and is consumed in the flames.

There are a number of other poems scattered up and down the mythical books of Saxo's history: amongst them another monologue by Starkad, and a dialogue-poem in which he meets his death. Other slighter poems give love scenes in dialogue, and there are several "flyting" poems. These will be considered more fully later on.

V

Perhaps before concluding this brief survey of ancient Northern verse we should refer to the doggerel in which parts of the old Norwegian and Icelandic laws appear to have been chanted. Of these the truce-formula most nearly approaches the structure of verse, but it follows no known laws, and is chiefly interesting to us on account of its tendency to confine the alliteration within the single line, instead of using it to connect the two halves of a long line. Thus we have:

> Sem metenðr mátu
> ok telienðr tǫlðu
> ok domr ðǿmði.

This was no doubt a popular tendency, and it is interesting to trace it in the three-stressed line of chant-metre, which has no caesura.

VI

We have glanced at what is left of the earliest Scandinavian literature, and have seen that but for the vestiges of verse in Runic inscriptions we might substitute the term "Icelandico-Norwegian" for "Scandinavian." But it is essential to remember that the absence of literary monuments from Denmark and Sweden merely mean that these countries lacked a literary colony, such as Norway possessed in Iceland, to preserve and transmit their literary achievements. But for the accident of Iceland we should know little more of Norwegian poetry of early times than we now know of Swedish or Danish. Recent investigators—Olrik for Denmark, Schück and Nerman for Sweden—have shown that literature flourished in Denmark and Sweden in the period before about 800 A.D. and that a great number of stories now preserved in Icelandic and Anglo-Saxon tradition belonged originally to Danish and Swedish literature. The question for us to answer is: Were these poems of Eddic type? It is a question which will almost answer itself in the later part of this book, when we have reached some conclusion as to what kind of themes lent themselves to Eddic treatment, but in the meantime there are certain facts to go upon.

Skaldic verse was evidently common to Sweden and Norway, if not to Denmark. For Sweden the evidence of the Rök inscription is conclusive. It vouches for the use of kennings, and for the existence of genealogical poems somewhat similar to the Norwegian *Ynglingatal*. Its description of Theodoric, seated on his steed in all the panoply of war, whether inspired by a statue or a carving, recalls the skaldic habit of seeking inspiration in pictures[1].

We cannot, then, deny Sweden certain forms of skaldic verse. Can we deny her Eddic verse? There is such a close community of ideas between Sweden and Southern Norway when history begins that it is difficult to believe that one country could have had a popular form of poetry of which there were no traces in the other. Forms of Runic lettering specifically Swedish

---

[1] Olrik suggests a pictorial origin for the description of the twenty slain kings which occurs in another part of the inscription (Bugge, *Der Runenstein von Rök*, p. 94).

are found in Norway[1]. And it is perhaps significant that the Eddic description of a woman riding a wolf should find its counterpart in the carving of just such a figure on a Runic monument from Skane[2], and be implicit in the Rök kenning which calls the wolf the "steed of the warrior-maiden." Carvings depicting scenes of the Sigurd story are as common in Sweden as in Norway.

Professor Sophus Bugge has pointed out a number of resemblances between the Rök inscription and the Eddic *Vafthrúðnismál*[3], and even if we do not accept them all enough remains to be at any rate suggestive. Thus where the Eddic poem has Seg þat et eina, Seg þat annat—"Say that the first—the second," and so on, the Rök stone has "That I say (the first), the second, the twelfth, the thirteenth" (Sakum annart, etc.). The Rök stone speaks of the horse of the greatest Hreidgothic king: *Vafthrúðnismál* gives the name of the best horse among the same people. These resemblances, however, even if not merely accidental, do not prove the existence of Eddic poetry among the Swedes, but only the influence of Swedish culture on Southern Norway, an influence almost inevitable, and certainly accepted as a tradition by the Norwegians, who regarded their Vestfold kings as immigrants, descended from the Yngling dynasty of Upsala. As regards the actual existence of verse other than skaldic in Sweden we have to fall back on the scholion to Adam of Bremen's History, written not so very long after the Swedes had abandoned their heathen customs. This scholion says that the *neniae*, magic songs or dirges, which accompanied ritual celebrations at the temple of Upsala, were of many kinds and *inhonestae, melius reticendae*[4]. A poem like the original *Hávamál* (The Sayings of Odin) might well be recited in a temple, and parts of it would certainly deserve the strictures of the canon of Bremen or his monkish scholiast. Or we need only imagine a more freely treated poem on the subject of *Skírnismál*, to include the meeting of Frey and Gerð, to realise that the strictures

---

[1] S. Bugge, *Norges Indskrifter med de ældre Runer* (1902), p. 18.

[2] Wimmer, *Danske Runemindesmærker*, III. pp. 24 ff.

[3] The researches of Prof. Schück, *Studier i Ynglingtal* 1905–10, and *Studier i nord. Litt. och Relig.*, reveal what we may call a common stock of traditions among the South Norwegians and the Swedes.

[4] Bk. IV. Schol. 137.

might very well apply to poems of the Eddic type. That the natural *dénouement* of this poem, the meeting of the lovers, was actually the subject of poetical treatment in South Norway is rendered probable by the finds of gold plates representing such a scene[1]. The cult of Frey appears to have had its centre at Upsala, so that it is not improbable that episodes in Frey's life should have formed the subject of *neniae* there. These are, however, suggestions and nothing more. All that is certain is that poems were recited at the temple of Upsala, and that the epithets applied by Adam: *multiplices, inhonestae, melius reticendae*, make it impossible that they should have been of skaldic type. It is conceivable that they were of Eddic type. If they were not, then they must have been a form peculiar to Sweden which has disappeared without leaving a trace.

The question as to the existence of poems similar to the Eddic in both Sweden and Denmark would be solved if it could be proved that the poem *Bjarkamál*, reproduced by Saxo, is indeed the work of a tenth century Danish poet, as Professor Olrik[2] maintains. There was, as we have seen, a closer literary connection between Sweden and Norway than between Norway and Denmark, so that if Denmark had poems of the type we know as Eddic, Sweden must almost inevitably have had them too. But even if the case for *Bjarkamál* be pronounced unproven, we can still reckon it as probable that Sweden produced poems of Eddic type[3], and possible, at least, that Denmark did so too. Norway may have been original in borrowing the Nibelungen story and in clothing it for the first time in Northern dress, but it is doubtful whether her originality extended further than this. It is highly improbable that she alone should have created so varied a literature[4].

---

[1] M. Olsen og Haakon Schetelig, De to Runestener fra Tu og Klepp paa Jæderen, in *Bergens Museums Årbog*, 1909.

[2] *Loc. cit.*

[3] For the whole question of early Swedish literature cp. Birger Nerman, *Studier över Svärges hedna litteratur*, Uppsala 1913.

[4] Cp. Schück, Fornnordisk Diktning och Europeisk, in *Samtiden* (Christiania), 1905, 16 Årg. pp. 302 ff.

VII

It is easier to deal with the wider question of the relation in which Scandinavian poetry stands to the remains of other early Teutonic poetry.

In structure it seems more primitive than either English or German, for it has clung to the strophic form, whereas only vestiges of strophic structure are to be found in the earliest poems of the other literatures. Unfortunately it is impossible to decide whether the chant-metre, like the strophe, perpetuates an ancient Teutonic mode, lost elsewhere. We certainly seem to catch a glimpse of a similar metre, used, as in the Edda, for direct speech, in the very early Anglo-Saxon fragment called the *First Riddle of Cynewulf*. At present we cannot decide whether the dialogue form of so much Scandinavian verse is a legacy from primitive Teutonic times, or a specifically Scandinavian development. Here we are fumbling in the dark. But one thing stands out clearly. At the dawn of history we find the English and, so far as we can see, the German peoples with a remarkably homogeneous literature. The epic metre and the epic style hold the field, and it has often been pointed out that this literature is the product of an aristocratic society. It is dignified, spacious, much concerned, like Homer, with the outward ordering of an aristocratic life, and as careful as Homer to avoid coarseness.

In Scandinavia we find something resembling this stately epic style used on mainly borrowed subject-matter, like the Nibelungen story, but there exists besides, both in the Edda and in Saxo, a mass of verse which we can only describe as popular. It is quick and vivid in style—in fact to us moderns its *verve* is its most attractive feature—and it is obviously addressed to an audience whose taste was tickled by crude repartee and coarse jokes. There is not the faintest trace of such scurrility in the extant Anglo-Saxon or early German literature, nor in Norwegian skaldic verse, which we know to be of aristocratic origin. Among the heroic poems of the Edda the Helgi Lays alone contain scenes in this style, with a somewhat incongruous effect. But for these passages the heroic poems are absolutely untainted by it.

Wherever early verse of this type can be traced, it is found to originate, not with the aristocracy—though they may find entertainment in it—but with the people. It is at least probable that the scurrilous poems of the Edda are no more the product of purely aristocratic circles than is the French *fabliau.*

But this is not the only anomaly in early Northern literature. In form, too, there are two extremes: the purely narrative skaldic poetry on the one hand, gaining its effects by means which we may describe as pictorial, and on the other hand a purely dialogic or monologic form, showing from the first, through the medium of direct speech, a high order of skill in its presentation not only of character but of action, but neglecting the outward aspects of things. "The eye is not the organ with which these poets regard the world," to quote Professor Heusler's words again. Skaldic verse, however, forbids us to account for this peculiarity by denying to the Northmen all interest in scenic accessories. On the contrary we have to admit that the Northern muse of the ninth and tenth centuries loved more than any other to dwell on the stately pageant of Court life, and had a real gift for reproducing impressions of colour and form and movement. The authors of later Eddic poems, such as *Rígsthula* and the *First Lay of Helgi Hundingsbane*, have been able to exploit this gift, even though the skalds of their day had lost the vivid pictorial touch which characterized the ninth and tenth centuries. There is no explaining the aloofness of the earlier Eddic poems from all this world of colour and movement, unless we assume some traditional difficulty, some traditional limitation of form, which forbade the attempt to incorporate it. We have seen that the style of even the most narrative Nibelungen poems suggests that the "mixed" poem, containing narrative verse as well as direct speech, was a new form in the North. If we could believe, with Müllenhoff, that the dialogue or speech-poems had preserved an ancient traditional form, it would be easier to account for the gulf between the Edda poems on the one hand, bare of description or comment, and the skaldic forms, which consist of nothing else, on the other.

Our line of enquiry is thus clearly marked out for us. Where the Edda poems diverge most markedly from the form of other early Teutonic verse is in the tendency, observable in them all, to give the story through the medium of the direct speech of their characters. This tendency cannot be explained from the outside, as due to foreign influence, and we have seen that the form of skaldic and runic verse throws no light on it,—in fact rather deepens the mystery. We are therefore thrown back on the Edda poems themselves. There the tendency is of course most marked in the chant-metre poems, which consist of nothing but direct speech. To us therefore these are all-important. We must begin with them, and we shall very likely end with them.

There is one further point as to which we must make our position plain. In researches which aim at establishing the provenance of any given poem or group of poems, those on borrowed subjects afford as good material as those on native subjects. In fact they serve even better, for the modifications of the story afford some guidance, at least as to its previous wanderings. Thus the Nibelung poems in the Edda, the Ermanaric poems, and the Völund lay have all proved a particularly rich mine for scholars. But when it is a question of *form* the position is reversed. Poems on borrowed subject-matter may of course be wholly clothed in native dress. But it is not safe to found deductions on such a basis, for it is at least equally probable that with the foreign substance something of the foreign form remains. In rejecting the evidence of such poems we are merely following the example of the anthropologist who seeks to establish the physical characteristics of a people. He studies the native, but dismisses the alien, however well naturalized. It is for this reason that the Eddic poems on the Nibelungen and Ermanaric cycles are so little considered in the following pages. The stories are naturalized in the North, but they are still dependent on the country of their birth and they cannot serve us as a guide to the native form. Our business lies with the native poems, and first of all with the poems in chant-metre.

CHAPTER IV

THE CHANT-METRE POEMS

WHEN we find some scholars assigning a poem like *Alvíssmál* to the tenth century, and others maintaining it to be from the twelfth, it seems at first as if all attempts to fix the chronology of the Edda poems must be in vain. But as a matter of fact such wide differences of opinion are only found in a few cases. Divergences of anything up to half a century must be admitted to be frequent —perhaps because it is still premature to attempt to fix dates within a score or so of years[1]. If however, instead of accepting the actual dates assigned to the several poems by various authorities, we content ourselves with classifying the chant-metre poems as pre-Christian or Christian, we shall find a surprising consensus of opinion about them. As representative of the latest views we will take the utterances of Professors Finnur Jónsson, Mogk, Sijmons, and Schück, adding the opinions of other scholars as to individual poems. Of these authorities only Finnur Jónsson and Mogk have expressed themselves as to the dates of all the poems. Before giving their views on this point it will be well to state their general attitude towards Edda problems. Professor Finnur Jónsson allows Iceland no share in the mythological part of the Edda, except for *Völuspá in skamma,* "the Short Prophecy of the Sibyl," a work of the twelfth century which a late MS. incorporates in *Hyndluljóð.* All the others he regards as Norwegian. This view reacts somewhat on his chronology, for the interest in heathen mythology is known to have waned more rapidly in Norway than in Iceland after the introduction of Christianity. Hence he is compelled to assume somewhat earlier dates than are usually accepted for certain of the mythological poems. Professor Mogk, on the other hand, assigns to Iceland all poems showing anything like a systematic interest in mythological questions. He pays perhaps

---

[1] So Sijmons, *Einleitung,* p. cclxxv.

too little heed to the fact that the mythographic tastes of thirteenth century Iceland need not necessarily have been the tastes of the Icelander of the tenth century[1]. For historical reasons he holds that only the period 930—1000 was suitable for the composition of mythological Edda poems. These limits Sijmons regards as somewhat too rigidly drawn.

If we take the year 1000 as approximately representing the date of the introduction of Christianity the chronological table for the chant-metre poems works out as follows[2]:

FINNUR JÓNSSON		MOGK	
Heathen	*Post-heathen*	*Heathen*	*Post-heathen*
Hávamál		Hávamál[a b]	
Vafthrúðnismál		Vafthrúðnismál[a b]	
Grímnismál		Grímnismál[a b]	
Skírnismál[a]		Skírnismál[a b]	
(Hárbarðsljóð)		(Hárbarðsljóð)[b]	
Lokasenna		Lokasenna[b]	
Alvíssmál[b]			Alvíssmál[a b]
The ⎧Reginsmál[a]		⎧Reginsmál[a b]	
Sigurd ⎨Fáfnismál[a]		⎨Fáfnismál[a b]	
Trilogy ⎩Sigrdrífumál		⎩Sigrdrífumál[a b]	
Hrímgerðarmál			Hrímger-ðarmál
Svipdagsmál[c]		Svipdagsmál[c]	
I Grógaldr		Gróg.[a]	
II Fjölsvinnsmál		Fjöls.[a]	

[a] Heusler regards these as the earliest chant-metre poems, *ZfdA*. XLVI. (1902), p. 214. Ranisch regards Reg. and Fáfn. as "sehr alt," *Völs. S.* Berl. 1891, p. ix.

[b] So also A. Olrik, *Nordisk Tidskr.* 1897, p. 341; and Magnus Olsen, in *Maal og Minne*, 1909, p. 92.

[c] "From the last days of heathendom or the first years after the introduction of Christianity." *Litt. hist.* I. p. 219.

[a] Sijmons, *Einleitung*, §28.
[b] Schück, *Illustr. Sv. Litt. hist.* I. pp. 88 f.
[c] Falk, *Arkiv N.F.* v. p. 331, ascribes *Svipdagsmál* to the thirteenth century and Heusler associates himself with this view: *Arch. f. d. Stud. d. neueren Sprachen*, 116, p. 266.

[1] Professor Heusler, also, considers that the "antiquarische Gelehrsamkeitsdichtung" is of necessity Icelandic—a view against which Bugge issues a warning in *Der Runenstein von Rök* (1910), p. 254.

[2] This table does not concern itself with interpolations or fragments of parallel poems in old-lore metre. I do not include the poem *Sólarljóð*, found in the seventeenth century paper MSS. of the Edda: it is not included in the Edda collection by Sijmons, nor by Hildebrand-Gering. It is a Christian vision-poem cast into the old heathen form. Cp. B. M. Ólsen, *Safn til Sögu Islands*, v. i. 1915.

It will be seen that all scholars regard the bulk of these poems as pre-Christian. The chief difference of opinion concerns *Alvíssmál*, in which Thor questions a dwarf as to the names given to various common objects and daily phenomena by the gods, dwarves, giants and elves. The answers of the dwarf contain a number of fanciful expressions not otherwise met with—thus the giants are said to call the sea "eel-home," and so on. These expressions have caused the poem to be regarded as a mere *heitatal*, or collection of poetic terms. Thus Sijmons appears to associate himself with Gering's description of it as " a versified chapter of skaldic poetics." The expressions, however, do not resemble the type favoured by the skalds, and it has even been suggested that the idea of renaming common objects is borrowed from a Welsh source[1]. But Professor Axel Olrik has shown that a number of the terms must have belonged to a long extinct "tabu-language" used at sea, and that some of them are still actually in use in the tabu-language used by the Shetland fishermen[2]. There is some evidence for the existence of such a language in ancient Norway: a few survivals of it are still in use, and it seems to be the source of a similar tabu-language among the "Sea-Finns" of the sixteenth century in Northern Norway[3].

The poem cannot therefore be of Icelandic origin, since there is no trace of a tabu-language in that country. But a mythological poem of this type could hardly have been composed in Norway after about 1000, even if the memory of the tabu-language survived. Accordingly it seems safest to ascribe it, with Olrik and Magnus Olsen, to the tenth century.

Hrímgerðarmál, a " flyting " in chant-metre inserted into the *Lay of Helgi Hjörvarðsson*, is regarded as late by Mogk. We shall

---

[1] Heusler, *Arch. f. d. Studium der n. Sprachen*, 116 (1906), p. 266.

[2] Olrik, *Nordisk Tidskrift*, 1897, p. 341. See also J. Jakobsen, *Det norrøne sprog på Shetland*, pp. 82–99 and, for N.E. Scotland, W. Gregor, *Notes on the Folk-Lore of the North East of Scotland*, 1881, pp. 199 ff. The words used for the sea in Shetland are almost identical with those in *Alvíssmál*. Traces of a tabu-speech are also found in some parts of Sweden. Cp. Rääf, *Beskrifning Öfv. Ydre Härad i Östergötland*, Linköping, Del I. (1856), pp. 36 f.

[3] M. Olsen in *Maal og Minne*, 1909, pp. 91 f. Olrik points out that the astuteness ascribed to Thor in this poem is contrary to later Icelandico-Norwegian tradition, but is an original characteristic of the god, preserved in Swedish folk-lore (*Danske Studier*, 1905, pp. 129 ff.).

presently see that it contains traditional features which might suggest an early date.

Svipdagsmál is considered to be very late by Falk, who shows that *Fjölsvinnsmál*, its second part, reveals imitation of many of the other chant-metre poems. Heusler is of the same opinion. If their view is correct, it proves nothing more than that the poem is a late imitation of an obsolete form, of the same type as *Sólarljóð*, the twelfth or thirteenth century jumble of Christian ideas which its Icelandic author clothed in the antique heathen form[1], or as the chant-metre verses which occur occasionally in the *Fornaldar Sögur* or Legendary Sagas.

The chant-metre Edda poems may thus fairly be said to terminate with the heathen age. Is it only a curious coincidence that, as Finnur Jónsson[2] observes, the Court poetry of Norwegian skalds is silenced for ever on the death of Eyvind skáldaspillir, about 990? Or does it not suggest that the chant-metre verse, too, was Norwegian, and unlike the skaldic poetry never took root in Iceland—except in a late imitative work or two, composed after the Eddic collection had been committed to writing? Certainly this metrical form can never have flourished in Iceland, or it would have survived the year 1000, which in that country was of no such fatal import to heathen poetry as it was in Norway. It is noteworthy that Icelandic poets were so little accustomed to compose in this metre, that they interpolate old-lore metre strophes into such a poem as *Grímnismál*.

Of the twelve chant-metre poems in the Edda Sijmons allots nine to Norway. To these we must in all probability add *Alvíssmál*. The two remaining chant-metre poems, *Vafthrúðnismál* and *Grímnismál*, are assigned to Iceland on no better grounds than that they aim at imparting mythological information[3]. In point of fact almost all the extant chant-metre poems are careful to impart mythological information. *Fáfnismál*, which is surely incontestably Norwegian[4], even encumbers the death-scene of the dragon with mythological irrelevances, which it is rash to ascribe

---

[1] Cp. B. M. Ólsen's newly published edition of the poem in *Safn til Sögu Islands*, v.
[2] *Litt. hist.* I. p. 325.   [3] But see F. Jónsson, *Litt. hist.* I. p. 323.
[4] Heusler calls it one of the oldest of the Edda poems.

to Icelandic interpolaters. And the Swedish Rök stone displays as eager a desire to impart, if not mythological, then at least legendary lore as any poem in the Edda[1]. The only incontestably Icelandic Edda poem which sets out to impart mythological lore is *Völuspá*[2], in old-lore metre, and it does so in the connected and straightforward style we should expect from the creators of the Saga. In this respect it forms a marked contrast to all that we know of the Norwegian didactic manner.

There is thus good reason for regarding chant-metre as a mainly Norwegian verse-form dating from heathen times.

It is generally considered to be especially adapted for didactic and gnomic verse. But though its use is limited to direct speech, it is so successfully employed to mirror the incidents of Skírnir's quest that we can safely deduce that *Skírnismál* was not the only chant-metre poem to reproduce scenes involving action and a change of scene. In fact there are enough fragments left in the metre to justify such a conclusion. Its use in the heroic part of the Edda is so rare that it is worth while observing that here also—in the Sigurd trilogy—it is employed to depict stirring scenes, a circumstance, as Professor Mogk observes, all the more striking since all the following poems on heroic legend are composed exclusively in old-lore metre[3].

With the possible exception of this trilogy all the poems in chant-metre deal with native subjects. Even in the trilogy, if the central figure is borrowed, the whole setting, and all the other personages, are native. But is it so certain that the central figure is borrowed, or at any rate borrowed from the Burgundian Nibelungen story?

It is generally agreed that what we know as the Nibelungen story was formed by the combination, at a very early period, of a Sigfrid or Sigurd tale and the Burgundian story of the Gjukungs. Panzer has adduced some evidence to show that the hero's upbringing by a dwarf, his fight with a dragon, the winning of the giant's treasure and his deliverance of an enchanted maiden are

---

[1] Cp. S. Bugge, *Der Runenstein von Rök* (1910), p. 254.

[2] Regarded as Icelandic by almost all scholars, except Finnur Jónsson.

[3] *Grundriss*, II. 629: "um so auffallender...als alle folgende Gedichte aus der Heldensage nur in fornyrðislag gedichtet sind."

not isolated episodes arbitrarily combined, but a coherent whole based on the folk-tale of the bear's son, in which these episodes occur[1]. At any rate we may take these incidents as the nucleus of the Sigurd story, as apart from the Nibelungen story. Now the chant-metre Sigurd trilogy gives just these incidents, and contains no single word which can reasonably be taken to allude to the Sigurd of the Burgundian story. In fact the poem contains several features which commentators have found very difficult to reconcile with the poems which follow[2].

There are a few highly significant facts to be considered in this connection. Firstly we may note that the numerous English and Scandinavian Sigurd carvings depict almost exclusively scenes from this part of the story. The otter-skin, the smithing of the sword, the slaying of the dragon, the birds watching Sigurd roast the heart, Sigurd killing Reginn—these are the scenes which occur over and over again, on Manx crosses and North English monuments, on thirteenth century church portals in South Norway, on Runic stones in Gotland and in central Sweden[3]. There is one representation only of the cutting out of Högni's heart. Gunnarr playing the harp in the snake dungeon occurs three or four times in England and Scandinavia, but this appears to be an addition to the story only found in these countries[4].

The Norwegian carvings all belong to Telemarken and the surrounding districts. This is just where Sigurd's early exploits are still sung. Professor Olrik has collected much folk-lore material to show that Sigurd *or Sigmund* and " Guro " (Gudrun) still survive in Telemarken as spirits who ride the countryside at night at the head of a troop of ghosts[5]. Now the Anglo-Saxon poem

---

[1] *Studien zur germ. Sagengeschichte*, II. *Sigfrid* 1912.

[2] Observe the efforts made by scholars to connect the utterances of the valkyrie in *Sigrdrífumál* with Sigurd's subsequent career. They have not only had to assume interpolations on a very large scale, but also to suggest far-fetched explanations of the strophes they retain.

[3] Schück, *Sigurdsristningar*, in *Nordisk Tidskr.* (1903), pp. 193–225. Schück observes that these scenes are by no means the most important in the Nibelungen story, and he can only explain their prevalence on the supposition that they are all copied from English models (probably on tapestry). But why should England have depicted only these scenes unless the original Scandinavian story had contained them and ignored the Nibelung part of the story?

[4] Cp. carving in Oseberg ship.

[5] (Norsk) *Hist. Tidskrift*, 3 R. III. Bd. p. 184 ff. Olrik observes that this Guro is

Beowulf attributes the dragon-slaying and winning of the hoard to *Sigemund* and not to Sigurd or Sigfrid; and Moorman has shown that certain place-names in England afford evidence for a mythical dragon-slaying hero Sigemund[1]. Is it not possible that this story has found its way into Beowulf (and England) from Scandinavia, whence, after all, Beowulf garners all its traditional lore[2]? As Olrik truly observes, it is very remarkable that the peasants of Telemarken should have taken their local ghosts from poems on foreign potentates who were known to have died in the Rhine country[3]. The tradition would however be perfectly explicable if this Sigurd or Sigmund were an older, localized hero, who, like Beowulf, slew a dragon, and like half a dozen other Scandinavian adventurers, won himself a valkyrie as a bride[4]. This is by no means a new suggestion. Following entirely independent lines of reasoning both Heinzel and Detter have reached the conclusion that the fusion of the "Sigfrid-myth" with the Burgundian story took place on Northern soil. Their arguments are re-inforced by the significant fact that the reference in Beowulf to Sigemund tallies with the alternative form Sigmund in Telemarken folk-lore, and that all the original chant-metre part of the Sigurd trilogy is innocent of the least trace of the German story.

If we may allow ourselves to believe that the Sigurd of the trilogy is indeed the hero of an older story, we shall at least be able to remove the slur on his reputation which the troth-plighting with the valkyrie in *Sigrdrífumál* has hitherto inflicted on him. Whatever the name of this valkyrie, it has been all too clear to commentators from the thirteenth century onwards that she was not Brynhild[5]. No doubt her name was Gudrun, and in Northern

---

at once a strange elfin figure in whom the terror of the midnight ride is centred and the mortal heroine of the Sigurd folk-songs.

[1] *English Place-names and Teutonic Sagas*, in *Essays of the English Association*, vol. v. (1914).

[2] It is possibly significant, too, that Beowulf l. 879 uses *fyrene* of the exploits of Sigemund and Fitela, and Hhu 1. and *Völs. S.* (Bugge's ed. p. 97) use the word *firen verkum* of Sinfjötli.

[3] Olrik says: "Det viser et Bondefolk, over hvis Fantasi Sang og Digt har større Magt en den ydre Virkelighed."

[4] It is noticeable that Beowulf is acquainted with other episodes which do not appear in German tradition: Sigemund's journeys alone with Fitela—(Sinfjötli).

[5] See the introduction to *Sigrdrífumál* and the prose comment (after str. 4) which is founded on lost verses (Sijmons, *ZfdPh.* XXIV. 1892, p. 7); *Grípisspá, Skáldskaparmál*

story this name has ousted the name of Kriemhild, Grimhild, for Sigurd's wife. But this older Gudrun has left other traces. The prose introduction to the *First Lay of Gudrun* records a tradition that she had eaten of Fáfnir's heart—which implies that she (and not Brynhild nor "Sigrdrífa") must have been on the spot at the time of the dragon-slaying. Evidently this is a totally different form of the story, a form in which Brynhild plays no part. So too, a Norwegian ballad recounts how Sigurd slew a flying dragon in the presence of Gudrun[1].

After the fusion of the native and the Burgundian stories this earlier Gudrun has yielded her pride of place to Brynhild and her name to the sister of the Gjukungs. But even if *Sigrdrífumál* were not an enduring monument to her, she would not have lived in vain, for she has flung round the figure of Brynhild the glamour of her own valkyrie attributes.

We do not claim that this earlier Sigurd story is purely Scandinavian: in its ultimate origin it is probably the common property of the Teutonic peoples[2]. But Beowulf's reference to its hero by the name Sigemund, preserved in Telemarken folk-lore, forces us to regard the story as fairly established in Scandinavia several centuries before the composition of the Sigurd trilogy as we know it, and before the introduction of the Burgundian story. It is with this Norwegian tradition that the Sigurd trilogy in chant-metre deals.

We must now glance at the fragments of poems in chant-metre which have survived in Snorri's Edda. There are seven of them. The first is the command uttered by Hár (Odin), to Gylfi:

> Stand up   while thou askest
> he shall sit who answers.

The second is the charming little dialogue between the god Njörð and his wife Skaði, in which each complains of the other's choice of residence. The third is a scrap of "incantation-metre" (a varia-

---

(longer redaction), ch. 39–42. *Völsunga Saga* avoids the difficulty by making Sigurd plight himself twice to Brynhild.

[1] Landstad, *Norske Folkeviser*, p. 124.

[2] This pre-Brynhild part of the story I describe as the Volsung story, using the word Nibelungen for the Burgundian or imported story.

tion of chant-metre), in which the god Heimdall is made to
say:

> Of nine mothers I am the son,
> Of nine sisters I am the offspring.

Snorri tells us that these lines come from a poem *Heimdallargaldr*, dealing with the adventures of Heimdall and Loki in
their search for Freyja's necklace. The fourth is an excerpt from
a poem which must have dealt with Frigg much as *Skírnismál*
deals with Frey. Her messenger Gná is seen in the sky, and one
of the Vanir asks who flies there. She replies:

> I fly not,   though I fare
>   and flit through the air
> on Hófvarpnir,   whom Hamskerpir
>   gat on Garðrofa.

The next fragment is from a poem about Balder's death, and is
addressed to Odin by the giantess Thökk:

> Thökk will weep   with dry tears
>   the obsequies of Balder;
> Neither quick nor dead   did man's son aught avail me
>   Let Hel keep what she holds!

The remaining two strophes presumably come from one and the
same poem on Thor: in one Thor addresses a river which he is
fording, and in the other he tells how once he had to exert his
full might.

We do not know who uttered the remaining fragment, a half-
strophe to the effect that:

> Glasir stands   with golden leaf
>   before the halls of Sigtýr.

But it is clearly a piece of mythological lore similar to that imparted by other poems in chant-metre. It might well come from
Grímnismál, although it does not appear in our redaction of the
poem.

Enough of these fragments remains to show that at least four
more poems about gods must once have existed[1], all of them containing as much action as *Skírnismál* (Skírnir's Quest), and that

---

[1] I do not reckon the Njörd-Skaði dialogue as part of a separate poem, as it is
sometimes thought that the extant strophes formed the whole poem. Saxo quotes them,
but assigns them to different (human) speakers.

they were all in chant-metre. There is hardly enough of the fragments to give any indication of date or place of origin.

Two other strophes of chant-metre remain to be discussed : one in the *Second Lay of Helgi Hundingsbane*, and the other in *Hamðir's Lay*. The latter follows a speech-metre strophe (28) in which Hamðir has expressed the opinion that he and Sörli might not have been overcome by superior force if they had had with them their half-brother Erp, whom they slew on the way. In the speech-metre poem Sörli replies (str. 30) "we have fought a good fight,...whether we die to-day or to-morrow," but the chant-metre strophe is inserted first:

I think it beseems us not, that we two should each set on the other, after the fashion of wolves: like the hounds of the norns, who raven, reared in the wilderness[1].

This strophe evidently does not belong to the context at all: it is in the present tense and should be in the past. Moreover the dual number, "we two," does not fit the case of the trio of brothers—Hamðir and Sörli united against Erp. And, further, as we have the tradition there was no reciprocity in the fight: the two fell on Erp and killed him. All that we can say is that the strophe may refer to any fight between two persons connected by blood or marriage, or by such a bond as that of foster-brotherhood[2].

The remaining chant-metre strophe, in the *Second Lay of Helgi Hundingsbane*, clearly belongs to a poem on the same subject as that dealt with in the extant poem. In str. 28, as we have seen, Helgi tells Sigrún how he has slain her father and brother, ending with the words: "This slaughter was no work of thine, but thou wast fated to be the cause of strife among the mighty[3]." A prose

---

[1]   Ekki hygg ek okr vesa   ulfa dæmi
                    at vit mynim sjálfir of sakask
              sem grey norna   þau's gráðug eru
                    í auðn of alin.

[2] Niedner regards it as from the old *Káruljóð*, but it cannot be said to fit the circumstances of that poem unless the words are wrested from their apparent meaning.

[3] Str. 28 3 of the extant poem seems to paraphrase the first half of the chant-metre strophe, apparently intentionally modifying the intimation contained in the latter that Sigrún was to blame. The suggestion of Edzardi, *Germania* 23, p. 116, that the chant-metre strophe can be transposed into old-lore metre and was probably originally composed in it, is not convincing, since there is no motive which could have induced anyone to remodel one strophe in chant-metre in a poem in old-lore metre.

"aside" adds: *Sigrún wept*—and then follows the chant-metre strophe. Helgi says:

Take comfort, Sigrún   a Hild hast thou been to me,
Kings cannot withstand Fate.

Sigrún said: Fain would I that some should live   who now are dead
and yet would I clasp thee in my arms[1].

We must postulate a lost, and therefore probably an earlier poem, on the loves of Helgi and Sigrún, and in this we have the support of Professor Sijmons. In a significant passage in his monumental Introduction to the Edda Poems he observes that the fragments of the Helgi lays have preserved the dramatic manner of the dialogue poems, though in taking over the metre of the narrative poems they have suffered an approximation to the style[2]. Thus he evidently regards the chant-metre strophe as a fragment of an older poem in that metre.

To judge by the very full prose comments supplied to the extant Lay the older poem must have contained supernatural features obliterated in the Lay. On learning that she has been betrothed to Hoðbrodd Sigrún "*rode with valkyries over air, over water, to seek Helgi...*" After strophe 18 we are told: "*Helgi collected a great fleet and went to Frekasteinn, and was overtaken by a perilous storm at sea: lightnings played above them, and the flashes struck the ship. They saw that nine valkyries rode in the air and they recognized Sigrún: then the storm abated and they came safely to land.*" In the prose after str. 29 we learn that "*Dag Högnason sacrificed to Odin that he might avenge his father* (whom Helgi had killed): *Odin lent Dag his spear.* Dag found his brother-in-law *at the place called Fjöturlund* (Fetter Grove): *he drave the spear through Helgi...*"

Professor Sijmons[3] regards the prose of this Lay as the composition of a later compiler. Odin's lending his spear to Dag he considers to be a deduction from str. 34, which attributes all the tragedy to Odin because he put "runes of strife" (sakrúnar) between

---

[1] Str. 29.   Huggask þú Sigrún!   Hildr hefr oss verit;
               vinnat skjǫldungar skǫpum!

       Sigrún kyaþ: Lifna mundak kjósa   es liðnir 'ru
               knǽttak þó þér i faþmi felask.

[2] *Einleitung,* p. cccxliv.

[3] *Zur Helgi Sage,* Beitr. IV. p. 168, and *Einleitung,* p. clvi.

kinsmen. But it is difficult to see why a late compiler should read into these lines the lending of a spear as an answer to a sacrifice by Dag. He regards the late *First Lay of Helgi Hundingsbane* (str. 26) as the source of the sea-storm paragraph, but this strophe describes, not a storm, but a sea-battle. It therefore seems safer to assume that the compiler of the prose founded it on reminiscences of the older poem. The obliteration of supernatural scenes is characteristic of the heroic style which has worked over the Lay, but all the supernatural scenes have their counterparts in Scandinavian story. Kára hovers over a battle-field in the guise of a swan in the lost poem *Káruljóð*; Dag's sacrifice to Odin has its parallel in the Balder story.

We have now reviewed all the poems and fragments of poems in this metre, and can distinguish a homogeneous group of poems composed in pre-Christian times, apparently in Norway. They are in a native metre, unknown outside Scandinavia, a metre which seems never to have flourished in Iceland[1], and which fell out of use in Norway on the advent of Christianity. Their form, the pure speech form, is a native form, and they deal with native traditions. In most of them gods and other supernatural beings are the protagonists, but even the heroic poems of the group seem to have been religious in the sense that divine or semi-divine beings interfere in the action and sway the destinies of the human actors. Moreover the human hero enters into relations with a supernatural bride.

With regard to the metre in which these poems are composed we may quote Professor Schück. "Singing verses, as distinct from spoken, were called *ljóð*. It appears that there was, anyhow in the North, a special term to denote the sung verse as distinct from the spoken verse; the former was termed *ljóð*. A special metre, *ljóðaháttr*...seems to have been developed for this sung verse, and it was presumably the customary one for hymns, oracles, spells, incantations and the like; or, in other words, for poems in

---

[1] The indifference of Icelanders to this metre is thus explained. As their native poets never composed in it (until after the classical period) they did not appreciate it, and sensitive as they were to fine points of metre, their disregard of this metre was such that they were capable of the barbarity of interpolating passages in old-lore metre into poems in chant-metre.

which a singing or chanted mode of recitation was adopted[1]."
Such ancient spells and incantations are actually preserved in
some of the *ljóðahåttr* poems, notably in *Hávamál*, *Skírnismál*
and in *Sigrdrífumál*, the last part of the Sigurd trilogy.

The strophic form of this verse seems also to speak for an
origin in chant or song. Whereas epic metre was either non-
strophic, as in Germany and England, or only arbitrarily strophic
as in the North, this chanted verse is strophic by the nature of
its structure. It falls naturally into two divisions of four lines.
Now strophic verse in all countries is intimately associated with
song, and usually with dance.

Our group of heathen Norwegian chant-metre poems is thus
taking a definite shape. They all deal with supernatural happen-
ings, and in distinction to the other Eddic poems, they are in a
metre intended to be sung or chanted. The speech of divine
persons (and of the human beings whose destinies they control)
is apparently represented by a kind of recitative. It is at least
a probable inference that where and while this convention was
in force, Edda poets would not compose poems in which divine
beings play a part, except in this metre. At least it may be
worth while to enquire into the date and provenance of such
poems in the spoken (old-lore) metre as introduce the direct
speech of gods. We should rather expect them to be either non-
Norwegian or post-heathen, for it would be a little surprising to
find heathen Norwegian poets using old-lore metre in such cases,
so long as a special type of chanted verse was in vogue, restricted
to native poems with religious or supernatural associations. From
this point of view it is significant that the only two Norwegian
skaldic poems to introduce the direct speech of gods, the tenth
century dirges *Eiríksmál* and *Hákonarmál*, are in chant-metre,
and that the only other trace of chant-metre in skaldic verse is
in *Hrafnsmál*, where a valkyrie is made the mouthpiece of the
poet.

---

[1] *Svenska Litteraturhistoria*, 2 Uppl. Bd. 1. p. 16. "Åtminstone nordiskt synes
man hafva en särskild term för att beteckna sångversen till skillnad från talversen, den
kallades *lioð*. Ett särskildt verslag, lioðahattr...synes hafva utbildats för denna sångvers
och var förmodligen den vanliga för hymner, orakelspråk, trollsånger, besvärjelser
o. d. eller med andra ord för de dikter, vid hvilka man begagnade sig af ett sjungande
eller halft sjungande föredrag." Cp. Sijmons, *Einl.* p. ccxxxvii.

We will first consider the pure speech-poems in old-lore metre, since the poems of the narrative type, such as the *Lay of Thrym*, may be considered to belong to a different class.

If, with Finnur Jónsson and Niedner, we are to regard *Hárbarðsljóð* as a mainly speech-metre poem interpolated with fragments of chant-metre, we must at once confess that it forms an exception to the rule enunciated above. But the results achieved by Finnur Jónsson in purging the poem of all prose have not convinced the majority of scholars, most of whom would agree with Sijmon's verdict that the work is not versified, but consists of free rhythmic prose, occasionally alliterative, and is perhaps an imitation of early improvised flytings. The language is not poetic but colloquial. Strictly speaking, therefore, it is not a poem at all, and it can therefore be set aside.

CHAPTER V

THE MYTHOLOGICAL POEMS IN OLD-LORE METRE

I. THE PURE SPEECH-POEMS

THE pure speech-poems in old-lore metre in which supernatural beings appear are: *Völuspá*, *Völuspá in skamma*, and *Hyndluljóð*. To these may be added the *Lay of Vegtam*, which is all but a speech-poem. In the second part there is the *Hel-Ride of Brynhild*, in which the interpellation of a giantess serves Brynhild as an excuse for a retrospective monologue. This poem is attributed by Mogk, Sijmons, and Finnur Jónsson to the eleventh century. Mogk and Sijmons regard it as Icelandic: Finnur Jónsson is disposed to attribute it to a Greenland poet. Thus in any case it falls outside the limits of our enquiry.

Among the mythological poems *Hyndluljóð* is the only pure speech-poem in which divine beings are made to talk old-lore metre. This in itself suggests that it would be wise to follow Mogk, Sijmons, Schück and Neckel in assigning the poem, in its present form, to late post-heathen times in Iceland (twelfth century). The title *ljóð*, however, suggests that it may be founded on an older poem in chant-metre, the measure of the *ljóð*. Olrik has demonstrated the probable existence of a poem on this subject in Norway at least as early as the tenth century[1].

The *Lay of Vegtam*, in which Odin communes with a sibyl, cannot be classed with the narrative poems: it is a dialogue-poem with a rather suspicious[2] introductory strophe in narrative. It is accepted as an early poem by Finnur Jónsson, is looked upon with suspicion by Sijmons and Heusler[3], and definitely declared

---

[1] (Norsk) *Hist. Tidskr.* III. R. Bd. III. p. 175 ff.

[2] Cp. Mogk, *Litgesch.* p. 582. This introductory strophe is practically the same as a strophe in *Thrym's Lay*.

[3] *Einleitnng*, p. cclxviii; Heusler, *Archiv f. d. neueren Sprachen*, 116 (1906), p. 269.

to be late by Schück[1], Neckel[2] and von Unwerth[3]. All these last assign it to Iceland[4].

As regards *Völuspá*, but for the fact that the sibyl or völva addresses Odin in the course of her monologue, we might fairly reckon her as a mere mortal, for we know that such prophetesses walked the earth. But though *Völuspá* is from the heathen period, it is generally admitted to be Icelandic[5].

The only other mythological speech-poem in old-lore metre, the *Short Prophecy of the Sibyl*, or *Völuspá in skamma*, is assigned by all to a very late period in Icelandic literature.

Thus none of the mythological speech-poems in old-lore metre are generally attributed to Norway. We now turn to the "mixed" poems, those containing an admixture of narrative verse.

II. "Mixed" Form—Narrative-Plus-Speech

Whereas we can trace at least fifteen poems in chant-metre, in all of which divine beings appear, we know only of three mythological poems in the "mixed" narrative-plus-speech form, *Rígsthula*, the *Lay of Hymir*, and the *Lay of Thrym*. With these we must include two poems which form a transition stage between the mythological and the heroic poems : the *Lay of Völund* and the *Song of the Quern* (Gróttasöngr).

Of these five poems the *Lay of Hymir* is attributed to Iceland by all scholars except Finnur Jónsson, who allows that country no part in the mythological poems. It is of a pronouncedly skaldic type.

The *Song of the Quern* contains some narrative verses[6], but is mainly a chant by the giantesses Fenja and Menja. They are condemned by King Fróði of Denmark to grind gold from the magic quern, and at last, weary of their unremitting toil, they prophesy their master's defeat and death, and grind out armed men. It is usually considered an early poem, but Mogk is doubtful

---

[1] *Studier i nord. relig. och litt. historia*, II. 27.
[2] Neckel, *Beiträge zur Eddaforschung* (1908), p. 63.
[3] *ZfdPh.* 1916, p. 103 (in a review on Neckel's *Studien*).
[4] Mogk (*Litgesch.* p. 582) regards it as dependent on *Völuspá*.
[5] Except by Finnur Jónsson.
[6] Neckel, *ZfdA.* XLVIII. 168 f., maintains that these are later additions.

as to this, and regards it as the work of an Icelander who had visited Denmark. Sijmons regards it as tenth century Norwegian. Finnur Jónsson, while dating it c. 950–975[1], observes that its language precludes its being ascribed to an early period. His reason for assigning this date is that str. 19 says: "A fire I see to eastward, war-spies watch, those are called beacons." The Norwegian King Hákon the Good ordered beacons to be set on hills about the middle of the tenth century. But the explanation— "those are called beacons"—seems better to fit the theory of an audience who were totally unacquainted with such bonfires, than of a Norwegian one, every child in which would know what a war-beacon was.

One peculiarity of the poem has hardly received the notice it deserves. Fenja and Menja declare themselves in str. 9 to be the kin of the giants Hrungnir and Thjazi, and go on to describe their way of life in words which suggest upheavals of the earth's surface; such as were familiar to Icelanders alone of the Scandinavian races:

> As maids we toiled at mighty labours
> and tossed about the terraced mountains.
>
> 12. And rocks we rolled o'er giants' dwellings
> so that the earth thereat went trembling[2].

Then (str. 13) they appear as valkyries, or norns, foreknowing fate:

> We fore-wise twain did follow armies[3].

The next lines suggest the amazon of late legend:

> We baited bears and battered shields
> and rushed through ranks of grey mailed warriors.
>
> · · · · · ·
>
> 15. Fame we earned for feats in battle:
> With sharpened spears we sheared asunder
> bleeding wounds while brands we reddened.

Giantesses—prophetesses—valkyries—amazons—bond-maidens —it looks as if a late tradition had woven all the romantic female

---

[1] *Litt. hist.* I. p. 217.

[2] Eiríkr Magnússon's translation (*Gróttasöngr*, Viking Club, 1910).

[3] E. Magnússon, *Gróttasöngr*, observes (13. 22): "hereby the giantesses give themselves the character of *völur*, or even *nornir*, sorceresses, and repeat it again in v. xiii., where they figure further in the guise of *valkyrior*."

figures of the past into these two beings. The identification of valkyries with giantesses is especially suspicious. Olrik, who regards
the poem as of tenth century Orkney origin[1], reconciles these
varied activities of the giantesses on the ground that they personify
mountain streams, which first carry huge boulders down the valley,
and are then used to turn these, when they are fashioned by men
into mill-stones. Even so, however, he has to regard str. 14 and
15 as interpolations. If his view is taken, the poem cannot possibly be of Norwegian origin, since water-mills were unknown
there in the tenth century.

The Orkneys still have a memory of Fenja and Menja ; and
as regards the localisation of the legend we are in complete accord
with Professor Olrik. But why should personifications of mountain
streams have prophetic gifts ? And is it necessary to cut out the
otherwise unexceptionable str. 14 and 15 ? It seems to us simpler
to regard the poem as a late treatment of an old story. But
this is inessential. The point of importance for us is that it is
probably non-Norwegian.

The *Lay of Völund* and *Rígsthula* can profitably be classed
together, for scholars regard them both as showing foreign influence. *Rígsthula* is only a fragment, but it contains some fifty
strophes, and is remarkable among the Eddic poems in that it is
devoid of dialogue, the apostrophe of a bird to the hero being the
only direct speech contained in it. It is generally regarded as
betraying Celtic influence, and most scholars attribute its composition to one of the Scandinavian colonies in Great Britain or
Ireland. Its date is a subject of controversy.

The first part of the *Lay of Völund* recounts Völund's relations
with supernatural swan-maidens in a purely narrative but somewhat confused style. The second part tells, largely in speech-form,
of Völund's capture by King Niðuð, his imprisonment on an island,
and his final escape by flying after he has taken a terrible revenge.
Only the first part of the poem can really be said to deal with
supernatural beings, for though Völund is called the "King of the
elves" in both parts, he shows no supernatural attributes[2]. His

---

[1] *DH.* i. pp. 280 ff.

[2] For instance he cannot fly away until he has provided himself either with wings
or with a "flying" ring: the poem is not clear on this point.

great skill at the forge is a capacity associated in the North with dwarves rather than with elves.

The introductory part with the supernatural maidens resembles the more lengthy mythological introduction which is all we have of *Rígsthula*, in that it contains no direct speech. Just as *Rígsthula* has been suspected of Celtic affinities, so this introduction has been declared to be a loan from some such tales as are contained in the *Mabinogion*[1]. For the second part, Bugge has pointed out resemblances between its phraseology and the references to Wayland in the Anglo-Saxon poem *Deor's Lament*, and has suggested that both learnt the tale from a common Anglo-Saxon source. The form *Völund* is held to indicate a loan from Anglo-Saxon, whether through poetry or oral tradition[2]. On the other hand the place names and the name *Thakkráðr* (Tancred) point to German sources[3]. The poem is generally held to be early.

There remains the *Lay of Thrym*, which is usually regarded as a Norwegian poem of about 900. It narrates the ruse by which Thor regained his hammer from the giant Thrym. But before we discuss this poem in detail we may pause to make some general reflections on the form of the Norwegian Eddic poems. The mass of the mythological poems are, as we have already seen, in chant-metre, that is to say in dialogue form. Of the five mythological poems in mixed narrative and speech-form two show strong foreign influence; one is probably ultimately of Orkney origin, and one is from Iceland. That is to say, with the possible exception of Thrym's Lay *all the mythological poems composed in Norway on native subjects are in pure speech-form.* Among the heroic poems also the poems on native subjects—the Helgi lays and the Sigurd trilogy—are in pure speech-form[4]. Only in the poems of foreign

---

[1] Schück, *Nordisk Tidskr.* 1903, p. 222. He regards the introductory part as an independent poem; so also Neckel, *Beiträge*, p. 281, who casts doubt on the antiquity of either part.

[2] Mogk, *Litgesch.* p. 609.

[3] Peculiar to this Lay is the short speech of a half-line—Göngum baug sjá, which has no counterpart in Northern Eddic verse. Also the broken line: "'Vel ek' kvað Völundr," which is equally unique. Such short remarks are permissible in German poems: cp. Heusler, *ZfdA.* XLVI. pp. 236 ff.

[4] The strophe and a half of narrative verse in Hhu II. is admittedly from a later

origin—those on the Nibelungen and Ermanaric cycles—do we find the mixed form of narrative verses interspersed with speech. The evidence of the Edda is borne out by Saxo, who knows no heroic poetry which is not in the pure speech-form, and also by the poets of the *Fornaldar Sögur* or legendary sagas. When these later poets set about imitating what they regarded as typical Eddic verse, they adhere rigidly to the dialogue form. Both Saxo's poems and those of the *Fornaldar Sögur* deal only with Scandinavian stories.

Thrym's Lay is thus the one possible exception to the rule that Norwegian Eddic poems on native subjects are invariably in pure speech-form. Is it feasible to maintain that this Lay alone represents the traditional form of the Eddic poem, an archetype from which nearly a score of other poems on native subjects have mysteriously diverged? Surely its resemblance in form to the poems on borrowed subjects renders a different conclusion almost inevitable. It is an attempt by a fairly early poet to use the new form on a native subject; and its style, closely examined, may be detected as dependent partly on the *Fragmentary Sigurd Lay*, one of the earliest[1] of the poems on the foreign model, and partly on a skaldic poem. Its position as a Norwegian poem will also be found to be far from unassailable. But since these points do not affect our argument we will relegate their discussion to the excursus following this chapter.

Instead of assuming a perverted taste which led the Norwegians to clothe so many poems in dialogue form, it will be wiser as well as more just to conclude that until the great influx of foreign material the Norwegians were unacquainted with the epic style of mingled narrative and speech. The speech-form was the traditional Eddic type, and in it they treated the homespun stuff of native tradition until the vast mass of foreign material became available, and with it the foreign form of narrative interwoven with speech, in which these tales presumably reached the North

---

poem : so also the half-strophe in Hhj. Heusler, *Dialog.* pp. 190 ff., does not reckon these poems as containing narrative verse.

[1] So Heusler, who in his *Lieder der Lücke*, pp. 26 ff., points out much evidence in favour of an early date for this poem.

Not for the first time in literature would the style have been borrowed with the subject-matter.

At the dawn of history we find the Northerners with two extremes in literary modes; the speech-poem and the purely narrative skaldic verse. The former is evidently of native origin: the latter has often been suspected of Celtic affinities. However this may be, it is instructive to observe that the poets never succeeded in fusing the two into an epic style, even with foreign models to help them. Even the most narrative of the later lays is modified by the hand of ancient tradition.

The short epic lay, the form in which most of the Nibelungen and the Ermanaric poems appear in the Edda, is usually regarded as the matured product of the Heroic Age. It cannot surprise us that Norway should not have participated in the earlier creative stages of this literary activity. For the Norwegians play no part in the stories of the Heroic Age. They are outside it, as the Ionians are outside the purview of the Homeric Age. The parallel may perhaps be pushed a little further. During the Heroic Age and the century following it the Norwegians were probably too poor to attract the foreign Court minstrel with all the heroic songs of Teutondom stored in his memory. But when, on the decay of the Frisian sea-power, the Norwegians won a sudden affluence, we may imagine that foreign minstrels were glad to frequent the courts of her kings. It was a time when the rise of a new world, and the reaction after generations of ceaseless activity, were beginning to dull the ears of the English and German nobility to the music of their forefathers' songs, while Frankish heroic poetry had died with the death of the old Frankish tongue.

Thus it came about that an alien heroic poetry was grafted upon Norwegian literature, and flowered a second time in Norway and in Iceland. There is a curious likeness in the lot of these peoples and that of the Ionians[1]. Both were the means of transmitting to posterity, in a style and metre they did not invent, the heroic poetry of an age in which they played no part. They glorify their own greatness by bringing a finer art to bear on the exploits of an age in which they were unknown and unsung, just

---

[1] The parallel here expressed was suggested to me by Professor Chadwick.

as the author of *Beowulf* honours his Anglo-Saxon king by stories of a heroic age in distant Scandinavia.

EXCURSUS TO CHAPTER V

Thrym's Lay

The *Lay of Thrym* is universally considered to be a Norwegian poem of an early period—from between 850 and 900. Its simplicity and vigour are sometimes alluded to as early characteristics, but the real reason for assigning an early date to it appears to be in the metrical form of certain lines. Instead of a minimum of four syllables, two lines in the poem contain only three. These are *þrúðugr áss* 17² and *þege þú Þórr* 18³. It is pointed out that both would become normal four-syllabled lines if we read the older forms **ǫsur* for *áss* and **Þóarr* for *Þórr*. These are by no means the only three-syllabled lines in the Edda[1]: it only happens that they are susceptible of being made into four-syllabled lines by inserting archaic forms. But if the form *Þóarr* be assumed in the three-syllabled line in this Lay, it must also be assumed in the later *Lay of Hymir* (dáðrakkr Þórr 23²). There is one other passage where it must certainly be substituted for the shorter form. This is in the *Þórsdrápa* of Eilíf Guðrúnarson, an Icelandic skald who composed his poem on Thor about the year 1000. Curiously enough we have no earlier instance of the skaldic use of this form. It is evidently one of those archaic forms permitted in poetry where metre demands it. And there is no reason to suppose that the other line—*þrúðugr áss*, "doughty god"—should be anything different. It has all the air of a fixed formula. We should note that the metre precludes the use of the older form in str. 2.—"*áss er stolinn hamri.*"

As far as these forms are concerned, the evidence may be said to be as much in favour of the conscious archaism of a later poet as of an early date. Is it only a coincidence that the Lay shares the use of the form **Þóarr* only with Icelandic poets[2]?

There is one other circumstance which points in the direction of a later date; namely the deliberate end-rhyme employed in the first half-strophe:

> (v)reiþr vas Vingþórr   es *vaknaði*
> ok síns hamars   *of saknaði;*

The nearest approach to such a marked rhyme occurs in the late Greenlandic *Atlamál*, where we have *þrír tegir* rhyming with *víglegir*; and in another poem suspected of Greenlandic origin, the *Short Sigurd Lay*[3]. Intentional

---

[1] Sievers, *Altgerm. Metrik*, §45. 2.

[2] It is perhaps significant that Vigfússon and F. Jónsson (*Litt. Hist.* p. 147) assume the *Lay of Thrym* to be by the same author as the *Lay of Vegtam*, which is definitely assigned to Iceland by many scholars.

[3] Sig. sk. 3, ætti: knætti.

rhyme such as this occurs very rarely in the mythological poems : once in *Völuspá*, once in a fragment of mnemonic verse, twice in the *Lay of Hymir* and once in one of the interpolated passages in old-lore metre in *Hávamál*. It also occurs in what Sijmons regards as interpolated strophes in *Skírnismál* and *Vafthrúðnismál*[1]. *Völuspá*, the Hymir Lay and the mnemonic verse are certainly Icelandic.

Curiously enough Thrym's Lay also contains one of the few cases of intentional assonance—or so Sijmons regards it :

> 24. Einn át oxa   átta laxa.

Such assonance seems intentional twice in *Völuspá*, but nowhere else in the mythological poems[2], so that this again is apparently an Icelandic feature. There is of course no inherent impossibility in the Icelandic origin of a poem dated about 900.

Jessen has said that it is "self evident" that the epic form in which this lay is cast is older than the dialogue form of *Skírnismál*, in which there is an equal amount of incident. Since the *Lay of Thrym* is the only pure example, among the mythological poems, of this supposedly earlier type, it will be interesting to examine the relation in which it stands to such a poem as *Skírnismál*. There are some remarkable parallels between the two[3]. At the outset we may observe that since so much rests on this one poem, it is a pity that it is itself so far on the way to becoming a speech-poem. Without adding any more "stage directions" than in *Skírnismál*, we can get the whole story in speech-form. We print the narrative parts in a separate column, and in another column we note affinities to other poems.

Thrym's Lay

Narrative	Speech
1 Wrath was Ving-Thor when he awakened and found his hammer not at hand. He shook his beard and tossed his locks, the son of Earth groped about him.	[*Thor awoke one day and missed his hammer. He was very wrath and said:*]
2 And of words this was the first he spake:	Hearken, Loki, hear what I tell : It is not known on all the earth nor yet in high heaven: Thor is reft of his hammer !

---

[1] Sijmons, ccxlvi.

[2] Sijmons, ccxlvii. It also occurs in Sig. sk. 3: ungi: kunni.

[3] Niedner, *ZfdA.* xxx. p. 149, postulates an earlier *Skírnismál* in epic style like the *Lay of Thrym*.

3 They went to the fair
   dwellings of Freyja
   and of words this
   was the first he spake:

Wilt thou, Freyja
lend me thy feather-coat
that I perchance
may find my hammer?

(*Skírnismál* 8.)
Skírnir said:
Give me the steed
that will bear me safe
thro' the flickering flame
and the sword which wages
war of itself
against the race of giants.

4   *Freyja said:*

I would give it thee
tho' 'twere of gold,
and grant it
tho' 'twere of silver.

9 *Frey said*:
I give thee the steed
which will bear thee safe
etc.

5 Flew Loki then
   the feather-coat re-
      sounded
   until he came outside
   the Aesir's dwellings
   and came within
   the lands of the giants.

10 *Skírnir said to his horse*:
It is dark without.
'Tis time for us, I ween
to fare over the damp fells
over the giant folk:
Together we shall win
   through,
or together he'll take us,
that awful giant.

6 Thrym sat on a howe
   the lord of giants
   for his hounds
   he plaited golden leashes
   and of his steeds
   he smoothed the manes.

[*Loki flew* into Jötun-
heim. He *flew* to where
Thrym sat on a howe
(plaiting leashes for his
hounds and combing the
manes of his steeds)].

Prose: *Skírnir rode* into
Jötunheim *to the dwelling
of Gymir. There were fu-
rious hounds before the gate
in the enclosure where
Gerð's hall was.* He *rode
to where the shepherd* sat on
a howe *and greeted him:*

7   *Thrym said:*

How goes it with Aesir
how with the elves?
Why art thou come alone
into Jötunheim?

17 *Gerð said:*
Who art thou, of elves
or of Aesir's sons
or of the wise Vanir?

             Loki said:

Ill goes it with the Aesir
ill with the elves:
hast thou hidden
the hammer of Hlórriði?

18
Of elves I am not
nor of Aesir the son,
nor of the wise Vanir.

8   *Thrym said:*

I have hidden
the hammer of Hlórriði
eight leagues
below the earth:
It no man shall
win back again
unless he bring me
Freyja to wife.

9 Flew Loki then
   the feather-coat rustled
   until he came outside
   the lands of the giants
   and came within
   the Aesir's dwellings:
   Thor he met
   midway in the court
   and of words this
   was the first he spake:

[*Then* Loki flew *home.*
Thor *was standing without
and he* (*greeted him and*)
asked for tidings:]

*Then Skírnir rode home.
Frey was standing without,
and he greeted him and
asked for tidings.*

10

Hast thou tidings
to equal thy toil?
Say thy long tale
here in the open
oft he who speaks sitting
tells a stumbling tale
and he who speaks recum-
bent
oft utters a lie.

40 Tell me, Skírnir
ere thou cast saddle from
the steed,
or stirrest one step forward,
what thou didst win
in Jötunheim
of my will and thine?

11   *Loki said:*

I have had toil
and also good tidings:
Thrym has thy hammer,
The lord of giants,
It no man shall
Win back again
Unless he bring him
Freyja to wife.

Hhj. 5. I have had toil
and no good tidings

12 They go to seek
The fair Freyja
and of words this
was the first he spake:

Gird thyself, Freyja
In bridal linen,
we two shall drive
into Giant-land.

13 Wrath was Freyja
she snorted
the whole hall of the
Aesir
trembled thereat:
the great Brísing torque
burst asunder.

[*Freyja said*]
Thou shalt know me
most wanton of women,
If I drive with thee
into giant-land.

14 Straightway the Aesir
Met all in council
And the goddessess
All in parley
And took counsel to-
gether
The mighty powers
How they might win
The hammer of Hlórriði.

Cp. Völuspá. 6. 9. 23. 25.

15 Then said Heimdall
The whitest of Aesir
—Well could he foretell
Like other Vanir—

[*Heimdall said*]
Let us gird on Thor then
the bridal linen,
let him wear
the great Brísing torque!

16 Let us from him
hang the jingling keys,
And women's weeds
let fall round his knees
on his breast
the broad stones
and with skill the wimple
let us bind round his head!

17 Then said Thor
   The valiant god :

              [*Thor said*]
       Womanish they
       will call me, the Aesir,
       If I let myself be girt
       in bridal linen.

18 Then said Loki
   Laufey's son :

              [*Loki said*]
       Utter not, Thor
       such words as these:
       straightway will the giants
       come dwell in Asgard
       Unless thou fetchest
       thy hammer to thee.

19 They girt on Thor then
   the bridal linen,
   and the great
   Brísing torque,
   they hung from him
   the jingling keys,
   and women's weeds
   let fall round his knees
   on his breast
   the broad stones
   and with skill the wimple
   they bound round his
     head.

20 Then said Loki
   Laufey's son:

       I also with thee
       will be thy wench
       we two maids will drive
       into Giant-land.

21 At once the goats
   were driven home,
   harnessed to the poles
   well should they run :
   Rent were the mountains
   earth was aflame
   Odin's son drove
   Into Giant-land.

                                                        Thjóðólf's shield-song :
                                               The whole vault of holy
                                       heaven blazed before the
                                       path of Ull's stepfather
                                       (Thor): but down below the
                                       earth was whipped with
                                       hail, when the goats drew
                                       the chariot-god to the tryst
                                       with Hrungnir (i.e. to giant-
                                       land): the earth was all but
                                       rent. The cliffs quaked, and
                                     the hills brast asunder.

22 Thus spake Thrym
   the lord of giants:

              [*Thrym said:*]
       Rise up, ye giants,
       And strew the benches
       Now ye bring me
       Freyja to wife,
       Njörd's daughter
       from Nóatún.

                                                        Alv. i. [Deck] the benches
                                       now a bride with me
                                       shall wend her homeward
                                     way.

23

       There wander in my yard
       Gold horned kine
       Oxen all swart
       To pleasure the giant,

                                                         Sk. 22. Gerð (the giantess)
                                       said

Much store have I of trea-
sure,
Much store of jewels
Meseems I lack
Nought but Freyja.

I lack not gold
In Gymir's courts,
Nor to share my father's
wealth.

24 Swiftly drew
the day to evening,
and ale was borne
before the giants:
Alone he ate an ox
eight salmon
all the dainties
set for the women
The husband of Sif
drank three tuns of mead.

(*At the feast Thor ate
and drank a great deal.
Thrym said:*)

25 Then spake Thrym
the lord of giants.

Where saw ye a bride
more sharply set?
ne'er saw I wenches
eat more heartily
nor a maiden quaff
so deeply of mead.

26 The crafty maid
sat beside:
who found an answer
to the giant's speech:

[*Loki said*]
No whit ate Freyja
For eight nights
So eager was she
for Giant-land.

27 *He bent under the wimple,*
he longed to kiss
but started back
the length of the hall:

(*Thrym bent to kiss Freyja but started back and said:*)

Why is so fierce
the glance of Freyja?
meseemed from her eyes
flames are darting!

28 The crafty maid
sat beside,
who found an answer
to the giant's speech:

[*Loki said:*]
No whit slept Freyja
for eight nights,
so eager was she
for Giant-land.

29 In came the wretched
sister of giants,
who dared to ask
for a bridal gift.

[*The giant's sister said:*]
Take from thine arms
the ruddy rings
if thou would'st win
my love
my love
and all favours.

30 Then spake Thrym
the lord of giants:

[*Thrym said:*]
Bear in the hammer
to hallow the bride.

Lay Mjöllnir
on the maiden's knee;
let Vár hallow
our clasped hands !

31 The heart of Hlórriði
laughed in his breast,
when the doughty one
knew his hammer once
    more;
first he slew Thrym
the lord of giants
and lamed all
the race of the giant.

32 He slew the ancient   [*Thor took the hammer and*   (*Vafthrúðnismál* leaves
sister of giants   *said:*   the slaying to be under-
she who had begged   Cuffs shall ye gain   stood.)
for a bridal gift;   in place of coins
cuffs she gained   and blows of the hammer
in place of coins   for wealth of rings.]
and blows of the ham-
    mer
for wealth of rings:
So came Odin's son
by his hammer again.

The narrative parts of this poem are inessential.   In fact in certain passages they actually retard the action, as where Loki having urged the recalcitrant
Thor to obey the will of the gods, says he will also dress up and go with him
—evidently to induce Thor to consent to his own metamorphosis. This point
is lost entirely if the 14 lines of narrative telling how Thor was dressed up
(merely repeating Heimdall's speech) are inserted here.   Several of the
narrative passages suggest versification of prose "asides."   Thus the strophe:

    5. Flew Loki then   the feather-coat rustled
        until he came outside   the Aesir's dwelling-place
        and came within   the lands of the giants,

or: str. 9.   until he came outside   the lands of the giants
        and came within   the Aesir's dwelling-place,

looks like a laborious conversion into verse of a prose statement:

        Then Loki flew to Jötunheim—or back to Asgard.

The methods of introducing the speakers is often somewhat clumsy

        and of words this   was the first he spake,

occurring four times; and in str. 12 we are still left in doubt as to the
speaker. The lines introducing Heimdall—"well could he foretell like other
Vanir"—are out of place, since his prophetic powers are hardly in question
here.
    Str. 6, describing Thrym sitting on a howe, plaiting the gold leashes for
his hounds and—apparently at the same time—grooming his horses, might

well be inspired by a prose paragraph like that in *Skírnismál*, which also mentions the howe and the hounds.

Str. 21 cannot fail to remind us of the magnificent description in the ninth century shield-song by Thjóðólf, of Thor driving his goats to meet the giant Hrungnir. Here too the mountains are rent, and Thor's path is one of flame. Which description is the earlier? It is to be noted that in the skaldic poem Thor is driving in his own proper person, and Hrungnir is expecting him and not Freyja. Is all the sound and fury quite so much in place when Thrym is to believe that Freyja, and not Thor, is on the way? Are we to suppose that he does not know Thor's chariot, since he is apparently quite at ease on seeing it (str. 22) and at once decides that it contains, not Thor (whom he might equally expect), but Freyja—Freyja who has other means of locomotion at her disposal? There is another interesting point in this passage. The Norwegian skald remembers Thor's connection with the thunder, and in fact it is still remembered in Norway : the sky is ablaze, but on earth there is a furious storm, and what we may take to be the crashing of thunder. The author of the Lay, too, makes Thor drive from Asgard to Jötunheim, he too makes the mountains quake—but with him it is the *earth* which is aflame. The tumultuous passage of the Thunder-god's chariot across the sky has called up other images to his mind—scenes of rending mountains and the solid earth afire. Where could he have looked on such a scene but during a volcanic eruption in Iceland?

If we might hazard a conjecture as to the genesis of the Lay, we should say that it was composed on a well-known myth by an early Icelandic poet who sought inspiration from a chant-metre poem like *Skírnismál* and from Thjóðólf, and that so far from being nearly the last of a long line, it owes its charm and vigour, as well as a marked inequality of style, to the fact that it is one of the first poems in a new mode.

The resemblances of this Lay to the *Fragmentary Sigurd Lay* now become extremely significant. Heusler[1] ascribes this *Fragmentary Lay* to the ninth or tenth century, and regards it as the earliest of all the Nibelungen poems and the one nearest to its German sources. Once grant that this Lay is earlier than *Thrym's Lay* (which Heusler would clearly allow, since the latter is usually ascribed to about 900) and the close resemblances between the fragment and the *narrative parts only* of *Thrym's Lay* betray whence our Lay has adopted the new form of narrative plus speech. The resemblances have been pointed out by Heusler. In the first strophe *Thrym's Lay* adapts a rather unusual phrase from the Fragment :

13. (his) he began to toss his legs	fót *nam at* hræra	
he began to mutter many things	fjǫlð *nam at* spjalla	

Thrym's Lay has :

1. he began to shake his beard	skegg *nam at* hrista	
he began to toss his locks	skör *nam at* dyja.	

---

[1] *Lieder der Lücke*, p. 80.

More remarkable is the reproduction of the sound, but not the meaning of another phrase, which must be given in the original :

Fr. S. Lay. 10.   Hló þá Brynhilðr   bær allr dunði

Thr. 9.   Fló þá Loki   fjaðrhamr dunði.

One of these means : "Laughed then Brynhild, the whole building resounded" —the poet is describing her shrill mirthless laughter when she heard of Sigurd's death—and the other may be translated: "Flew then Loki, the feather-coat resounded." There can be little doubt that *Thrym's Lay* is here the borrower. So also with the phrase:

And of words this   was the first he (she) spake[1].

This is very finely used in the Fragment. The Gjukungs have slain Sigurd, and are returning to their hall.

6. Gudrun stood without,   the daughter of Gjuki
   and of words this   was the first she spake,
   "Where is Sigurd,   the lord of men
   since my kinsmen   lead the van?"

Gudrun's instantaneous perception of something amiss is well indicated by the words underlined.

The *Lay of Thrym* had few models for its "inquit"-formulas, and, as we have seen, it uses this no less than four times.

This close resemblance between the only early narrative mythological poem and what is perhaps the first extant Nibelungen lay in the foreign form is surely not to be put down to accident. The poet of *Thrym's Lay* was inspired to compose a mythological poem in the new style, and he did not achieve his purpose without a few cases of slavish imitation of his model. We shall show later, not only that the dialogue verses in the Lay have characteristics peculiar to the chant-metre poems, but also that it closely resembles them in other particulars.

There is thus a good deal of evidence going to show that *Thrym's Lay* was (1) modelled on an older chant-metre poem, (2) indebted to one of the Nibelungen Lays for its narrative style, and (3) composed in Iceland.

---

[1] Ok hann (hon) þat orða   alls fyrst um kvað.

CHAPTER VI

LOST POEMS IN CHANT-METRE

IT will be well to recapitulate the line of argument followed in the preceding chapters. Firstly we observed the consensus of opinion among scholars as to the pre-Christian date of the mass of the chant-metre poems. The deduction that the metre fell out of favour about the year 1000 suggested that it never took root in Iceland[1], and this idea was confirmed by observing that the Icelanders constantly interpolate strophes in old-lore metre into poems in chant-metre. Secondly we discovered that the use of chant-metre is limited to poems in which supernatural beings play a part, and that the pure speech-poems in old-lore metre treating of such beings are those which are generally admitted to be Icelandic.

It was now clear that the chant-metre speech-poem must be of an ancient traditional type. On examining the other mythological poems, those which contain narrative verses as well as speech-verses, we were struck by the fact that with the exception of *Thrym's Lay* they either showed foreign influence or were composed out of Norway. The inference was forced on us that the original type of mythological poem in Norway was exclusively in chant-metre—that is to say, in speech-form. Turning to the heroic poems we found that there also the poems on native subjects were in dialogue form, while those on borrowed subject matter were mainly in the mixed narrative-plus-speech-form.

We have thus reached a stage in our investigations at which we can affirm that certain mythological poems in the Edda are almost certainly of the heathen Norwegian period. It will be convenient to set a list of these by the side of those which we can definitely set aside as not belonging to the old Norwegian tradition.

---

[1] It is employed in twelfth and thirteenth century imitations of Eddic verse in Iceland.

Heathen Norwegian poems	Post-heathen Norwegian, Icelandic or Western[1] poems
Hávamál	
Vafthrúðnismál	Völuspá
Grímnismál	Lay of Hymir
Skírnismál	Lay of Thrym (in its present form)
Lokasenna	Hyndluljóð (in its present form)
Alvíssmál	Song of the Quern
Sigurd Trilogy	
Chant-metre fragments	

We have classed *Thrym's Lay* and *Hyndluljóð* in the non-Norwegian group on the grounds given above. But for *Thrym's Lay* we have seen reason to postulate an earlier chant-metre form, and this form must have been Norwegian. For *Hyndluljóð*, too, we must assume an earlier tenth century prototype, and this too must have been in chant-metre.

Hárbarðsljóð we have left out of account, as being imperfectly versified. Here again, however, we must reckon with the possibility that fragments of an old chant-metre poem have been filled up by a later author with rhythmic prose.

Can we trace any other mythological poems which must have belonged to the Norwegian group? Snorri's memory has preserved for us various fragments of mythological poems, and it will be well for us to establish their provenance, so far as this is possible. Some of them are merely *heiti*—versified lists of horse- and ox-names and other scraps of information in old-lore and speech-metre. They do not concern us here, for they can hardly be regarded as integral parts of a real poem. The first of the chant-metre fragments, too—Hár's bidding to Gylfi—may also have been a stray verse not incorporated in a poem, and the same is sometimes held to apply to the second fragment, the dialogue between Njörð and Skaði. This verse is cited by Saxo, who attributes the words to other and merely human speakers. But about the remaining chant-metre fragments there can be no manner of doubt. They are fragments of longer poems, and since they are in chant-metre, these poems must have been Norwegian.

---

[1] I.e. composed in a Scandinavian settlement on the coasts or islands of Great Britain.

We may well regret the *Heimdallargaldr*, the Spell-Song of Heimdall, from which the third fragment is taken[1], for it seems to have given a lively picture of Heimdall's adventures. Snorri says[2]: "It is said that he was pierced through by a man's head (used as a missile): that story is told in verse in *Heimdallargaldr*; and since then a head is called the 'bane of Heimdall.' Heimdall is the owner of Gulltopp; he is also 'he who visited Vágasker and Singasteinn'; that was when he fell out with Loki about the Brísing torque; he is also called Vindlér. Úlf Uggason composed a long piece in *Húsdrápa*[3] on that story, and it is there mentioned that they (Heimdall and Loki) were in the likeness of seals."

We cannot tell how much of all this came into *Heimdallargaldr*, but as it describes the slaying of Heimdall, it must clearly have been a poem of incident.

In the next fragment "one of the Vanir" asks Gná what she is, as she rides through the air on an errand for Frigg. This must surely have formed part of a poem of the same type as *Skírnismál*, in which Skírnir performs his mission for Frey.

The next fragment is of unusual interest. In the extant strophe the giantess Thökk refuses to weep for Balder. But the alliteration of the conversation reported by Snorri as between Frigg and Loki (the latter disguised as a woman), is obviously from a dialogue-poem[4] on Balder's fate, presumably the same. After the scene between Loki and Frigg follows the slaying, and then the grief of the gods. We can guess that a good deal of what Snorri gives in narrative or indirect speech was originally

---

[1] Heimdall says:

> "Of nine mothers I am the offspring
> Of nine sisters I am the son."

[2] *Skáldskaparmál*, ch. 8.

[3] Str. 2 of this poem runs: "The very wise, famous watcher of the paths of the gods goes with Farbauti's cunning son to Singasteinn: the valiant son of nine mothers comes first into possession of the gleaming stone: this I make known in one section of my poem." (F. J.) *Skjaldedigtning*, B., I. 128. The poet is describing the pictures on the wall.

[4] Gylf. ch. 48: þá mælti Frigg: "eigi munu *v*apn eða *v*iðir granda Baldri: *ei*ða hefi ek þegit af *ǫ*llum þeim." þá spyrr konan: "hafa *a*llir hlutir *ei*ða *u*nnit at *ei*ra Baldri?" þá svarar Frigg: "*v*ex *v*iðarteinungr einn fyrir *v*estan *V*alholl; sá er mistileinn *k*allaðr: sá þótti mér *u*ngr at *k*refja *ei*ðsins."

in dialogue[1]: all the passage describing the grief of the gods and
Odin's woe shows the alliteration very clearly, as also Frigg's
request that some one should go to Hel. The funeral scene offers
a curious mixture of comedy and tragedy: the gods cannot
launch the ship, and a giantess comes to their help: her steed,
a wolf, is so restive that it has to be felled and held down by
four berserks. Thor wants to kill the giantess, but is restrained.
Nanna breaks her heart and dies, her body is flung on to the
pyre, which Thor solemnly consecrates, incidentally kicking a
dwarf into the flames. Odin is present with his ravens, Frigg
beside him: Frey drives his boar, Freyja her cats: Heimdall is
mounted on his horse Gulltopp. Besides the gods many of the
frost-giants and mountain-giants attend the ceremony.

Fragment 7, in which Thor addresses the river Vimur, as he
fords it with Loki, and 8, in which he tells how he once put forth
all his might, both belong to a poem recounting Thor's visit to
Geirröð, a giant. Snorri clearly bases his account on the *Thórs-
drápa* of Eilíf Gudrúnarson, an Icelandic skald who flourished
about the end of the tenth century, but this Eilíf no doubt drew
on the Eddic poem.

There are two other stories recounted by Snorri which must
in all probability have had a chant-metre basis, though no verses
are extant. One is the story of Thor's fight with Hrungnir, a
giant, told in *Skáldskaparmál*, ch. 17. Snorri gives the skald
Thjóðólf as his authority, but as Heusler observes, the direct
speech in the story must almost certainly go back to a poem of
the chant-metre type[2]. Hrungnir has challenged Thor to a
duel. To assist their champion in the combat the giants make
a huge figure of clay, but have hardly finished settling a mare's
heart inside this Trojan, who is called Mökkrkálfi, when Thor
arrives. Thor's henchman, Thjálfi, advises Hrungnir to stand
on his shield, which he does; the whet-stone hurled by the giant

---

[1] Cp. the passage beginning: þá er Baldr var *f*allin, þá *f*ellusk *o̧*llum *á*sum or*ð*tǫk
ok svá *h*endr attaka til hans, ok sá *h*verr til annars, ok váru allir með *e*inum hug til þess
er *u*nnit hafði verkit:...*e*ngi mátti *o̧*rum segja frá sínum harmi; en Oðinn bar þeim
mun verst *s*kaða, sem haun kunni mesta *s*kyn, hversu mikil *a*ftaka ok missa *á*sum var
í frá*f*alli Baldrs...þá mælti Frigg, ok spurði hverr...*e*ignask vildi allar *á*stir hennar ok
*h*ylli, ok vili hann ri*ð*a á *H*elveg ok *f*reista ef hann *f*ái *f*undit Baldr....

[2] Heusler, *Dialog*, p. 213. For convenience sake we will call this poem *Hrungnismál*.

meets Thor's hammer in mid-air and is shattered, but a fragment
enters Thor's head, so that he falls. But Hrungnir's skull is
crushed by the hammer, and he falls too, one foot on Thor's
neck. No one can stir this until Thor's infant son arrives. In
the meantime Thjálfi had accounted for Mökkrkálfi, who fell
with little glory[1].

The addition to the story, narrating Gróa's attempted removal
of the fragment of whet-stone in Thor's head, after his return to
Asgard, was probably not treated in the same poem, as it forms
a distinct episode.

The other story is given in *Skáldskaparmál*, ch. 47 (50),
and deals with the half-mythical Hjaðning battle. Heðinn takes
Hild, Högni's daughter, by force. Högni pursues him and in
spite of Hild's somewhat ambiguous mediation refuses to come
to terms. Before the battle, however, Heðinn again offers his
father-in-law much gold. Högni answers—and the old alliteration
of the verse is clearly visible in his words[2]:

> Too late hast thou offered this, if it is peace thou desirest, for I have
> drawn Dáinsleif, which the dwarves made, and which must be a man's bane
> every time it is bared; and never does it fail in its stroke, nor the wound
> heal which is struck therewith.

Heðinn retorts:

> Thou boastest thy sword but not victory: that alone I call good which
> is faithful to its master.

They fight, and during the night all who have fallen, and all
weapons, become as rocks and stones, but every day the dead
are raised again by Hild's magic arts, and the weapons return
to their shape; and so the battle will go on every dawn until the
crack of doom.

Snorri adds: "The skald Bragi made verses on this subject
in the *drápa* on Ragnar Loðbrók." Bragi's verses are still extant,
but we do not need them to know that the dialogue reported

---

[1] K. Helm, *Altgerm. Religionsgesch.* I., Heidelberg, 1913, pp. 196 f., thinks that the
poem did not include Mökkrkálfi and Thjálfi, giving as his reason that they are not mentioned by the skald Thjóðólf. This is however accounted for by the fact that skaldic
poetry tended to avoid burlesque incidents.

[2] "Of síð bauttu þetta, ef þú vill sættask, þvíat nú hefi ek *d*regit *D*áinsleif er *d*ver-
garnir gerðu, er manns *b*ani skal verða hvert sinn er *b*ert er, ok *a*ldri *b*ilar i hǫggvi,
ok *e*kki *s*ár grær, ef þá *s*keinisk af." þá segir Heðinn "*s*verð hælir þú þar, en eigi *s*igri, ..."

above cannot be free from the pure narrative verse of the skalds. It must be from an Eddic poem, and since the poem is wholly lost, we may assume that it was not Icelandic. If it was Norwegian, we should expect it to have been in chant-metre. We have already suggested that the chant-metre strophe in *Hamðismál*, which is certainly out of place there, might belong to a lost poem on this subject. It would fit in perfectly where Heðinn calls to his father-in-law just before the battle, and offers him terms and much gold in compensation for the wrong done. At this point he might well urge:

> Surely it beseems us not   that after the fashion of wolves
>   we two should attack each other
> like the hounds of the norns,   who raven,
>   reared in the wilderness.

We will call this poem *Hjaðningamál*. Like the Sigurd trilogy, it is heroic saga interwoven with supernatural elements.

What of the other heroic poems? We have dismissed those dealing with the Nibelungen and Ermanaric cycles as owing their substance, and therefore possibly their form, to foreign models. There remain the two earlier Helgi Lays—the *Second Lay of Helgi Hundingsbane* and the Lay of *Helgi Hjörvarðsson*.

We have seen that the *Second Lay* originally contained supernatural elements which bring it into line with the chant-metre Sigurd trilogy, and the assumption, made by Sijmons, that this earlier poem was in chant-metre is supported by the presence, in the present poem, of a chant-metre strophe. The possibility that this strophe may be a late interpolation may be regarded as disposed of when we remember that chant-metre does not appear to have been a popular metre in Iceland, and that though the Edda poems are full of interpolations in old-lore metre, there is no case of obvious interpolation in chant-metre[1].

Professor Sijmons holds the same view with regard to the Lay of *Helgi Hjörvarðsson*, in its present form also in old-lore metre. The worst preserved of all the Eddic poems, this poem tells its story so confusedly as to be barely intelligible. It seems in fact a jumble of elements from more than one story,

---

[1] It will be seen later that the implication in the chant-metre strophe that Sigrún was responsible for the slaughter shows a link with ancient Norwegian ideas.

and it is suspected of being made up of fragments from several poems. At least it may be said that the story belongs to Scandinavia, probably to Denmark. Mogk follows Bugge in regarding it as of Western origin—composed in Great Britain or Ireland. Finnur Jónsson attributes it to Norway.

There are two points which in the light of our previous investigations corroborate Prof. Sijmon's theory that this poem, like the *Second Lay of Helgi Hundingsbane*, is based on an earlier chant-metre poem. One of them is that the prose paragraphs contain supernatural features—the heroine, Sváva, is a valkyrie who protects Helgi in battle: one of the characters is metamorphosed into an eagle; a troll-woman riding a wolf appears and fatally influences the course of the story, so that she cannot be dismissed as an invention of the prose commentator. The second is that the poem actually contains, in the episode of Hrímgerð, nineteen strophes of chant-metre, which there is no reason to dismiss as a late interpolation. It is the only one of the three heroic "flytings" to use chant-metre, and is at the same time the only one to introduce a supernatural element—the giantess Hrímgerð—so we may safely regard it as an integral part of the old poem. We have already traced in the rest of the Lay the blurred outlines of the supernatural, overlaid, it is true, with prose[1], but still a marked feature of the plot. It seems safe to assume that the whole Lay had a chant-metre prototype, and that the Western or Icelandic poet who recast it in the heroic style, purging it of the supernatural as best he could, did not trouble to remodel the flyting episode, which he would probably regard as unworthy of a heroic poet. Yet we can see from Saxo's stories that it was customary for heroes to engage in recrimination of this type.

Another heroic poem, now lost, is referred to in the prose conclusion in the *Second Lay*:

Sigrún soon died of grief and misery. It was the belief of men in old times that people were born again, but that is now reckoned an old wives' tale. It is said that Sigrún and Helgi were born again: he was then Helgi Haddingjaskati, and she Kára Hálfdan's daughter, as is recited in Káruljóð; and she was a valkyrie.

---

[1] There is an allusion to the supernatural intervention of the valkyrie in str. 26 (*Hrímgerðarmál*).

Fortunately a late legendary saga, that on Hrómund Greips-son, preserves the outline of this story. Helgi fights for the two Haddings, kings of Sweden. In a battle against one King Óláf in Denmark Helgi swung his sword so high that it struck his love Lára (Kára), who was fluttering above the battle-field in the form of a swan. Lára fell dead, and his antagonist Hrómund killed Helgi, whose previous successes in the fray are put down to Lára: "she chanted such mighty spell-songs that none of Óláf's men thought of defending himself."

The title of the poem—*ljóð*—chant, and its supernatural elements, render it more than probable that it was in chant-metre, and that it should be added to the group of native Norwegian poems.

CHAPTER VII

ICELANDIC TRADITION AND THE NORWEGIAN POEMS

THE result of these investigations justifies us in formulating, at least tentatively, the rule: *The Norwegian Eddic poems on native subjects all contain supernatural elements, and all were originally in chant-metre.* This brings us to the end of a definite stage in our investigations. We gain, for instance, a far more adequate idea of the influence of the Nibelungen poems on old Norwegian literature. We can understand that the chant-metre recitative, weighted with its religious associations, was not deemed suitable for the new subjects, about which there clung no flavour of the supernatural. They were composed in a measure used by Court poets to glorify great men, the "old-lore" metre of runic inscriptions, of genealogical poems and battle-lays, a metre identical with the epic metre of England and Germany, whence the new songs came to the North. After a time the two styles re-acted on one another. The native dialogue style was used on the new material—in fact from the first the native poets had found a difficulty in the introduction of a due proportion of narrative verse, and an insuperable difficulty in representing the progress of events in narrative. On the other hand, they began to recast the ancient heroic poetry in the new semi-narrative style. Finally—but, it would seem, not until they reached Iceland—they retold some of the old tales about the gods in narrative style and in old-lore metre[1].

To reach this point of our argument we have not had to offer any startling new theories on the date of a single Eddic poem. It has only been necessary to concentrate our minds on the poems treating of obviously native subjects. If the reader once grants that poems on borrowed subjects are not likely to give the most

---

[1] Or, still more frequently, in skaldic verse.

faithful reflection of the native form, he can hardly refuse to follow us all the way.

There is one other point which should be dealt with here. It will be observed that all the lost mythological poems of which we have any knowledge must be classed under the head of incident-poems, poems which depict a lively series of scenes such as Thor's fight with Hrungnir, his visit to Geirröð, the stirring adventures of Heimdall, and Gná's quest. The proportion between incident-poems and what we may term the conversation-poems (though those too work up to a dramatic climax) is thus very different from that prevailing in the extant Eddic collection. The following is a list of all the poems which we venture to regard as Norwegian, arranged under these two heads.

An asterisk denotes a poem for which we postulate a Norwegian prototype in chant-metre. Poems surviving only in fragments of one or two strophes are in round brackets. The titles of poems of which no verse is extant are given in square brackets.

Conversation-poems	*Incident-poems*
Hávamál.	Skírnismál.
Vafthrúðnismál.	⎧Reginsmál.
Grímnismál.	⎨Fáfnismál.
Lokasenna.	⎩Sigrdrífumál.
*Hárbarðsljóð?	*Thrym's Lay.
*Hyndluljóð.	⎧*Lay of Helgi Hjörvarðsson.
	⎩Hrímgerðarmál (19 str. in chant-metre).
	*Second Lay of Helgi Hundingsbane.
	(Gná's errand.)
	(Balder's death.)
	(Thor's visit to Geirröð.)
	(Heimdallargaldr.)
	[Hrungnismál.]
	(Hjaðningamál) 1 chant-metre str. (?).
	[Káruljóð.]

But does even this list give an idea of the true proportion between incident-poems and conversation-poems? Before we can answer this question we must consider by what agencies the poems have been transmitted to us.

A people without a script cannot possess a greater literature than the memory of one generation can carry. The selective process perpetually at work is like that which winnows the possessions of a people fleeing in haste from an enemy, when every individual throws aside the least useful or the most bulky articles in his burden, and there is apt to be considerable unanimity as to what is flung aside and what kept. When the burden is a literature, what is lost can never be replaced by things of the same pattern; it is lost irretrievably. This process goes on in all traditional literatures: it is inevitable. But the Norwegian poems which have come down to us have been through a still more rigorous winnowing. Elsewhere the communities which create the literature are also those whose unuttered judgment decides what shall be kept and what jettisoned; and, since a native literature is very tenacious of life, we may always hope to find what has been discarded by the main body has been preserved by the jealous care of some section of the population. But Fate decreed that the arbiters of life and death for the Norwegian poems should not be the inhabitants of Norway. The struggle for survival was to take place, not in the valleys where the poems had been created, and where the thoughts and customs reflected in them were firmly rooted in the soil, but in a different atmosphere, in a society which was more enlightened if only because it was the result of so much fusion. In Iceland a family from the Lofoten islands might be settled next to a family from Telemarken : each would listen to the other's stock of poems, but there would be much in them that they would not understand, and would therefore not care to remember. The most characteristic poems, those rooted most firmly in local tradition, would be the first to disappear, or the first to be subjected to the hand of the *remanieur*.

The disintegrating effect of the migration is clearly seen in another connection. We know that there existed in Norway, and still exists, a very great number of semi-ritual rustic customs, varying locally, observed at harvest-time, at Christmas, in May and at Midsummer. Yet in Iceland, from the settlement to the present day, there is no trace of such ritual customs, no dancing round May-poles, no mock battles between Winter and Summer, no festivities at Midsummer bonfires.

Of course the configuration of the new country, which only allowed of scattered settlements, must have contributed to this result. But in the realm of literature a still more destructive force must soon have shown itself. The Icelanders were not only lovers of literature but also prolific creators of it. Every people likes its own songs best, and the multitude of new poems must have contributed greatly to the crowding out of the old ones. Of these only such would survive as were especially interesting to the Icelanders. To a certain extent these would include poems in which plot and motive were intelligible and striking and clearly worked out. But another factor must have operated in the selection. The very existence of the class of skalds depended on the preservation of traditions concerning the heathen cosmogony, and no doubt the greater the reputed age of poems dealing with such subjects, the more considerable their vogue. Hence the survival of such a large proportion of poems ranging over a wide mythological field: *Grímnismál*, essential as a store-house of epithets for Odin; *Vafþruðnismál* and *Alvíssmál*, for a general view of the world, and such flytings as referred to a considerable number of episodes in the lives of the gods. Poems dealing with but one episode, and containing action, would obviously be less valuable, especially as Norwegian tradition had not furnished them with any verse narrative, so that much of the action was obscure to the Icelander, if not to the Norwegian, without the help of comments to be furnished in prose "asides" by the reciter. To do the Icelanders justice, we must admit that the old Eddic fashion of telling a story is somewhat baffling. There was all the less reason for preserving these poems since the skalds seem to have made it their business to give the contents of them in their own vivid and pictorial style. Why trouble to remember the dialogue-poem on Thor's journey to Geirröð, or his fight with Hrungnir, when it was told so much more comprehensibly by the skalds Thjóðólf and Eilíf Guðrúnarson? The subject of the lost *Heimdallargaldr* was probably covered by Úlf Uggason; the lost poem on the story of Heðinn and Hild and Högni is dealt with at length by Bragi the Old, and these poems survived. We must remember that the Icelanders could compose "mixed" narrative-plus-speech-poems, so that they were likely to be impatient of the old stories all in dialogue, with the reciter interrupting himself from time to time in order to explain what was only indicated in the verse.

Some of our losses must however be put down to the twelfth century collector of the poems in our Elder Edda. He also had his idiosyncracies. The most unfortunate for us was that which forbade him to include mythological poems which are not fairly complete in themselves. Apparently he would not stoop to piece together a number of fragments, even if he could have filled up the lacunae with prose. Now a didactic poem could be incomplete without being rendered meaningless. There are almost certainly missing passages, as well as interpolations, in most of the didactic poems, but these lacunae do not obtrude themselves. On the other hand gaps, however small, are very conspicuous in incident-poems, and are difficult to gloss over, so that our collector would deny his pages to poems of this type even if they were actually far more complete than the didactic poems he admitted. We can even see the Icelander at work. *Grímnismál* lacks all its verse intro-duction explaining the action, and in both it and *Hyndluljóð* the action is left so obscure in places[1] as to make it practically certain that verse or prose has been omitted. But the Icelanders preserve these poems as compendiums of ancient lore, not as dramatic tales, and they are heedless of such lacunae. On the other hand they are quick to suspect lacunae where none exist, but this is where the information imparted appears to them to be incomplete. If the poet has not given a complete list of the names of Odin, or of the South Norwegian kings, or valkyries, or of rivers, as they have learnt them from their skalds, they hasten to repair the omission; and they care so little for the artistic form of the poem that they do this in another metre.

The Eddic collector or an earlier collector had made a kind of access to a Sigurðarsaga[2] which made it easy for him to piece together fragments, and he also included a good deal that is only arbitrarily connected with the Nibelungen story. But we must not blind ourselves to the probability that other heroic poems still survived which had not yet been attached to the Nibelungen cycle, and which have thus perished entirely.

These considerations make it clear that oblivion must have exacted a far larger toll from the group of incident-poems than from the didactic poems. There is no reason why the latter group

---

[1] See p. 104 below.
[2] Cp. F. Jónsson, Sigurðarsaga og de prosaiske stykker i Cod. Reg., in *Aarbøger f. n. Oldkyndighed*, III R., VII. Bd. (1917), pp. 16–36.

should not have survived intact, whereas we possess little more than vestiges of the other type.   But we may congratulate ourselves on the chance which has preserved for us one complete incident-poem, *Skírnismál*, without which the fragments would be of little use.   And short fragments from so considerable a number of poems are probably more useful than two or three longer pieces.

It will be our next task to examine the group of ancient Norwegian poems in search of any peculiarities of style and structure which may throw light on the nature of the poems and the aims of their authors.   In the following pages it will appear that the whole group shows similarities of style and structure which mark these poems off from the rest of the Edda and which go far to prove that they all belong to an ancient and homogeneous form of literature.

CHAPTER VIII

CHARACTERISTICS OF NORWEGIAN EDDIC POETRY

TRACES OF POPULAR ORIGIN

§ 1. *Style and Subject-matter.*

WE have already observed that the Edda collection comprises two types of literature. Such poems as *Völuspá* and the Nibelungen lays were composed for an intellectually enlightened audience, while the mass of the mythological poems and the Sigurd trilogy had in view a public not too critical or refined, nor too much troubled with inner questionings as to the ultimate significance of human life. We can now differentiate a little further. Roughly speaking, it is the poetry influenced by borrowed material that shows the aristocratic and enlightened tendencies : and it is the old chant-metre verse which regards the world in a less sophisticated fashion.

Of course the Helgi lays, which are modelled on older chant-metre poems, achieve tragic pathos in their catastrophic endings, a pathos and a dignity quite equal to anything in the Nibelungen poems. But they do not keep to this high note throughout : in the earlier scenes they do not disdain triviality or even scurrility. And if we examine the tragic conclusions of these two poems more closely, we shall see that even here the psychology is far more direct, far less subtle, than in the Nibelungen lays. In both the poems the pathos is of a very simple type, well within the compass of a ballad. Sváva and Sigrún both mourn the death of their beloved : Sváva, only half-willing, allows herself to be brought to think of Helgi's brother ; while Sigrún rejoices to clasp her lord in her arms, though he be but a ghost. Her meeting with Helgi is told with unapproachable restraint and dignity, but we have here something very different from the clash of motives—jealousy and love and wounded pride—which the Nibelungen lays depict with such psychological insight.

The same simplicity is traceable in the prose accounts of the other heroic poems in chant-metre—in *Káruljóð* and *Hjaðningamál* with their mingling of naïve superstition and tragedy.

Perhaps we may even see the influence of popular tradition in such a minor point as the beverages granted to the gods. Wine was of course well known among the Norwegians of the tenth century, but it was an expensive luxury. In skaldic verse the drink which conferred upon Odin the gift of poetry is often termed wine. But in *Hávamál* it is described as a draught of precious mead (*Háv.* 140), and the mythological poems invariably describe the gods as drinking ale or mead, except in *Grímnismál*, where Odin's sole nourishment is said to be wine, while that of the *einherjar* is ale. In *Sigrdrífumál* the valkyrie offers Sigurd mead or ale (*bjórr*, str. 5). But in the lays of the Nibelungen and Ermanaric cycles wine is plentiful, as at the court of Jörmunrekk (*Hamðismál* 20 2) and at Atli's court (*Lay of Atli*, 2 2) where all the men-at-arms drink it. And in the skaldic poem *Eiríksmál* all the *einherjar*, Odin's warriors, drink wine, not only the god himself, as in *Grímnismál*.

With regard to Odin, too, these Eddic poems show the attitude of the common people and not of the aristocracy. It has been maintained that in Scandinavia Odin was pre-eminently the god of warlike aristocracies, and in the Court verse of the skalds his warlike propensities appear prominently in a great number of kennings: battle is the tumult of Odin; his ravens are the carrion-crows of carnage, his hall is the abiding-place of the slain, and so on. The only other attribute ascribed to him is the gift of skaldic verse. In the chant-metre Edda poems he wins the secret not of skaldic verse but of magic songs, and though his warlike qualities are not entirely forgotten, in some of the poems there linger memories of a time when he was not the god of the aristocratic slain, nor the ancestor of royal dynasties, but the furtive soul-stealing daemon, expert in charms and runes and auguries. It is significant that *Hávamál*, the self-glorification of Odin, contains no word of his activities in war: he is the rune-winner, the worker in spells, the secret lover, sometimes successful and sometimes flouted and foiled. In *Hárbarðsljóð* he uses language learnt from apparently disreputable ghosts, and he boasts as much of his intrigues with women as of his activities in battle. Indeed in speaking of war he seems in one instance in *Hárbarðsljóð*, and one in the *Second Lay*, to regard himself as the cunning sower of dissension rather than as a war-god proper. In *Reginsmál* he is the augur, in *Lokasenna* almost the peace-maker. In *Grímnismál* he shares the slain with Freyja: in *Lokasenna* the gift of fore-knowledge (which implies fore-ordaining) with the goddesses Gefjón and Frigg. In *Skírnismál* Frey seems to have usurped his place entirely : it is Frey who is called the ruler of the gods (*folkvaldi goða*); who seats himself in Hliðskjálf, whence all the world is seen, and who owns the magic horse, sword and ring which elsewhere belong to Odin[1]. In *Grímnismál* Odin yields his pride of place to Thor in a curious manner. The first strophe of his description of the divine world is devoted to Thor, a circumstance which Professor Finnur Jónsson regards as strange enough to warrant the excision of the lines from the poem, as an interpolation. But Odin himself in a later strophe confirms our inference that Thor, the first mentioned, is in this poem regarded as the first of the gods. After describing the six hundred[2] and forty doors of Valhöll, Odin goes on to the six hundred and forty halls of Bilskirnir, Thor's dwelling-place, and continues : " Of all gabled halls I know, I wot that my kinsman Thor's is the greatest[3]." How can Thor's dwelling be vaster than Valhöll, the abode of the innumerable victims of war?

But Valhöll itself is not as prominent in the Edda as contemporary skaldic verse would lead us to expect. That Balder must fare forth not to Valhöll, but to Hel, is of course an integral part of the story and cannot be quarrelled with. But it is quite obvious that all Eddic tradition sends Sigurd to Hel and not to Valhöll. This is clear from the *Hel-Ride of Brynhild*, but it is also implicit in the double burning. Suttee, such as Brynhild practises (though of course she is not Sigurd's widow), is not con-

---

[1] Cp. M. Olsen, Fra gammelnorsk myte og kultus, *Maal og Minne*, 1909, pp. 20 f.

[2] A northern " hundred " of course = 120.

[3] Str. 24   ranna þeira   es ek rept vita
                       míns veitk mest magar.

sistent with the belief that the warrior was about to enter Valhöll, where there is no admittance for women. Sigurd's place in Hel must have been all the more galling to him, if we may so phrase it, because his father Sigmund and his cousin and half-brother Sinfjötli appear in the skaldic *Eiríksmál* as honoured guests in Valhöll (this about 950). Yet Sigurd was better qualified to enter Valhöll than Sinfjötli, for he was slain by weapons, while Sinfjötli died by poison. Of course we cannot insist too much on consistency in such details as this[1], but it is at least significant that the skald should assign Sigurd's kinsmen to Valhöll while Eddic tradition is so clear as to his own presence in Hel[2].

The treatment of Helgi Hundingsbane is still more curious. It has been pointed out by Niedner[3] that the Valhöll references in the *Second Lay* have been super-imposed on an older tradition. Helgi's appearance, chill and blood-stained, his bitter complaint that Sigrún's tears fall like ice-cold drops of blood on his body, the maid's warning to Sigrún that night endues the ghosts of the dead with greater strength—all this belongs to a faith far older and more widespread than the Valhöll belief. It is this world which the poets of the Edda have in mind.

On the whole it is true to say that the older chant-metre poems represent a more primitive view of life than the later heroic lays or the mythological poem *Völuspá*. In metre and structure, too, they show clear traces of a popular origin.

§ 2. *Metre.*

It is characteristic of the kind of alliterative chant, more doggerel than verse, which we find in old Scandinavian legal formulas, that the alliteration is not invariably employed to connect two half lines divided by a caesura, as in old-lore and speech-metre and in the German and English epic metre, but is used to

---

[1] In Egill's *Sonatorrek* even those who are drowned or dead of disease are admitted to Valhöll; cp. *Egilssaga*, ed. F. Jónsson (1886–8), pp. 431 f.

[2] From the fact that Sigmund and Sinfjötli, not Sigmund and Sigurd, greet Eirík in *Eiríksmál* Schneider argues that Sigurd and Sigmund were not yet completely connected by 950 (*ZfdA*. XLII. pp. 340–1).

[3] *Zur Liederedda* (1896), p. 29.

give the effect of verse to undivided lines.   Thus in the very ancient truce-formula preserved in Icelandic we have such alliteratively independent lines as the following, sometimes in sequences, sometimes combined with the double line:

> *s*áttir ok *s*amværir
> á *þ*ingi ok á *þ*jóðstefnu
> at *k*irkna sokn   ok í *k*onungs húsi...

These doggerel chants, gradually formulated through centuries of usage, repeated and modified by the lips of many generations, are in a very real sense the true poetry of daily life, the true creation of the people.   It cannot be without significance that the chief characteristic of this doggerel, its tendency to use alliteratively independent lines without caesura, is equally characteristic of chant-metre, although the use of such lines is there regulated to fit the stricter requirements of verse.   In certain cases however, more especially in magic formulas, whole sequences of such lines are actually found at the end of chant-metre strophes; as for instance in *Hávamál* 134:

> þeims hangir með hám
> ok skollir með skrám
> ok váfir með vilmǫgum,

or 142:   er fáþi fimbulþulr
> gok gjǫrþu ginnregin
> ok reisti hroptr ragna,

or 149:   sprettr mér af fótum fjǫturr
> en af hǫnðum haft[1].

It is as if the verse still held a memory of a time when the rules of metre were less rigid, and it can still revert at moments to the earlier license.   We may note too that it is just in these alliteratively independent lines that so much latitude is allowed in the number of unaccented syllables; a latitude which is not found even in the earliest runic specimens of the old-lore metre.

But these chant-metre poems have preserved other features of popular verse.

---

[1] Cp. 162 7–9, 164 7–8, and *Grímn.* 49 7–8, 10, *Lok.* 23 7–8.

§ 3. *Incremental Repetition.*

The chain of questions and answers which is so characteristic of them suggests an origin in popular entertainments. The ready-witted answer or retort is obviously most interesting to the audience when it is unexpected, that is to say improvised, and the interest in this type of literature wanes as soon as question and answer are fixed beyond any possibility of variation. A characteristic almost peculiar to the chant-metre poems suggests that the period of improvisation lay not so very far behind. This is the frequency of repetition, and the linking of the strophes; devices which leave the improvising poet a moment to elaborate his question or his answer. *Vafthrúðnismál* is particularly full of examples. The giant Vafthrúðnir begins his first four questions with the lines[1]:

> Tell me, Gagnráð   since thou in the hall
>   wilt put thy credit to the proof...

The last line of the question-strophe becomes the third line of the answer-strophe[2]; the fourth and fifth lines of the question-strophe are as nearly identical with the first and second lines of the answer-strophe as the exigencies of alliteration will allow:

> Str. 11. Tell me, Gagnráð etc.
> .   .   .   .
>
>   what that steed is hight   which draweth each
>   day over mankind?
>
> 12 Skinfaxi is he hight   who draweth the shining
>   day over mankind.

In the next part Odin (Gagnráð) prefaces all his questions with:

> Say this the first (the second, etc.)   if thy wit avails
>   and thou, Vafthrúðnir, knowest,

the second line only varying with the requirements of alliteration, which usually rests on the number, *eina, annat, þriðja* etc. This opening is repeated eleven times[3]. The repetition in the answer-

---

[1] Str. 11, 13, 15, 17. For examples of repetition see Sijmons, *Einleitung*, pp. ccxi ff.

[2] 13 6=14 3; 15 5–6=16 2–3; 17 5–6=18 2–3.

[3] Str. 20, 22, 24, 26, 28, 30, 32, 34, 36, 38, 42 (Str. 40 only has repetition of the first line).

strophes is not so regular in this part, but we find str. 40 3–6 repeated in str. 41 3–6, and 42 3–4 repeated as 43 1–2.

After the twelfth question Odin enters on another series (already used in str. 3) with the beginning:

> Much have I travelled,   much experienced,
>   much have I tested the Powers...

which occurs six times[1].

Similar repetitions are found in the question-and-answer poem *Alvíssmál*:

> Tell me this, Alvíss!   all the fates of men,
>   meseems that thou, dwarf, knowest...

occurring thirteen times[2].

The device is equally characteristic of the first part of *Hávamál*, though this part of the poem is regarded as a monologue. Its structure suggests two persons capping verses, the second elaborating on different lines the thought uttered by the first.

Thus we have the strophe:

> 10   No burden better   bears a man on the road
>   than much mother-wit
>   better than gold   it seems in strange lands
>   and is a shield to the destitute.

The second bard (if so he be) takes up the theme:

> No burden better   bears a man on the road
>   than much mother-wit:
> he chooses the worst   provision for the way
>   who drinks too deeply of ale.

There are five other pairs of strophes[3] in the poem in which the preliminary statement is thus differently expanded: and there is also a sequence of three strophes[4] bearing the same relation to one another.

Skírnismál is full of this type of repetition[5]. Observe Skírnir's speech in str. 8 and Frey's answer:

---

[1] Str. 44, 46, 48, 50, 52, 54.

[2] Str. 9, 11, 13, 15, 17, 19, 21, 23, 25, 27, 29, 31, 33.

[3] Str. 24, 25; (26, 27); 36, 37; 42–3, 58–9, 76–7.

[4] Str. 54, 55, 56 (cp. the sequence 3—4—5).

[5] Cp. Sijmons, *Einl.* p. ccviii.

Skírnir said:

> The steed give me then   that will bear me through the murk
> through the magic flickering flame,
> and the sword which wages   war of itself
> against the Jötun folk.

Frey said:

> That steed I give thee   that will bear thee through the murk,
> through the magic flickering flame
> and the sword which will wage   war of itself
> if he be brave who wields it.

Str. 17, Gerð's question, is only slightly modified in str. 18, Skírnir's reply. The first line of str. 19, Skírnir's offer, is repeated in the first line of Gerð's answer[1]. The first three lines of str. 21 re-appear with but slight variation in Gerð's retort, str. 22. Skírnir twice repeats the threatening words:

> 23, 25   See'st thou, maid, the sword,   graven and slender
> which I hold in my hand?

A glance at *Lokasenna* shows a number of repetitions and linked strophes, which we need not discuss in detail[2].

The fragments of the chant-metre poem *Reginsmál* are so scanty that we can hardly expect to trace repetition in them, but we find it in the second and third parts of the trilogy[3].

---

[1] 19 1, Epli ellifo = 20 1.

[2] *Lok.* 1 6, sigtíva synir = 2 3.   3 5, gumna synir = 4 2.

> ⎧ 3 1–3 Inn skal ganga   Ægis hallir í | á þat sumbl at séa.
> ⎩ 4 1–3 Veiztu ef inn gengr   Ægis hallir í | á þat sumbl at séa.
> ⎧ 7 4–5 Sessa ok staði   velið mér sumbli at.
> ⎩ 8 1–2 Sessa ok staði   velja þér sumbli at.
> ⎧ 10 4–6 síðr oss Loki   kveði lastastǫfum | Ægis hǫllu í.
> ⎨ 16 4–6 at þú Loka   kveðira lastastǫfum | Ægis hǫllu í.
> ⎩ 18 1–3 Loka ek kveþka   lastastǫfum | Ægis hǫllu í.

23 6, 24 6 ok hugðak þat args aðal.

57 1–3, 59 1–3, 61 1–3, 63 1–3 þegi þú róg vættr !   þér skal minn þrúð hamarr
        Mjǫllnir mál fyrnema.

[3] *Fáfn.* 2 4–5 fǫður ek ákka   sem fira synir | geng ek einn saman.
        3 1–2 Veiztu, ef fǫður né áttat   sem fira synir.
        5 1 hverr þik hvatti?   6 1 hugr mik hvatti.
        10 6, 34 5, 39 6 fara til heljar   heðan.
        12 1–3, 14 1–3 Segðu mér Fafnir   alls þik fróðan kveða | ok vel mart vita.
        16 1 Ægishjálm bark....   17 1 Ægishjálmr bergr....
        23 6 þik kveðk óblauðastan alinn.   24 3 hverr's óblauðastr alinn.
        34 1 Hǫfði skemra láti hann = 38 1.

There are only two poems in old-lore metre which betray any tendency to make regular use of repetition[1]. These are, significantly enough, the *Lay of Thrym*, for which we have already suggested a chant-metre original, and the *Lay of Vegtam*, which may be modelled on the old chant-metre poem on Balder's death.

It is so important to establish the stylistic affinities of *Thrym's Lay* that we make no apology for dealing with this question in detail, although we have already treated the poem at some length in a preceding chapter.

The repetitions in *Thrym's Lay* are of two kinds: (*a*) in the narrative verses, (*b*) in the speech verses. (*a*) In the narrative verses most of the repetitions are not of the incremental type characteristic of popular verse, in which the repetition must follow almost immediately. They must rather be attributed to the helplessness of the poet when faced with narrative verse. We have already observed his frequent use of the inquit-for-mula:

> and of words this   was the first he spake.

So also with the repetition of the rather feeble str. 5:

> Loki flew then,   the feather-coat resounded
> until he came without   the dwellings of the Aesir,
> and came within   the lands of the giants

with a mere reversal of lines 3 and 6, in str. 9.

So also with the repetition in narrative form of the speech-strophe 16, in 19. Of these narrative repetitions the only one which stylistically resembles the chant-metre type is that in str. 26 and 28:

> The crafty maid   sat beside
> who found an answer   to the giant's speech.

(*b*) On the other hand the repetitions in the speech-strophes exactly resemble those of chant-metre poems, and are very numerous. Note the question- and answer-strophe 7:

Thrym said:

> How goes it with the Aesir   How with the elves?
> Why art thou come alone   into Jötunheim?

---

[1] The repetitions or refrains in *Völuspá* partake of the nature of skaldic refrains, cp. Sijmons, *Einl.* p. ccxii, and Brate, *Arkiv NF.* (1914), pp. 43–61.

Loki said:

> Ill goes it with the Aesir,   ill with the elves:
> hast thou hidden   the hammer of Hlórriði?

Str. 8.

Thrym said:

> I have hidden   the hammer of Hlórriði
> eight leagues   below the earth.
> It no man shall   win back again
> unless he bring me   Freyja to wife.

The last three lines of this strophe are repeated almost word for word in Loki's first words to Thor, str. 11.

Note also in str. 10:

> Hast thou tidings   to equal thy toil

repeated in Loki's answer, str. 11:

> I have had toil   and also tidings

Note also Loki's answers in str. 26 and 28 (but for the inserted narrative they would only be interrupted by the giant's half-strophe of speech, 27 7–8):

> Nor whit ate Freyja   for eight nights
> so eager was she   for Jötunheim;

which is repeated with the sole alteration of "slept" for "ate" in the first line[1].

In this respect—but in the speech-strophes alone—the Lay of Thrym shows close affinity with the most characteristic of the chant-metre poems, and a complete divergence from its model in narrative verse—the *Fragmentary Sigurd Lay. The Lay of Vegtam* shows the same tendency, though here there is no repetition in the introductory narrative verses which are usually considered a late addition. The völva or sorceress ends her answers with the two lines:

> Unwilling I've spoken   now I'll be silent.

Odin begins his questions with:

> Be not silent völva,   thee I would question
> till all is clear,   I will fain know more.

---

[1] Note also:
- 12 7–8 vit skulum aka tvau   í jǫtunheima.
- 13 9–10 ef ek ek með þér   í jǫtunheima.
- 20 3–6 vit skulum aka tvær   í jǫtunheima.

Also 15 6, 17 6, (19 2) brúðar líni.

We may also note the repetition of str. 8 ₅–₈:

> who will be   the slayer of Balder
> and who will deprive   Odin's son of life?

in the völva's answer in str. 9. If this poem is not founded on a scene in a chant-metre poem it has at least successfully imitated the style of that type of verse.

What is the significance of this kind of incremental repetition, where the last lines of the preceding strophe are modified to form the opening lines of the following strophe? We may legitimately deduce that this dependence on some already uttered phrase must ultimately go back to a tradition of improvisation, but it also seems to imply a tradition of two or more speakers uttering alternate strophes. One bard or reciter asks a question or makes a statement, and the other repeats the formula, taking what lies ready to his hand while he composes his own verses, and thus making equal use of his quick memory and of his gift of ready improvisation. No other hypothesis can account for this technique, especially as it is not used *in strophe sequences uttered by the same character.* Thus there is no trace of it in the monologue *Grímnismál*, nor in the series of strophes in *Hávamál* which are obviously supposed to be uttered by Odin himself[1], beginning with str. 138: "I know that I hung." Nor does it occur in the series of strophes uttered by Hnikarr (Odin) in *Reginsmál* and by the valkyrie in *Sigrdrífumál.* The tendency in these is to have a kind of refrain, if one may call it so, in the first line of the successive strophe, very often serving the purpose of a mere *memoria technica,* as in the seventeen strophes in the section of *Hávamál* already mentioned, all beginning with

> That I know the first, the second, etc.,

or in the eleven strophes in *Sigrdrífumál* beginning

> That I counsel thee the first, the second, etc.

---

[1] In my opinion the series str. 112–137, all beginning

> I counsel thee, Loddfáfnir,   accept thou my counsel
> thou wilt profit if thou accept them
> they will avail if thou win them

are uttered by various speakers, and perhaps the introductory str. 111:—

> "I saw and was silent   I saw and meditated
> I listened to the speech of men" (hlyddak á manna mál)

may be considered as an indication that there was more than one speaker.

But in some sequences the repetition of the first line is a little more artistic, as in the valkyrie's:

> Victory-runes　　must thou know
> Ale-runes　　must thou know
> Rescue-runes　　must thou know, etc.

in *Sigrdrífumál*. This may be called the first beginnings of stylistic variation, which is found so highly developed in the Teutonic epic. Professor Gummere somewhere complains that in the Teutonic epic "the zeal for variation has blotted out the primitive note of repetition," but the chant-metre poems of the Edda show that the device is not inconsistent with alliterative verse, as he appears to suggest. It is absent in the Teutonic epic, as it is absent in the Icelandic poems of the Edda, because in its final form the epic or the Icelandic lay was the deliberate creation of a single poet, whereas the Norwegian Eddic poems originated in part at least in the improvising skill of two or more speakers. They thus resemble the Danish *folkeviser*, or ballads used to accompany dances, of which Professor Olrik says: "For a dance verse any reference to the dancers' own circle may be used: a 'love ballad' sung by a maiden to a knight, or *vice versa*, or else a teasing or mocking duologue, carried on between a lad and a maiden in verse which was partly remembered and partly new-made in the excitement of the dance[1]."

§ 4. *Proverbial Expressions.*

The Norwegian Eddic poems resemble the ballads in one other particular, designed to help the improviser. In most popular verse in which the stage of improvisation has not been left very far behind, we usually find a certain number of stock phrases which help out the invention of the poet in dealing with certain stock situations. These are of course extremely common in ballads, but it should be observed that certain of them are found in the chant-metre poems[2], some of which, as Heusler has pointed out also make a free use of proverbial expressions[3].

---

[1] A. Olrik, *Danske Folkeviser i Udvalg* (Copenhagen, 1899), p. 8.

[2] Síns (þíns) um freista frama Háv. 2 6, Vaf. 11 3, 13 3, 15 3; mæli þarft eða þegi, Hav. 19, Vaf. 10; Segðu þat áðr...þú stígir feti framarr Skírn. 40 1–3; segðu þat...svá at þú einugi feti gangir framarr, Lok. 1 1–3; koma...salkynni at séa; Grímn. 9 2, 10 2; Skírn. 17 4, 18 4, cp. Vaf. 3 4. We may also note: Ærr ertu...ok örvita; Lok. 21, Hhu. 11. 34.

[3] In *Zs. d Verein Volkskunde*, XXV., XXVI. (1915 and 1916).

CHAPTER IX

CHARACTERISTICS OF NORWEGIAN EDDIC POETRY (*cont.*)

THE PROSE COMMENTS

HEUSLER and Sijmons have shown that the information conveyed by the prose in the Edda is not all of the same type, and we may roughly classify it under three heads: A, prose annotations; B, reproduction of forgotten verses; and C, prose "asides."

A. Prose annotations include introductions and conclusions to the poems, whether they simply explain the situation and introduce the speakers, or connect the poem with what precedes and follows. Such introductions and conclusions occur also in the narrative poems of the Edda in the Nibelungen lays. Under this head we may also class statements giving items of information not found in the poems themselves (as for instance in *Fáfnismál* the name of the sword, Riðill, with which Reginn cut out Fáfnir's heart) and also interpretations or amplifications of the verse, as in the *Lay of Völund*: " *Völund...was placed on an island close to the shore, called Saevarstað."*

B. Reproductions of the general drift of forgotten verses. A good deal of the introduction to *Grímnismál* should probably be classed under this head, and also much of the prose comments in the *Lay of Helgi Hjörvarðsson*, and of the *Second Lay of Helgi Hundingsbane.*

C. Prose "asides" descriptive of the action implied in the verse; as for instance in *Lokasenna*: *Then Viðarr stood up and poured a cup for Loki, but before he drank he pledged the gods.*

The Icelandic origin of types A and B is generally conceded, except by those scholars who look back to a "mixed" form of literature, a combination of prose and verse. But it is with type C that we are most concerned. It occurs in the following poems:

Grímnismál[1], *Skírnismál, Lokasenna, the Lay of Helgi Hjörvarðsson*, the *Second Lay of Helgi Hundingsbane*, and the Sigurd trilogy.

It is not surprising that this type of prose comment should be absent from the semi-narrative poems, for it merely elucidates action, and is not required except in poems devoid of narrative verses. But neither does it occur in the later speech-poems, such as the *Hel-Ride of Brynhild*, the *Lay of Vegtam*, the *Prophecy of Grípir*, or *Svipdagsmál*.

At first sight it seems tempting to deduce a Norwegian origin for such prose comments, since they only appear in poems of the chant-metre type. But further consideration will make us pause before we reach this conclusion.

We can, it is true, draw no conclusion from the fact that such comments are lacking in certain Norwegian poems—*Hávamál Alvíssmál, Hárbarðsljóð, Hyndluljóð* and *Vafthrúðnismál*. In *Hávamál* and *Hárbarðsljóð*, as we have them, there is no action; *Hyndluljóð* is fragmentary, and in *Vafthrúðnismál* the place of a prose "*Odin went to Vafthrúðnir's hall*" is taken by a narrative strophe in chant-metre, which can hardly be an original feature. The absence of comment in these poems cannot therefore be regarded as evidence against a Norwegian origin for the device.

On the other hand, we may at once dismiss, as an argument in favour of Norwegian origin, the absence of such comments in the Icelandic dialogue-poems, for the most cursory glance at them reveals that they contain no action, and very seldom any change of scene. All they need is a scrap of introductory prose, introducing the speakers.

Some positive results may however be obtained by observing the system on which the prose comments are inserted. Perhaps we should rather say the lack of system, for we note two apparently contradictory tendencies, both somewhat startling. Action which is self-evident in the verse, and needs no comment, is almost invariably supplied with one. On the other hand, where the action is obscure or liable to be overlooked, it will constantly be found that there is no prose statement to elucidate or emphasize it.

---

[1] Introd. *Agnarr gekk at Grímni ok gaf hánom horn fult at drekka*, and part of the prose conclusion.

We cannot bring such a serious charge against the authors of the prose comments without adducing evidence. First as to the prose "asides" which are entirely superfluous. *Lokasenna* contains the most flagrant instances of this type; in fact all the prose comments in this poem could be dispensed with, whether they describe action or indicate change of scene.

After str. 5, we have: *Then Loki went into the hall. But when those who were present saw who was there, they were all silent.* Loki has just told Eldir, in the verse, that he will enter the hall; and as he goes on to say:

> Thirsty I am come,   I, Lopt, to this hall

the first sentence is superfluous. But so is the second, for the next strophe twits the gods with their silence.

The next statement runs : *Then Viðarr stood up and poured mead for Loki, but before he drank he pledged the gods.*

The first clause is rendered unnecessary by the strophe immediately preceding, in which Odin has bidden Viðarr give place to Loki (str. 10) and the second is sufficiently clearly indicated by the formula immediately following: "Hail gods, hail goddesses," etc., which was evidently used for toasts[1].

After str. 52 we have: *Then Sif went forward and poured mead for Loki in a crystal goblet and said:*

> 53   Hail to thee, Loki,   and take the crystal goblet
>   full of ancient mead...

Here the prose merely amplifies the verse. After this strophe we might be credited with the conclusion that Loki would drink the mead. But no! we are told: *He took the horn and quaffed it.*

In str. 55, Beyla says :

> The fells are quaking   Surely the Thunderer
>   is on the way from his home,
> he will cause to hold his peace   him who slanders here
>   the gods all and men.

After this speech we only need the usual *Thor said* to introduce Thor: we hardly need to be told: *Then Thor arrived....*

Heusler[2] has already pointed out that most of the "asides" in *Fáfnismál* are hardly more than paraphrases of the verse. In

---

[1] Cp. *Sigrdr.* 3, 4.   [2] *Dialog*, p. 208.

Sigrdrífumál, too, we may note that the prose tells us that the valkyrie *took a horn full of mead and gave him* (Sigurd) *a memorial cup*. The two following strophes[1] begin with the customary invocation, and another speaks of " signing " the cup, so that the situation is perfectly clear without the addition of the prose. So also in the *Second Lay of Helgi Hundingsbane*[2], where Sigrún's speech:

> Here for thee, Helgi, I have heaped a bed

is prefaced by the remark : *Sigrún prepared a bed in the grave-chamber.*

On the other hand our prose commentators have passed over a number of passages in which action is not obvious in the verse, and where in consequence a little guidance would be welcome. The reference to the cup brought by Sigrún to Helgi[3] has escaped their notice, because it is not very clearly worded. In *Skírnismál*, while paraphrasing in prose part of Skírnir's speech to the shepherd, our commentator fails to observe that Skírnir causes his horse to leap over the raging fire which surrounds Gerð's dwelling. This must occur immediately after Skírnir's gallant speech in str. 13, where he refuses to be daunted by the shepherd's warning. Since he could not pass through the gateway guarded by the dogs, he leaps the magic wall of flame. The incident is referred to in Gerð's first speech :

> 17 Why didst come alone, over the raging fire
> to visit our homestead?

In her speech to the maid she has just alluded to the thunder of the horse's hoofs as it alights. Moreover there is a reference to the leap in the earlier part of the poem, where Skírnir asks for, and is given, the horse that will ride the magic flame. But our commentator was not very attentive, and the whole incident appears to have escaped his notice.

---

[1] The second strophe is surely spoken by the valkyrie herself, as she takes the horn from Sigurd. If so, the author of the prose has overlooked it.

[2] In this poem the commentator seems definitely to have misunderstood the verse; he has taken the poetic and ceremonial plural used by Helgi as a real plural, and so involved himself in the belief that at Helgi and Sigrún's meeting there is an audience of men and maids. The prose after str. 49 seems altogether doubtful.

[3] Hhu. II. str. 46.

A few prose comments would greatly have facilitated the task of understanding *Hyndluljóð*, which contains a good deal of action. But we cannot help suspecting that this action was quite as obscure to the Icelandic collector as it is to us, and further that he was less concerned about it than we are, or ought to be. He wrote down the poem for the sake of the genealogical information contained in it, and for no other reason. Certainly he can have had no prose comments to help him, but we cannot lay much stress on this, since the poem is only preserved in a fourteenth century MS.

Grímnismál is another poem in which we should have been grateful for a few additional prose "asides." Clearly some action is implied in str. 42:

> The favour of Ull   and of all the gods
>   he has who first touches the fire
> for the worlds lie open   to the sons of the Æsir
>   when they raise the cauldrons[1].

Possibly the strophe depends on str. 45, which should probably directly follow it:

> I have raised my countenance   to the sons of the war-god
>   thereat shall help appear,
> to all the gods   "that" shall come in
>   on Ægir's benches
>   at Ægir's banquet[2].

The last half-strophe appears to be corrupt, so we are helpless. But it is important to observe that the commentators do not help us in a difficulty like this.

It may be said that our failure to understand these passages does not greatly detract from the general effect made on us by the poem as a whole. We are, after all, only left in the dark as to

---

[1] Bing, "Ull," in *Maal og Minne*, 1916, p. 107 f. thinks that this str. shows that the god Ull is represented as present between the cauldrons. Prof. Magnus Olsen concurs in this view. If so, the poem must have contained much more action than we have any trace of. (For the magic significance of a boiling pot, see the English dramatic game "Mother, mother, the pot boils over": A. B. Gomme, *Traditional Games*.)

[2]   Svipum hek nú ypt   fyr sigtíva sonum
             við þat skal vilbjǫrg vaka;
           Ǫllom ásum   þat skal inn koma
             Ægis bekki á
             Ægis drekku at.

the significance of some dramatic by-play. But sometimes our commentators leave us without prose comment at a far more important juncture. Let us look at *Vafthrúðnismál* and *Alvíssmál.*

Vafthrúðnismál has the entirely superfluous narrative strophe, probably founded on a prose comment, to the effect that Odin repaired to Vafthrúðnir's hall. The author of such "asides" means to give all proper guidance, and he does so in this detail.

But he appears to have been blind to the whole dramatic significance of the poem. Vafthrúðnir declares in str. 7 that Odin will not leave his hall alive unless he prove the more learned. And a phrase in Vafthrúðnir's last speech shows that the penalty of ignorance was to be the same for both, and that his own death followed immediately upon his failure in knowledge. The disguised god has asked him what Odin whispered in Balder's ear before he was placed on the pyre. Vafthrúðnir recognises the god and replies:

> There is none that knoweth   what in days of yore
>   thou spak'st in the ear of thy son ;
> with a fey (doomed) mouth   I uttered my ancient lore
>   and (told) of the doom of the gods.

It is obviously implied that the scene ends with the giant's death at the hands of Odin, and we should expect the commentator to supply us with a prose account of this, somewhat as the prose at the end of *Grímnismál* tells of Geirröð's death. But the dramatic catastrophe has apparently escaped his attention.

We find the same curious indifference to the dramatic conclusion of *Alvíssmál*, though in this case the verse is more explicit. Thor has lured Alvíss, a dwarf, to the display of his knowledge, of which the dwarf is so proud that he does not heed the passage of time. Finally Thor observes:

> 35   In one breast   Ne'er did I see
>   more abundance of ancient lore ;
> great wiles, I declare,   I have used to lure thee :
>   Day has caught thee, dwarf, above ground,
>   Now the sun shines into the hall !

Of course the inference here is fairly plain : a dwarf caught above ground turns into stone, but when we consider with what care the commentator frequently supplies a prose paraphrase of actions that are actually described in the verse, we cannot help feeling that he was really indifferent to the dramatic conclusion of this poem.

The guidance of the prose commentators is therefore super-fluous in a majority of cases, and where it is not superfluous it is inadequate. It is impossible to credit the original authors of the poems with such a combination of officiousness and helpless-ness. We know that the Icelanders did not themselves practise the art of presenting incident in dialogue, and we may perhaps conclude that the prose comments were for the benefit of Icelandic audiences.

Were there, then, no prose comments until Icelandic tradition supplied them? The absence of explanation in passages where explanation is obviously needed certainly points to this conclusion, for it shows both that the Icelandic commentators could overlook references to action in the verse unless they were extremely clear, and that they had no means of elucidating such references beyond the help afforded by the text itself.

In this conclusion we seem to be in accord with expert opinion reached on somewhat differing lines. Heusler regards the Eddic collector as responsible for the greater number of the prose com-ments, and both he and Sijmons[1] repudiate the idea that these are an integral part of Eddic literature.

At first sight, however, there is one very serious objection to this view, an objection which has been hardly sufficiently regarded. It is easy to understand why the Icelanders should have found it necessary to annotate the old poems, adding prefaces and intro-ductions and paraphrasing lost verses. But if we attribute to them also the prose "asides," interpreting action and explaining the change of scene, are we not, on the one hand, crediting the Nor-wegians with preternatural acuteness, and on the other denying the Icelanders even an ordinary modicum of perspicacity? If the Norwegians could understand every hint of action, every change of scene, without prose explanations, why should the Icelanders require each indication of movement on the part of the characters to be underlined for them, as it were, by a running commentary of prose? For there is no denying that they appear to need more

---

[1] *Einl.* § 23: pp. cliv ff.

explanation, more prose "asides," than even the modern reader would demand.

> Here for thee, Helgi,   I have heaped a bed

says Sigrún in the *Second Lay*.   No modern audience, listening to the poem, would require the reciter to interrupt himself to state: *Sigrún prepared a bed in the grave-chamber*.

> Hail to thee, Loki,   take now this crystal goblet
> full of ancient mead

says Sif in *Lokasenna*.   A modern audience would not be grateful to a reciter who should preface this remark with—*Then Sif went forward and poured mead for Loki into a crystal goblet*, and follow it with: *Loki took the horn and quaffed it*.

There are however cases in which a reader might interpolate brief statements of action as frequently as it is done in *Lokasenna*, even though these were in no way necessary to explain the verse. Suppose he were reading passages from a play: would he not pause at intervals to enable his audience to visualize the action, adding a "Here Thor comes in," "Here Sif comes forward and hands him a cup," "Meanwhile Sigrún busies herself with making a bed," even where the speeches of the characters make it quite plain that some such action is taking place?   Have we not here the explanation of the prose "asides"?

We have only to suppose that these dialogues were *acted* in heathen Norway, even in the rudest pantomimic style, to understand why prose "asides" would be superfluous for the Norwegians, while for the Icelanders, who did not see them acted, they would be necessary not so much to *explain* the verse as to *illustrate* it. A literary parallel lies ready to our hand in the mediaeval miracle or mystery plays, where the stage directions are of just the same type as in the Edda.   "This wyndowe I will shutte anon," says Noah; *Then shall Noye shutte the wyndowe of they Arcke*. Abraham says: "A sword and fier that I will take": *Here Abraham taketh a sword and fier*.   "Thou must be bounde both hande and feete" he says to Isaac: *he taketh hym and byndeth*.   Isaac begs: "About my head a carschaffe bynde"...*Here Abraham...bynds a charschaffe about his heade*[1]. Or in the scene between Adam and Eve:

---

[1] Chester play.

>Eve. Byte on boldely, for it is trewe
>we shall be goddis and knawe al thyng.

>Adam. To wynne that name
>I shall it taste at thy techyng.
>*Accipit et comedit*[1].

If these prose asides are put into the past tense they are the very counterparts of the prose comments of the Edda.

We have seen that the incremental repetition found in the alternate strophes of dialogue in the Norwegian poems, and nowhere else, not in the monologue sequences, finds its readiest, and indeed its only explanation, in the theory that the dialogue strophes were originally uttered by two speakers, who had behind them a tradition of improvisation. We now find that the only complete explanation of the peculiarities of the prose comments is that they were composed in Iceland to elucidate action, change of scene, etc. which must have been perfectly clear to the original audience. We must therefore assume, not only that in the original home of the poems different speakers uttered the strophes assigned to different speakers, but that these speakers also acted—that is to say they moved about the scene in accordance with the actions indicated in the poem. We have already briefly alluded to a tendency to explain the scene in the speeches of the characters, a tendency which is typical of primitive drama, with its limited resources, and which may be found again in mediaeval plays in an even more naïve form than in the Edda. "Now hens woll I fast owt of this town," says a messenger in the Digby *Mary Magdalene* on being sent by Pilate to Herod, and he immediately addresses the latter: "Heyll! soferyn kyng onder crown!" On a par with this technique we have the care taken in the Eddic verse to show the whereabouts of the characters. The strophe in which Frigg bids Odin farewell, in *Vafthrúðnismál* is followed by the strophe in which Odin says:

>Hail to thee, Vafthrúðnir!   Now am I come into thy hall
>to look upon thyself....

So in *Lokasenna* the fact that it is a hall which Loki enters is emphasized in the verse:

>Thirsty I've come,   I, Lopt, to this hall.

---

[1] Broome play.

In *Alvíssmál* the hall is indicated more dexterously: the poem opens with the dwarf's words: "Deck the benches...." So when a river comes into the scene various devices are used to represent it. In *Reginsmál* Loki asks:

"What kind of fish is that   which swims in the stream."

And in the fragment on Thor's visit to Geirröð the god shows that he is fording a river by addressing it:

Wax not, Vimur,   for I needs must ford thee.

These indications of scene must be said to be well done on the whole and less clumsy than such indications often are. The Edda poets are distinctly more dexterous than say the Elizabethan Greene, in the scene where he makes two characters meet in a street, and one bids the other accompany him out of the town. The other replies: "Now we are at the townes end. What say you now?[1]"

This superiority is partly due to the fact that the Edda poets have elaborated a special technique for the indication of change of scene. The methods of the Elizabethan stage, with its sign-post "This is a tavern, a castle," etc. were not open to them, and instead they attained a really high degree of skill in the use of what we may call the human sign-post, the supernumerary character, whose whole *raison d'être* is to show the movements of the main characters and the change of scene. Thus in *Vafthrúðnismál* Frigg is really a supernumerary character, introduced to let us see Odin's start for the giant's hall. In *Lokasenna* there are a couple of such characters, first Eldir, who stands outside the hall of Ægir and has a conversation with Loki, then Beyla, who announces a new arrival:

All the fells are quaking   I think that Hlórriði
must be on the way from his home.

In the fragment on Gná's journey we see this favourite device employed to show us Gná riding in the air, "One of the Vanir" asks:

Who flies there,   who floats there
and rides through the air?

But the highest level of skill in this use of supernumerary persons is reached in *Skírnismál* and the *Second Lay of Helgi Hundingsbane*.

---

[1] *The Pinner of Wakefield*, Act IV, Sc. iv.

When Skírnir is finally persuaded to undertake the mission
we might expect a few farewell words from Frey to indicate that
the emissary is about to start.   But no! that has become too
commonplace a trick for our poet.   Far more vivid, far more
dramatic, is the introduction of a new, supernumerary character,
this time a mute one.   The dangers of the journey are set forth
for us in Skírnir's words to the horse:

> Dark 'tis without   'tis time for us to fare
>   over the reeking fells
>   over the goblin folk
> Together we'll win through   or together he shall take us
>   that mighty giant.

Another supernumerary figure, the shepherd on the cairn, is introduced in order that Skírnir's question to him may show the scene
outside the giant's dwelling.   Skírnir's reply to the shepherd's
discouraging answer shows us the fiery barrier, and his successful
leap over this obstacle is made clear by the introduction of yet
another supernumerary personage, the maid, who tells Gerð of
the man outside who has leapt from his steed, and lets it crop
the grass.

In the *Second Lay of Helgi Hundingsbane* Sigrún's maid serves
the purpose of both the shepherd and the maid in *Skírnismál*.   It
is she who greets Helgi, describing his arrival on horseback, and
on her return to Sigrún she indicates that the following scene will
take place within the burial mound.   This is also carefully mentioned by Helgi: "a bride is housed in the grave chamber."   After
Helgi's departure the maid is again used, but this part of the poem
is fragmentary.

It would be difficult indeed to explain these traditional supernumerary figures, the shepherd and the maid, without resort to
the hypothesis of a dramatic origin.

CHAPTER X

I. STOCK SCENES

WE shall more clearly realise the character of the older poetry if we compare it with the newer. *Völuspá* and the *Lay of Hymir* among the mythological poems, the *Lay of Völund* and the heroic poems on borrowed subjects—these may be classed as the less primitive Edda poems. But when we have made this statement, we can proceed little further with their classification, except to observe that they are either pure speech-poems or of a mixed speech and narrative type. We can, if we like, further subdivide them into poems containing incident and what are called "situation-poems," the latter to include prophecies like *Völuspá*, and retrospective laments like those of Gudrun and Brynhild. But further than this we cannot go; for the poets who shaped them were evidently perfectly free to treat of what episodes they chose. *Völuspá* is a long monologue ending at the point where prophecy can go no further. The *Lay of Hymir* elects to combine several episodes and to leave off where Thor returns with the cauldron. The *Lay of Völund* closes with Völund's triumphant flight and Böðvild's shamed confession. In the longer poems from the Nibelungen story it was natural for the poets to treat of the main incidents, ending either with Brynhild's approaching death or with the slaying of Atli, and so in the Ermanaric poems. But they were evidently free to choose what episode they liked. The *Hel-Ride of Brynhild* contents itself with the dialogue between Brynhild and a giantess; the *Prophecy of Grípir* ends with Sigurd's departure to seek Brynhild and to dree his weird; the First and Third *Lays of Gudrun* each treat of one episode, and end, in the one case with Gudrun's tears, and in the other with her acquittal from the charge of infidelity. The *Second Lay of Gudrun* is a retrospective lament; the *Egging of Gudrun* closes in like manner, after her sons have ridden away to attempt revenge on Jörmunrekk.

All this freedom of choice is altered when we turn to the old native poems of Norway. In style there is more variety among these than in the later poems, which are all in the heroic manner, with the one exception of *Hymir's Lay*. The older poems oscillate between the didacticism of *Grímnismál*, a childlike delight in picturesque incident, such as Thor's crossing the river or Loki catching the pike, and the idyllic charm of *Sigrdrífumál* or *Skírnismál*. But as regards structure the conventions are very rigid: in fact every Norwegian poem, except the gnomic *Hávamál*, belongs to one of three fixed forms:—

I. *Poems which culminate in a death or slaying.* (This may include funeral, and, reappearance as ghost.)

Such are *Grímnismál, Vafthrúðnismál, Alvíssmál, *Thrym's Lay, Balder's death, Thor's visit to Geirröð, Heimdallargaldr, Hrúngnismál, Hjaðningamál, Káruljóð*. If the giantess is destroyed by fire in **Hyndluljóð*, as seems probable[1], we must add that poem to the number.

II. *Poems which culminate in a wooing or love-scene:*

Skírnismál, the Sigurd trilogy, the **Second Lay of Helgi Hundingsbane*, the **Lay of Helgi Hjörvarðsson*.

III. *Flytings.*

Lokasenna, *Hárbarðsljóð (?).

It will be at once observed that several poems contain scenes belonging to another type. Thus the second part of the Sigurd trilogy ends in a slaying, and *Hrímgerðarmál*, in the *Lay of Helgi Hjörvarðsson*, combines the flyting and the slaying. The last extant strophe of *Hyndluljóð* may well indicate a love-scene between Freyja and Óttarr, in which case the poem would rather belong to Class II. More interesting perhaps is the combination of the love-scene and the death-scene found in *Káruljóð* and the *Lay of Helgi Hjörvarðsson*; or the combination of the resurrection scene

---

[1] Cp. str. 48: Freyja flings fire round the giantess, "so that thou escape not hence": svá at þú igi kømsk á braut heðan—the rest of the strophe is lost. Gering and Hildebrand, for metrical reasons, amend á braut to óbrend, unburnt.

(as a ghost) with the love-scene, as in the *Second Lay* and (probably) in *Hjaðningamál.*

Besides *Hávamál,* the only poem we have failed to place is the brief colloquy between Njörð and Skaði, or as Saxo would have it, between Hadding and his wife. These are regarded by Sijmons as mere stray verses; and if they did belong to a longer poem its contents are too doubtful for us to venture an opinion on them. The extant strophes might have formed the opening verses of a flyting.

It may possibly be regarded as accidental that the Norwegian Eddic poems all conform to one of these three types. Let us look at the poems of Saxo. No doubt they are not as old as the older Edda poems, but they must at least represent Scandinavian tradition. Of the dozen more or less independent poems[1] translated by him we find the following belong to our types:

I.   *Poems which culminate in a slaying:*

Ingeld's Egging (VI. 204); Starkad's death (VII. 269); Asmund and Hadding (I. 26); Bjarkamál (II. 59); Hildiger and Halfdan (VI. 224); Ole-Grim-Gunn (VII. 251).

II.   *Poems which culminate in a wooing or love-scene:*

Hadding-Harthgrep (I. 20); Svanhvit and Regner (II. 42); Othar and Syritha (VII. 226).

I and II.   *Combination of slaying and love-scene:*

Gram-Gro (I. 13); Gram-Signe (I. 191); Signe and Hagbard (VII. 231 ff.); Halfdan and Gyuritha (VII. 245).

III.   *Flytings:*

Fridleif and the giant (VI. 178); Grep and Erik (V. 132 f.); Gotvar and Erik (V. 139).

The only longer poem in Saxo which fails to correspond to one of these types is that in which Starkad wounds the goldsmith who has aspired to Helga's love (VI. 191). The Erik-Olmar dialogue is obviously incomplete[2], and the *Lay of Bravalla Battle,* given by Saxo in prose, cannot by any possibility have been of Eddic type. It is a skaldic lay.

---

[1] Olrik regards as possibly "Oldkvad" all poems which are comprehensible without Saxo's prose. This criterion would admit a number of poems of the *Eddica Minora* type, and would exclude fragments of more ancient poems.

[2] The verses on the Huns' battle in Hervararsaga, with which these have affinity (cp. Heusler and Ranisch, *Eddica Minora,* XVI.), end in the death of one brother.

Poems of class I are naturally of frequent occurrence in any primitive literature, but it is none the less significant that an ending of this type is given to poems of the question-and-answer type such as *Vafthrúðnismál* and *Alvíssmál*.

Class II deserves a word of comment. We find a love-scene at the end of the Sigurd trilogy, at the end of the *Second Lay*, at the end of the *Lay of Helgi Hjörvarðsson*. But when we examine the Nibelungen Lays we find a singular absence of real love-scenes. Both Gudrun and Brynhild mourn for Sigurd in a number of poems, but actual love-scenes are entirely absent from the extant Eddic poems of the Nibelungen cycle, and, to judge by Heusler's brilliant study, they were far from conspicuous in the lost poems of the lacuna[1]. The Northern Nibelungen poets never seem to have chosen a love-scene as their central theme, nor to have made it the culminating point of a poem. It is therefore all the more important to observe the strong tendency of the older dialogue-poems to conclude on this note, and the number of love-scenes among Saxo's poems.

The continual recurrence of stock scenes is of course a characteristic of primitive drama. We hardly need to be reminded that the flyting, the love-scene, the slaying and the resurrection are to this day the main scenes of folk-drama. We have already noted the traces of improvisation by two speakers, and the method of indicating change of scene, both typical of early drama. The Norwegian Eddic poems bear the unmistakable stamp of dramatic origin, however superficially obscured by their survival for a couple of centuries of oral tradition in a country where they were not represented dramatically. As Professor Ker says, they had lost their vogue and freshness before they came to be written down, and they had probably been preserved in the faithful memory of peasants rather than by the more aristocratic settlers and their descendants. Yet these poems are not the remains of folk-drama in the modern sense of that word. Modern folk-drama is a degenerate descendant of ancient religious drama, whereas these poems are the actual shattered remnants of ancient religious drama.

---

[1] *Lieder der Lücke, loc. cit.*

II. Theriomorphic Personages and Disguise

We have already seen that even the heroic poems of the old Norwegian type are placed in a supernatural setting quite foreign to the poems on the Nibelungen and Ermanaric cycles. The Sigurd trilogy shows us an otter and a pike[1], birds, dwarves, gods, a dragon, and a valkyrie ; the Helgi Lays introduce Odin, valkyries and a giantess ; *Hjaðningamál* and *Káruljóð* both obviously contain supernatural elements. It is perhaps worth noting that the chant-metre type of poem betrays a special fondness for beast and bird characters. In *Hyndluljóð* we have a boar and a wolf; in *Skírnismál* we must almost call the horse a personage ; in the *Lay of Helgi Hjörvarðsson* there is the mysterious bird which talks to Atli and demands worship as the price of its secret; and in the prose, there is the troll-woman riding a wolf. In *Reginsmál* a pike converses[1], and if the poem were complete it would probably make the otter a speaking part. In *Fáfnismál* we have the dragon and more talking birds. In the poem on the death of Balder, besides the giantess' wolf, the steeds of all the gods are present: Frey's boar, Freyja's cats, and Heimdall's horse, while Odin is accompanied by his ravens; and we also have a motley crowd of shaggy giants. In the poem on Hrungnir we should doubtless find the grotesque figure of Mökkrkálfi, a monster made of clay.

Such bird and beast personages are characteristic of primitive literature, and have been discarded by heroic poetry, whose interest lies with man and his relations with other men. There are no such characters in the Nibelungen and Ermanaric lays ; and though *Beowulf* preserves the Scandinavian tradition in Grendel and the dragon, these beings are not permitted to play a speaking part, and the emphasis of the poem is all on Beowulf's relations with other men. We must regard these beast and bird personages in the chant-metre poems as an additional indication of their popular origin.

Less explicable, perhaps, is the delight manifested in the older

---

[1] Olaus Magnus tells us that in his times in Sweden fishermen used to wind themselves up in nets to represent fish in the Carnival masquerades (Bk. XIII. ch. 41). That this was an ancient disguise is perhaps indicated by the story of Kráka, in *Krákumál*, who comes to Ragnar clothed in a fishing-net.

type of poem for disguise of any kind. Odin disguises himself in
Vafthrúðnismál, in *Grímnismál*, in *Hárbarðsljóð* and in part of
Hávamál. In another part of the *Hávamál* collection a wandering
singer masquerades as Odin, or else Odin masquerades as a
wandering singer. In *Reginsmál*, too, Odin disguises himself, this
time as Hnikarr. In *Hárbarðsljóð* Thor seems to be dressed in
garments not befitting a god; and in *Thrym's Lay* he and Loki
get themselves up as women, a device which Loki again adopts
in the poem on Balder's death. In *Hyndluljóð* Freyja disguises
her lover Óttarr as a boar[1]. In the *Lay of Helgi Hjörvarðsson*
Franmarr is metamorphosed into an eagle. In the *Second Lay*
Helgi is presumably disguised in some way in the first strophe,
and in the next scene we see him clad as a bond-woman.

In *Sigrdrífumál* there is a trace of the reverse form of disguise.
The prose shows us Sigurd mistaking the sleeping form of the
valkyrie for a man, until he removes her helmet. If the skaldic
Húsdrápa re-tells the story of *Heimdallargaldr*, Heimdall and
Loki must have disguised themselves as seals in this poem. In
the lost poem *Káruljóð* Kára takes the form of a swan; and in
the late Saga founded on this poem we find Helgi's opponent,
Hrómund, putting on a goat's beard before going into battle[2]. No
motive is assigned for this remarkable act, which no doubt reflects
an ancient tradition.

In the light of these instances it seems more than probable
that Sigurd is in animal disguise when he slays Fáfnir and replies
to the dragon's enquiry as to his name that he is called "Gǫfugt
dýr," "stately animal[3]."

It is interesting to find traces of this predilection for disguise
in Saxo's poems. It appears to be a fixed convention of his
wooing-scenes, so constantly does the motive appear in them,
though in various forms. In the Gram and Gro poem (II. 13) Gram
is disguised: so also in the Gram and Signe poem (I. 19). In

---

[1] Professor Finnur Jónsson maintains that the last three lines of str. 7 (which allude
to Óttarr as a boar) are an interpolation. *Lit. hist.* I. pp. 196 f. We shall however find
later on striking confirmation of their genuineness.

[2] *Hrómundar Saga Greipssonar*, ch. 2.

[3] Cp., in Danish tradition, the "shaggy breeks" which Ragnar Loðbrók uses in his
fight with the vipers, and the ox-hides donned by Frode and Fridleif to attack their
dragons.

Harthgrep's colloquy with Hadding (I. 20) she intimates that she can alter her shape at will. Regner is disguised when he woos Svanhvit (II. 142) and in the prose narrative following Othar's address to Syritha (VII. 226) we find that Syritha is disguised. Hagbard is disguised as a woman in the first scene of his wooing of Signe (VII. 231 ff.) and apparently Hálfdan is disguised in the scene with Gyuritha (VII. 245).

But disguise is not limited to the love-scenes in Saxo. Starkad is disguised as a charcoal-burner when he comes to Ingeld's court to rouse that slothful king to vengeance (VI. 204), and he is similarly in disguise when he delivers Helga from the smith (VI. 191). We may also note that while Saxo has no explanation of Bjarki's sleep during the great fight depicted in *Bjarkamál*, Icelandic tradition maintained that Bjarki was really fighting all the time, in the guise of a huge bear. Odin is disguised as Vagn-hofde in the Asmund-Hadding poem (I. 24, 27).

Disguise is certainly not a typical feature of the later or Icelandic Edda poems. In fact it only occurs in the *Lay of Vegtam*, where Odin presumably disguises himself in order to conceal his identity from the völva. It plays no part in the extant Nibelungen poems. In the lost poems the shape-changing between Gunnarr and Sigurd can hardly count as disguise, but in the old Northern part of the story Signý disguises herself for her visit to Sigmund. We may perhaps compare this scene with the wooing poems of Saxo where disguise is mentioned.

Such a marked tendency towards masquerade, especially in cases where there seems no motive for the disguise, as in some of Saxo's love-scenes, and in the case of Hrómund in *Káruljóð*, surely points in the same direction as certain other Eddic characteristics which we have just been discussing—to an origin in popular drama.

CHAPTER XI

EVIDENCE FOR INDIGENOUS DRAMA IN SCANDINAVIA

THESE mystery-plays of Norwegian heathendom throw light on many obscure points of Scandinavian custom, and are in their turn vouched for by evidence from the most diverse sources of the existence of popular drama, obviously heathen and indigenous in character. Even without the evidence of the Edda, scholars have found it necessary to postulate the existence of ritual drama both in Sweden and Norway. Thus Professor Schück explains certain stories in the Norwegian skaldic poem *Ynglingatal* (which celebrates prehistoric kings of Upsala) as originating in heathen dramatic representations on the lines of the mock fights between Winter and Summer so common in Sweden[1]. But we have other evidence than this. Saxo tells us that his hero Starkad left the Swedes after living with the sons of Frey, "because when stationed at Upsala at the time of the sacrifices he was disgusted by the effeminate gestures and the clapping of mimes on the stage and by the unmanly clatter of the bells[2]." Mogk[3], Hammerstedt[4], Schück[5] and Leffler[6] take this passage to mean that dances and pantomimic scenes of an erotic or obscene nature formed part of Frey's ritual at Upsala.

---

[1] H. Schück, *Studier i Ynglingatal*, II. pp. 60 ff.

[2] Elton's translation p. 228; Holder's ed. VI. 186: "effeminatos corporum motus scenicosque mimorum plausus ac mollia nolarum crepitacula fastidiret." Olrik in 1887 regarded this passage as merely indicating the presence of jugglers at festival time in Upsala (*Mindre Afh. af det phil. hist. Samfund*, 1887, pp. 74 ff.). But he gives a complete account of what is known of the early jugglers, and nowhere do we find any mention of their using bells, whereas bells were until recently hung on the "wedding tree" round which the newly-married couple dances in certain districts in Sweden (Hammerstedt, Kvarlefvor av en Frösritual, *Maal og Minne*, 1911, pp. 189 ff.).

[3] Menschenopfer, *Abh. d. phil. hist. kl. d. kgl. sächs. Gesellsch. d. Wiss.*, Leipsic, 1909, p. 637, note 9.

[4] *Op. cit.*   [5] *Svenska Folkets Hist.* Bd. I. p. 266.

[6] In *Maal og Minne*, 1911, p. 640.

Further evidence of such a pantomimic ritual marriage, with a human being personating the god, is furnished by a story in the Flateyjarbók version of St Olaf's Saga. A Norwegian, Gunnarr helming, tells King Olaf that while taking refuge in Sweden he was seized by the Swedes and in danger of being used as a human sacrifice. The god Frey was at that time on his yearly journey round the countryside in charge of a priestess called Frey's wife. This woman took in Gunnarr, and for the rest of the trip he personated the god, having fought with and overcome his image. Finally the priestess was seen to be with child, which was looked upon as a good omen for the crops[1]. The story is hardly comprehensible unless we assume the custom of a ritual marriage, with a human being personating the god. Such "bridals" persist in modern Scandinavian custom, though in later times the bridegroom has usually had to be dispensed with, as the final ceremonies are of such a nature that it was impossible to get any self-respecting girl to take the part of bride. A "Whitsun" bridal was however performed with full ceremony in Rönnebergs härad in Skåne in the middle of last century[2], and similarly at Ullensvang in Norway, in 1893[3]. In Gotland the ritual marriage used to be celebrated at Midsummer, two young men being dressed up in leaves and flowers to represent bride and bridegroom respectively[4].

There is also prehistoric evidence for this dramatic representation of a ritual marriage. In his researches on Norwegian place-names[5] Professor Magnus Olsen has collected evidence indicating that this was the central rite of a prehistoric fertility-cult. Ull was one of the gods connected with the cult, and close to Ullensvang church there is a large rock called Ulla-bersteinn on which people used until recently to gather on June 24, "Jonsokaften," and dress up a little girl as "Jonsokbrur"—"the Midsummer bride[6]." Evidently "Ullaber" is a corruption of Ullarberg—Ull's knoll. Professor Olsen has also pointed out

[1] *Flat.* I. pp. 327 ff.

[2] M. P. Nilsson, *Årets folkliga Fester*, Stockholm, 1915, pp. 81 ff.

[3] Frazer, *Magic Art*, II. 92.

[4] *Årsfesterna i ett gotländskt hem*, in *Fosterländska Bilder* (1877–78), p. 191.

[5] M. Olsen, *Hedenske Minder i norske stednavne. Skr. utgit af Vidensk. Selsk. i Kristiania*; II. *Hist. phil. kl.* 1914–15.

[6] *Ib.* 1915, p. 180.

the significance of the twenty-seven gold plates, of Norwegian
origin, representing a ritual wedding—the figures of a man and a
woman facing each other with, in the better examples, a leafy branch
between them. These plates appear to have been buried in the
soil[1]. As Professor Schück says: "We have only to imagine that
this ritual was performed dramatically—and that is the case with
all ritual—and we have just the popular play of which the main
traits occur in *Skírnismál*[2]." Professor Olsen sees a reflection of
this drama in the story of Hálfdan the Black carrying off his bride.
In Sweden the Year-drama, the May battle, has always been
prominent among the festivities of the year, and for the sixteenth
century Olaus Magnus witnesses that besides the slaying of the
Winter-Lord, clad in skins, and the winning of the bride by the
May-Lord, there was a flyting between youths and maidens.

But there is evidence for other types of dramatic performances
in Scandinavia. In the Icelandic *Ljósvetninga Saga*[3] we are told
that on his return from a visit to the Trondhjem district in Norway, where there had been great festivities[4], a man called Brand,
in the service of the Icelandic chief Thorkell Geitisson, instituted
various entertainments[5], "and it is said that he first invented the
Syrpuþingslög"—the "laws of Syrpa's *thing*." The saga tells how
folk came from far and near to this entertainment, and were very
noisy: it was a hindrance to the household work, and Thorkell
often found himself spending the evening almost alone, while his
guests joined in the entertainment. He complains to Brand, who
tries going to bed early, in order to discourage the visitors. "The
thingmen however came according to custom, but the 'thing'
could not be held when there was no 'chief man[6]'." Evidently the
Syrputhing was a dramatised burlesque of the ceremonies and
speeches of an ordinary "Thing," and Brand got the idea from
Norway, the name *Syrpuþingslög* being formed on the analogy
of *Frostuþingslög*, the laws of the district round Trondhjem. The

---

[1] Olsen and Schetelig, *Bergens Museums Aarb*. 1909. (A similar plate, so small
that the figures can only be made out with a magnifying glass, was recently found in
Bohuslän and is in the National Museum at Stockholm.) Cp. Olsen, Fra gammelnorsk
myte og kultus, in *Maal og Minne*, 1909, p. 32.

[2] *Illustr. Sv. Litt. Hist.* (1911), p. 90.

[3] The chief Thorkell Geitisson died about the year 987.

[4] Ch. 8.   [5] Ch. 9.   [6] *formaðr*.

ancient "Things," as we know, were solemnly opened by the priest-chief, the *goði*, with a religious sacrifice. The *Syrputhing*, too, has a "leader" and the ceremonial expression "heyja" for holding the Thing suggests that the representation was accompanied by religious observances, however scurrilous or ribald these may have been. The officiating priest would be a "play-priest," *leik-goði*, and this word actually occurs in the Icelandic Saga *Vatnsdæla*[1], applied to one Thórólf who lived in the heathen period and who does not belong to any of the known *goði* families, or indeed to any well-known family.

There are two different views as to the meaning of *syrpa*. Cleasby-Vigfusson's Dictionary states that it is the name of a giantess, and quotes Snorri, who knows it as a term of abuse for women. Heusler and Ranisch[2] think it is a witch-name. Fritzner, on the other hand, regards it as connected with *sorp*, rubbish[3]. As the term evidently came from Norway it will be perhaps best to look for its meaning there. Aasen, in his *Norsk Ordbog*, besides the fem. noun *surpa*, which he translates "mash, especially soft fodder," has a verb *surpa*, to stir together, to mix into fodder, also "affærdige i en hast," "to finish off, despatch in a hurry[4]." This suggests that the original meaning of *syrpu* in *Syrputhing* may have been "improvisation[5]." However it must have acquired a ritual or magic significance as well, for in the late Bósa Saga an old witch Busla forces the king to pardon Bósi by first reciting *Buslubæn*, which prevents the king from stirring, and then *Syrpuvers*[6], Syrpa's verse, "which is full of magic power, and it is not permitted to recite it after sun-down."

It appears then that the *Syrputhing* was a kind of improvised dramatic entertainment with a flavour of heathen rites about it.

---

[1] *Vatnsdæla Saga*, ch. 47.

[2] Heusler and Ranisch, *Eddica Minora*, Introd. p. c.

[3] According to Fritzner, *syrpa* in mod. Icel. means an album containing occasional verse. The word *syrpuvers* occurs once in the *Riddara rímur*.

[4] In Småland, Sweden, the meaning of the word *sörpa* is to cook food badly. *Rietz. Dial. lex.* sv. *Sörpa*.

[5] This has its bearing on such a work as *Hárbarðsljóð*, which might better be explained as an improvised flyting than as a very corrupt poem.

[6] *Herrauðssaga ok Bósa*, ch. 5 (*F. A. S.* III. p. 206). The verse is a kind of riddle, ending in a curse if it is not answered rightly.

Amusing though it evidently was, the chief Thorkell Geitisson does not condescend to be present at the entertainment, from which we may presume that already about A.D. 980 dramatic representations, even in Norway, were generally left to the lower classes. This would of course explain the silence of our sources about them.

It would hardly be possible to find a better proof of our hypothesis, based on quite other grounds, that popular drama existed in Norway while it hardly took root in Iceland. But a curious survival in Sweden shows that some kind of comic dramatic representation of proceedings at a *Thing* must have been widely prevalent in Scandinavia, since we hear of it there as well as in Iceland. After the close of the local *Thing* or assizes at Rättvik in Sweden it used to be the custom for the magistrate to invite the *nämnd* or jurymen to supper[1], and during this entertainment the jurymen are said to have amused themselves with acting a complete " sessions." The magistrate was naturally Chairman, plaintiffs and defendants were selected from among the company and the imaginary suits were called out and dealt with according to the legal forms[2]. In view of the occasion it is clear that the proceedings were of a comic character.

It will be remembered that the ancient Scandinavian *Thing* was a religious festival.

There is evidence that at an early date the Swedes found it natural to represent historical events dramatically. In Strelow's *Chronicle of Gotland*, published in 1633, it is stated that in 1361, when the Gotlanders heard of the Danish king's preparations to attack the island, instead of being alarmed they mocked him and made a game or play to be acted at all public meetings, especially in the Carnival season, "which is still commonly played at our Yule parties[3]." The players form a ring and "Valdemar" (the Danish King Valdemar Atterdag) has to try and creep within,

---

[1] Each guest presented a brace of blackcock to the host somewhat after the fashion prevailing at heathen festivals: cp. *Heimskringla*, ed. F. Jónsson; *Hákonar Saga góða*, ch. 14.

[2] In the introduction to *Tafvelgalleri från stugor i Dalom*, utg. af E. Bosæus, 3de Uppl. Stockholm, n. d.

[3] Strelow, *Guthilandiske Cronica*, 1633, pp. 168 f.

any player who allows him to do so being penalized. The chronicler gives the text of the song used in his day, in which the players taunt Valdemar with being better at playing the lute, etc., than at taking Gotland. Valdemar pleads to come in, and they reply: "Thou shalt surely stand outside"; "Here come the Gotlanders riding against thee," and so forth[1]. It has recently been suggested that the dramatic Yule game in Sweden in which "King Orre" figures originated in a representation of the defeat of King Erik of Pomerania[2].

For Denmark an English Franciscan monk, of the second half of the thirteenth century, has preserved for us a significant little cautionary tale, related to him, he says, by a Danish comrade, Brother Peder[3]. In his country, Brother Peder said, the lying-in of a woman is enlivened by her neighbours, who come in and divert themselves with songs and improper dances[4]. On one such occasion when a number of women were gathered together they collected a bundle of straw and gave it the likeness of a man with arms of straw, put a hood and belt on it and called it Bovi. Thereupon they began their ring-dance, two women leapt and sang with him between them, and in between the verses they turned round to him, *as was the custom*, with froward gestures and said to him: "Sing with us, Bovi, sing too, why art thou silent[5]? But at that moment the devil answered: "Yea, I will sing"—and uttered a yell which killed some of them with fright.

When this game was not interrupted by supernatural intervention "Bovi" was evidently represented as singing his part, and we must therefore regard the dance as a kind of drama. The introduction of a dummy is interesting, and may be paralleled in heathen times by the dummy giant Mökkrkálfi in the lost poem

---

[1] A similar representation occurs sporadically and much later at Lübeck, a town much influenced by Scandinavia. When the inhabitants of the town heard of the defeat of the Danes at Hemmingstedt in 1500, they made a dramatic representation of it at the Carnival, mocking the Danes. (Troels-Lund, *Danmarks og Norges Hist. i Slutningen af det 16de Aarh.* (1805), Bd. I.; Bog. VII. p. 197.)

[2] H. Jungner, Om Kung Orre, *Maal og Minne*, 1914, pp. 123 ff.

[3] *Danske Studier*, 1907, p. 175, from Paul Meyer, *Notices et Extraits des MSS.*, XXXIV. p. 433.

[4] Tripudia sua cum cantilenis inordinatis.

[5] Meyer's emendation: *quid taces*, for *quid faceret*.

on Thor's fight with Hrungnir[1]. In a modern Swedish game such a straw figure, called Job, appears, and the object of one of the two players is to upset "Job." The game has dramatic elements, for there is an amusing dialogue between the two players[2]. A stuffed figure plays a part in Christmas festivities in Southern Norway[3].

In an article entitled "Traces of Swedish popular drama[4]" the playwright Strindberg points out that while scholars have connected the folk-games and dance-ballads with an original popular drama in Sweden, they have ignored the far more dramatic "conversations" (*samtal*), printed copies of which are found in Sweden from the seventeenth century onwards[5]. It appears that about a dozen of these "*samtaler*" are still extant as flysheets from the seventeenth and eighteenth century, and most of them have servant girls or old women as chief speakers, so that they cannot be of literary origin. One of them, called Radänga, represents a wooing and has six characters. A similar dialogue from Skåne is a sort of flyting between two old women[6]. The popular origin of these *samtaler* seems to be vouched for by the fact that in Skåne up to the beginning of last century or later little plays were composed and acted at Christmas representing any remarkable action, generally of a reprehensible kind, by one of the neighbourhood. It was a form of reprimand if anyone was told that his behaviour was such that it would make the subject of a Christmas play[7]. Among the plays is mentioned one called *Träffenlo*, which represented a person then living who was discovered stealing seed. The representation was given in a corner of the main room, and showed a man very busy filling his sack

---

[1] See above p. 115. Perhaps the two "wooden men" who according to *Flateyjarbók*, I. p. 403, were buried with Frey, may be considered in this connection. One, we learn, was afterwards sent to Trondhjem, while the other was worshipped by the Swedes. Cp. also the wooden figure sent by the Danes to the Swedes after the Danish victory over Óttarr vendilkráka.

[2] L. Lloyd, *Peasant Life in Sweden*, London, 1870, p. 183.

[3] Ross, *Norsk Ordbog*, s.v. *jolestratt*.

[4] Strindberg, *Kulturhist. Studier*, Stockholm, n. d. p. 158.

[5] A list of these plays is given in the Appendix to P. O. Bäckström, *Svenska Folkböcker*, Stockholm (1845), pp. 158 ff. Many of them appeared in a number of editions.

[6] *Sv. landsm.* II. 9. pp. 83 ff.

[7] Lundell, in *Pauls Grundriss*, II. 2, pp. 1162 f.

with seed while in a monologue he expressed his fear lest day should dawn before he had finished, or that the night should conceal some eye-witness. He continually paused to listen, thinking he heard voices, and then settled to work again. Finally a cock crowed, and while he was hurrying to the door with his sack the owner of the grain leapt forth and pommelled him soundly, while he writhed and shrieked, to the great joy of the spectators[1]. In another play a man with a blackened face, carrying a horn, bursts in upon a gay group of merry-makers and card-players, calling out " Here I win[2]."

In this connection the very widespread play *Staffan Stalledreng* should be mentioned, for though it is ostensibly ecclesiastical in origin the importance given to the horse has led scholars to see in it heathen antecedents, only superficially modified by being attached to the story of St Stephen. Staffan and Herod are the chief actors. Staffan makes his speech mounted on his gray steed, which consists of two youths fastened so that they are back to back and each walking on both feet and hands—or rather on sticks held in the hands. This eight-legged horse[3] is draped with a gray cloth, and much of Staffan's speech deals with its incredible swiftness[4]. Another little play with a beast performer is found all over Scandinavia—the *Bukkevise*. The performers are three boys, two of whom personate "father and son," while the third is dressed up as a goat. The doggerel recited by the " father and son " is corrupt[5], but it recounts the slaughter of the goat and its resurrection, and this is accompanied by appropriate action on the part

---

[1] The form of this play has analogies with *Grímnismál.*

[2] Nicolovius, *Folklifvet i Skytts Härad i Skåne*, Lund, 1847, pp. 81 ff.

[3] The steed or animal represented by two men fastened together under a hide or cloth is so common that it must almost be assumed to be ancient. "Old Hob" in England is thus composite; so is the Scandinavian " Skymmelryttaren " and often the " Yule Goat " in Denmark (Nilsson, *Årets folkliga fester*, pp. 173, 268). Odin's eight-legged horse may well have been thus represented.

[4] G. Djurklou, Hvem var Staffan Stalledreng? *Sv. fornminnes-föreningens tidskrift*, II. pp. 335 ff.

[5] There is a curious reference to "Elias' top" and "Elias fjeld." "Elias" appears to have taken the place of Thor: cp. Hammerstedt, Elias, åskguden, in *Fataburen*, 1916. It is perhaps worth noting that among the Circassian Tatars in the seventeenth century a goat was sacrificed on " St Elias Day " (*Encycl. of Religion and Ethics*), s.v. *Animals*, I, p. 517.

of the third performer. The Norwegian verses appear to retain a memory of the partition of the goat-skin : "how much wilt thou give for the goat its skin?—wool?[1]"

We have here another case of the actual performances of a slaying and resurrection, with the additional primitive feature of a beast-skin disguise shed by the victim and at one time apparently allotted to one of the persons present. But in one district of Sweden a scene acted until recently included a mimic representation not only of a slaying and resurrection, but also of what we may call a love-scene. This folk-play preserves a feature lost in the May-Day performances in the English mumming-plays, for an element of sacrifice appears to linger about the mock slaying. Several youths with blackened faces and disguised persons are the chief performers. One of them represents the victim about to be immolated. The knife and other needful appurtenances are brought forward and he is put to death to the accompaniment of music and song. A woman officiates, hideously attired, and with a blackened face. She becomes the partner of the victim in the dance that follows, which ends, says our informant, with gesticulations so gross as to give reason to believe that the priestess and high priest (of the original ritual) were accustomed to terminate their sacrificial dances in the like manner[2].

We will defer the discussion of the dramatized ballads so common in Scandinavia, for we have quoted enough cases of popular drama in Sweden and Denmark[3] to show that in these countries it was not a mere degenerate descendant of Church drama, but an independent and living growth, which must go back to heathen times. Its origin therefore will be best elucidated by our examination of the plots and characters of the surviving Eddic drama.

Before entering on this part of our task we must acknowledge

---

[1] Nicolaysen, [Norsk] *Historisk Tidskrift*, III. R. Bd. III. (1895) pp. 212 ff.

[2] L. Lloyd, *Peasant Life in Sweden*, 1870, p. 181. Nilsson says that the traditional ritual marriage performed up to about 1850 in Rönnebergs härad in Skåne ended in such a way that no persons of any self-respect could be found to act the parts of bride and bridegroom (*Årets folklige Fester*, p. 81).

[3] Copies of two Danish popular plays exist : *Den utro Hustru* (ed. Birket Smith), 1874, and Rauchs *Karrig Niding*, composed before 1607 : cp. Kohler, *Germania*, XXII.

a change of method in our investigations. In the previous chapters the general consensus of expert opinion about the date and provenance of the poems formed the foundation of the argument, and in the whole course of the investigation it was never necessary to seek evidence outside the Eddic poems themselves and the records of Saxo and Snorri. But when we come to deal with questions of folk-lore and ritual we must necessarily proceed on another plan. We must combine the bare indications given by the poems themselves with such hints as can be gleaned from popular customs, archaeology, ancient tradition, and parallels from other times and countries. We build therefore on a less secure foundation, and our results are necessarily speculative in a sense in which it would be unjust to apply the term to the earlier stages of our enquiry. But there is one very re-assuring feature about the results attained in the following pages. In the first part of this book the conclusions of scholars form the premises of our argument. In the second part the premises are our own, but the results tally with the conclusions of all that band of scholars who have devoted themselves to the prehistoric religion and sociology of the North. Professor Chadwick, Professor Schück, and Professor Magnus Olsen have all approached this subject on entirely different lines, and using to a great extent wholly different material. Our own researches into the heroic drama of the North have led us to discern the same religious conceptions, the same historical facts, as Professor Chadwick has deduced from the wide fields of archaeology, history and comparative religion, Professor Schück from the philological study of *Ynglingatal*, and most recently Professor Magnus Olsen from the unpromising, but in his hands exceedingly productive soil of Norwegian place-names.

CHAPTER XII

PLOTS OF THE EDDIC DRAMAS

DIVINE PROTAGONISTS

SINCE all the native Norwegian Eddic poems originally contained supernatural elements the usual distinction—always a clumsy one—between "mythological" and "heroic" poems is no longer convenient, and it will be best to classify them according to their central themes—the slaying and the love-scene.

The poems which do not contain a love-scene are: *Grímnismál, Vafthrúðnismál, Alvíssmál, Balder's Death, Thor's visit to Geirröð, Heimdallargaldr* and *Hrungnismál*. The only two poems which form a kind of transition between this class and those containing love-scenes are *Thrym's Lay* and *Hyndluljóð*. In *Thrym's Lay* a wedding is at least simulated, but there cannot be said to be a love-scene in the poem, and we therefore class it with the plays in which the slaying is the central theme. So also with *Hyndluljóð*. Although there is reason to believe that the poem culminated in a betrothal scene between Freyja and Óttarr, the end of the poem as we have it shows the destruction of the giantess by fire, and it must therefore be classed with the slayings.

If we examine these plays more closely we shall find that they fall under two heads. I. Plays which represent the slaying of a god. II. Plays in which a god or supernatural being causes the death of his opponent. We will begin by considering type I.

I. *The slaying of a god.*

Of the two poems on this subject the slightest fragments only remain, but we know enough to recognise that neither flyting nor love-scene nor resurrection is combined with the theme of *Balder's Death*. Of *Heimdallargaldr*, the other poem representing the slaying of a god, we have still less information, but at least we have no traditions to suggest that in these respects the play was different from that on *Balder's Death*.

Curiously enough, while the human beings in the plays die but to rise again, there is at first sight no such clear indication as to the resurrection of the two gods who are represented as slain in our dramas, Balder and Heimdall. But we must remember that we have only one strophe of the poem on Balder, and two lines of that on Heimdall. Of Balder we can at least point out that it is hoped that he will return. The condition laid down is that everything on earth quick or dead shall weep for him. Snorri tells us that men and beasts weep, and the earth and rocks and trees and all metal. But the giantess Thökk will not weep, and she is the speaker of the one extant strophe of the poem. Snorri tells us that there is a great ship-funeral. All the gods are present, with the motley collection of their steeds— cats ·and a boar and horses. Odin has his ravens: there is a giantess on a wolf whose beast is so restive that when she dismounts four berserks have to fell it before they can manage to hold it. There is an officious dwarf, and mountain-giants— uncouth figures, no doubt—attend the ceremony. Balder's wife Nanna, dies of grief during the proceedings, and her body is flung on the funeral pyre. As we read Snorri's words, the whole proceeding seems rather like a game which Snorri had either seen himself or had had described to him[1]—for the dialogic poem could hardly have described all the spectators at the funeral.

The annual burning of a god in effigy or in the person of a human representative seems to have been practised by the Phoenicians and the Hittites[2]. The mourning over a god in effigy was part of the ritual of Adonis[3]. As these effigies, after being carried out to burial, were thrown into the sea or into springs, so an effigy of Balder may have been committed to the deep. On the shores of the Mediterranean we hear of the wailing and lamentation for Pan, for Adonis, or Tammuz and further afield for the grape-cluster[4]. In this last case universal lamentation is prescribed

[1] Professor Chadwick informs me that he has always regarded Snorri's account as founded on an annual dramatic game, which Snorri had seen or had described to him.

[2] Frazer, *Adonis, Attis and Osiris*, p. 155.

[3] *Ib.* p. 183.

[4] Frazer, *The Dying God*, p. 8. The laments for these gods seem to take place at Midsummer. Apparently Midsummer fires in Sweden were called "Balders bålar."

P.   9

under heavy penalties. Might not the drama of Balder's death and departure overseas have been enacted in the North with some idea that universal lamentation, and what we may call a royal send-off[1], would have an effect in inducing the god to return at the proper season?

A strange custom in Sweden, described by Olaus Magnus in the sixteenth century, may perhaps best be explained as a survival of some such pantomimic mourning. He says that "they dance at feasts, singing ancient songs of heroic deeds and then all of a sudden begin to sigh and sob and then follow laments, tears and loud wailings, and finally all fling themselves to the ground, followed by some of the bystanders[2]."

The other slain god is Heimdall. According to Snorri the poem *Heimdallargaldr* described the god's death; he was struck, Snorri says, by a human head, apparently used as a missile. Only two lines of the poem survive, but it is interesting that these two lines appear to allude to rebirth.

Heimdall says:

> I am the son of nine mothers,
> I am the offspring of nine sisters.

It is difficult to see what these two lines signify unless they allude to nine re-incarnations, the mothers who bear him successively being nine sisters. Both at Lejre in Denmark and at Upsala in Sweden there was a great festival every nine years, and we might possibly connect these words with such a nine-year cycle. But there is other evidence which probably bears more closely on the story.

In *Ynglingasaga* Snorri tells us of a Swedish king Aun[3], who sacrificed his nine sons, one every tenth year (Ari says every ninth year) in order to secure for himself long life, and when the Swedes refused to let him sacrifice the tenth and last son, he died.

---

[1] This send-off appears to include a sacrifice for a safe journey, an unnecessary precaution if the god be thought of as irretrievably dead. Snorri says that while Thor was consecrating Balder's pyre on the boat a dwarf ran in front of him and got kicked into the flames. A curious passage in the old Norwegian laws hints very plainly at a custom of human sacrifice at the launching of a vessel for a voyage, and the chronicler Dudo knows of such a practice among the Normans.

[2] Olaus Magnus, Bk. IV. ch. 8.   [3] *Yngl.* ch. 25.

Icelandic tradition has a similar tale about Hálfdan the Old[1]. This king performs a great sacrifice at mid-winter in order to live for three hundred years. His prayer is not granted, but he is told that for that space of time no scion of his race will be other than a king. He marries and has nine sons, all born at the same time, and all of whom fall in battle without issue. Then he had another nine, also all at a birth, and these were the ancestors of famous dynasties. In view of the other story there is something suspicious about the deaths of the first nine without issue. In both tales it is only the tenth son (or sons) who carries on the race.

All this looks like the dim memory of a time when the sons of a king were sacrificed in order to preserve his divine life, and only when he became very decrepit was a surviving son allowed to succeed him[2]. Probably the memory of such a ritual sacrifice is at the back of our poem[3].

Snorri says[4]: "A sword is called Heimdall's head: it is said that he was pierced through by a man's head:—that is narrated in *Heimdallargaldr*,—and since then a head is called the doom[5] of Heimdall."

A head is called the doom of Heimdall—that is natural, since he was killed by a head. But we must also note that a sword is called *Heimdall's head*—which implies that Heimdall's head killed some one just as he himself was killed by a head. This is of course just what we should expect in a case of re-incarnation. He slew and was slain by the same means; and his head, according to tradition, was the instrument of death.

It is a puzzling story, and could probably only be explained by some forgotten ritual to which we have no clue. The nearest analogy seems to be the procedure at the end of a viceroy's

---

[1] Snorri, *Skáldskaparmál*, ch. 26.

[2] Cp. Schück, *Stud. Yngl.* III. (1907), p. 99. According to Bugge's reading of the Rök inscription Vémóð is Theodoric reborn after nine generations (*Runenstein von Rök*, p. 87). According to a suggested reading by Professor Schück (*loc. cit.* pp. 101 f.), Theodoric is said to have lived for nine generations.

[3] If human kings required sacrifices, so would the gods, if in that remote time we may draw any distinction between gods and kings. Heimdall would be the guardian of the gods (*vörðr goða*) because by his death they would be preserved from danger.

[4] *Skáldskaparmál*, ch. 8.

[5] *mjǫtuðr*: a rare word, only used in poetry. Its original meaning is "ordainer," or "fate"; cp. A.S. *meotoð*.

tenure of office in remote Malabar. At the end of every five years the head of the king's deputy was cut off and thrown up in the air, and the man who was successful in catching it succeeded to the royal power[1].

If the funeral of Balder survived as a game in Norway or Iceland, perhaps we may fancy that the game of Haxey Hood, played with much pomp and circumstance at Haxey in Yorkshire, may have affinities with a dramatic representation of the mode of Heimdall's death. The game is played[2] on Plough Monday (the Monday after Epiphany), and the "hood" or head (Scandinavian *höfuð*) with which it is played is a heavy plum-shaped ball. The proceedings open at the foot of the old market cross, with a speech by "Billy Buck," the leader of the game, but the game itself is played on a rise outside the village, on what once was common ground, and "Billy Buck" is very particular to get in line with a certain tree. Young men dressed up in ribbons play a special part in the game, and are called "Boggins[3]." If one of the "boggins" touches the "hood," it is, so to speak, taboo, and has to be handed back to "Billy Buck"; but if another player can carry it off to any public-house within a mile's radius he is entitled to free drinks for the afternoon. In this point the game has its affinities with the Malabar custom just quoted.

In the Haxey game no element of sacrifice survives, and the "hood" is regarded as a prize rather than as a weapon. For us its interest lies in the fact that it is a very old game played with a

---

[1] Frazer, *The Dying God*, p. 53.

[2] This year (1915) the game was not played owing to the absence of the young men at the war: and it is probable that it will never be taken up again. The information with regard to it was furnished to me by Miss Maisie Marshall, of Lady Margaret Hall, Oxford, who saw the game played in 1914 and made enquiries about it. "Billy Buck" is dressed in a red cloak and has a staff of willow wands bound together. In the course of his speech he has to say: "We've killed two bullock and a half, but the other half we've had to leave roonin' in t' fëeld. We can fetch it if its wanted. It's. hoose agin hoose, toon agin toon, and if you meet a man, knock him doon." (Cp. Chambers, *Mediaeval Stage*, I. p. 150.) Besides *the* "hood," of leather and very heavy, there are half a dozen others of stuffed sacking. With regard to the red cloak it may be observed that red is the traditional wear in Sweden at various folk festivals.

[3] In Lincolnshire dialect a "boggin" means a ghost. It is curious that the masked and beribboned lads who carry about an effigy of Winter at Zürich are called *Böggen*.

"head," and that it must almost necessarily go back to a ritual performance. When it is remembered that at Abbots Bromley[1] in Staffordshire a solemn performance takes place once a year in which six men wear *reindeer-horns*, which have been kept in the church for unnumbered generations, it will be realised what a miraculous tenacity of life is possessed by games of what we may call a ritual type.

II. *Plays in which a god causes the death of his opponent.*

These poems depict an argument or a fight culminating in the death of the god's opponent—a giant or dwarf, or in one case, in *Grímnismál*, a king.

In *Vafthrúðnismál* the giant Vafthrúðnir is slain by Odin as the result of a wager that whichever of them fails to answer the other's questions shall lose his head. In *Hyndluljóð* Freyja apparently destroys the giantess Hyndla by fire. The other poems of this type have Thor for their hero. In *Alvíssmál* the rising sun achieves the god's purpose for him, for when the first rays shine into the hall the dwarf is turned to stone. In three other poems, *Thrym's Lay*, *Hrungnismál* and the *Visit to Geirröð* Thor shows himself as the doughty champion dear to Northern myth and legend. In *Thrym's Lay* there is a scene of disorder in which the god's hammer is wielded to great effect, the giant brood being caught unawares. In *Hrungnismál* the giant is killed in fair fight. In the *Visit to Geirröð* Thor breaks the backs of two giantesses who try to crush him against the roof, and he also kills their father Geirröð.

The exploits of the gods are emulated in two cases by heroes. In the *Lay of Helgi Hjörvarðsson* Helgi lures the giantess Hrímgerð to death by the same device as that which Thor adopts to rid himself of Alvíss. In the Sigurd trilogy Sigurd kills first the dragon Fáfnir and then the dwarf Reginn. As however these slayings are merely episodes in the poems, and do not form the final dramatic catastrophe, they do not properly find a place here.

What is the significance of these little dramas setting forth the slaying of monsters by the gods, or occasionally by heroes?

---

[1] Ordish, Folk-drama, *Folk-lore*, IV. p. 172.

To use Greek terminology, each play is an *agôn* in which the god's antagonist meets his death. But we must observe that the contest is not merely one of brute force. It is also one of wits. In *Vafthrúðnismál* the slaying is merely the climax of a contest of knowledge in which Odin has won. In *Hyndluljóð* Freyja imposes her will on the giantess and extracts from her the information she desires. And the same thing is true of Thor's contests, though here his companions sometimes supply the wits. In *Alvíssmál* Thor himself outwits the dwarf; in *Thrym's Lay* Loki's help is necessary to fool Thrym. In *Hrungnismál* Thor might not have won the day but for the guile of his attendant Thjálfi, who persuades the giant to stand on his shield.

These scenes represent in every case a victory of the god over some powerful enemy of the gods and the human race alike. The giants are evidently felt as a menace to both, for in *Thrym's Lay* Loki is made to point out that if Thor does not recover his hammer, the giants will take possession of Asgard. Among these hostile giants are the frost-giants (*hrímþursar*); and it is perhaps significant that the Norwegian people believed that the end of the world was to be brought about by cold. A *fimbulvetr*, a "chief of winters," would hold the earth in its iron grip, and in the darkness and famine and misery of that time all life would disappear[1].

Primitive drama is not composed solely with a view to entertainment. If the Norwegians performed a special type of dramatic representation in which a god, usually Thor, is victorious in a contest with a giant, we may suppose that they first did so as a means of securing that Thor should in fact always be successful in those encounters with a race which for ever threatened the security of the world. And if we may conjecture the season when such plays were performed, we should suggest the Yule festival, the time when darkness broods most heavily on the earth, and when evil spirits are most powerful.

Four of the extant plays make Thor the hero of the encounter. Odin appears as the victor in one, and Freyja in another. But many legends show that the people regarded Thor as pre-eminently the protector of mankind against these would-be invaders. He is called *Miðgarðs véurr*, the defender of the world.

---

[1] Olrik, *Ragnarök*, Aarb. f.n.O., 1902.

The story of Hrungnir illustrates the helplessness of the other gods when they rashly admit the giant to their citadel. As soon as their guest becomes unruly they realise that this is Thor's business, and summon him by uttering his name.

The dramatic poems of this type are thus closely connected with Thor; and the representation of his victories probably tended to ensure the safety of mankind against redoubtable foes. We may be allowed to note a similarity between the Northern Thor and the Greek Heracles of comedy and myth. Heracles kills the giants Antaios, Geryon, Cacus, Eurytion, Eryx, as Thor slays Hrungnir, Hymir, Thrym, Geirröð, and the nameless builder of Asgard, and wrestles with the world-encircling serpent. Heracles is always disappearing on some perilous adventure; so is Thor. Heracles visits the world of the dead, so does Thor on his visit to Útgarðaloki. Heracles fights Old Age, so does Thor. Heracles was invoked in marriages, so was Thor, and Thor's hammer consecrates the bride. Heracles in comedy is not above ribaldry and tauntings, nor is Thor. Heracles in comedy is a gigantic eater and drinker, so is Thor. In this, indeed, the Northerner beats the Southron: Heracles eats a whole ox at a sitting, but Thor can dispose of eight salmon as well. Heracles has *thiasi* or clubs named after him: personal names are compounded with Thor. Heracles is armed in primitive fashion with a club, Thor in equally primitive style with a hammer which the peasants of the North still recognise in the flint axes of the Stone Age. Thor never appears in heroic story: Heracles barely appears in Homer. Both have comic associations incompatible with heroic Saga. Their place is in drama.

Now it appears that Heracles was the mythical leader of the *kômos*, a festal procession. Aristotle tells us that Attic comedy originated with the revel-songs sung by the *kômos* under its leader or precentor. The satyric drama, in which Heracles played so large a part, was closely akin to comedy, if not from the same source. It is interesting that Thor, who corresponds to the Greek Herakles in so many respects, corresponds to him also in this further particular, that he is the chief character, the victorious Agonist, in what we may call the satyric drama of the North[1].

---

[1] A recent writer says of Heracles: "Observe that the myths, with whatever

The Fertility-Drama, having a human and princely hero, was capable of being treated in the "heroic" style and so made acceptable to an aristocratic society, while the combats between gods and giants probably lost their interest for the travelled and enlightened aristocracy of the Viking Age. No aristocratic influence, therefore, has been at work to purge these poems of the grotesqueness, the buffoonery, the occasional coarseness and the *naïveté* which belong to the drama of the country folk.

Naturally these representations did not survive Christianity, being far more obviously heathen than the folk-play successor to the old Fertility Drama. Of the two antagonists, the victorious god was doomed to disappear, while his opponent, vanquished in the conflict, yet survived, and may still be seen on village greens as the wicker-work giant of English folk-drama.

---

variety of detail, all have one plot, the combat or Agôn with the Agonist and the Victory of Heracles" (J. A. K. Thomson, *The Greek Tradition*, 1914, p. 130).

CHAPTER XIII

PLOTS OF THE EDDIC DRAMAS (*cont.*)

THE RITUAL MARRIAGE

WE have already seen that besides the folk-plays representing the Year-Drama, surviving in the fights between Summer and Winter for the May Queen, little scenes were commonly acted in Scandinavia representing merely a wedding. The object of both forms of drama is evidently originally the same—the promotion of the earth's fertility—but the ritual marriage is of a simpler type. It is of the essence of the Year-Drama proper that there should be competition for the bride, and we shall see that to win her it is invariably necessary for the bridegroom to slay some close kinsman either of himself or of the bride, a kinsman who is thought of as holding her in his keeping. Under literary treatment these plays therefore tend to be tragic. In the ritual marriage plays the ending is a happy one, for the only important point is that the forms of a wedding should be gone through, with more or less preamble in the way of wooing, and more or less difficulty to be overcome by the wooer. To this class we must assign at least two Eddic poems, the Sigurd trilogy and *Skírnismál*[1], and we can guess that *Hyndluljóð* in its original form belonged here too. The difficulties to be overcome are in each case different. Sigurd has to kill a dragon, Frey has to overcome the opposition of his bride and the dangers of her dwelling. In *Hyndluljóð* Freyja, apparently, has to satisfy herself that Óttarr is really the descendant of a royal line. In each case, it may be observed, the bride is of supernatural origin, even when, as in the Sigurd trilogy and *Hyndluljóð*, the bridegroom is mortal.

---

[1] A reference in Gerð's speech (str. 16) shows that this play originally belonged to the Year-Drama type, since Frey had killed Gerð's brother. It is worth noting that Iðunn, another goddess of fertility, is accused of union with her brother's slayer (*Lokasenna*, str. 17).

The Sigurd trilogy is unfortunately very fragmentary, owing to its forcible amalgamation with a poem in another metre dealing with the Nibelungen story. But it seems clear that the deliverance of the valkyrie depends in some way on the slaying of Fáfnir. According to our theory of the original Norwegian tradition, this nameless valkyrie is Gudrun, Brynhild being one of the later German accretions to the story. It is therefore highly significant that certain Norwegian ballads imply the presence of Gudrun during the fight with the dragon. Such a tradition survives also in the prose introduction to the Eddic *First Lay of Gudrun*: "It is a tale among men, that Gudrun had eaten of Fáfnir's heart, and therefore she understood the speech of birds." This can only refer to the original Norwegian form of the story in which Gudrun was the maiden to be delivered during the fight. This traditional form of the story, in which the liberation of the maiden depends on the slaying of the monster[1], reappears in the *Seyfriedslied*, a sixteenth-century reproduction of mainly Scandinavian tradition. It at once brings the play into line with the "St George" folk-plays in which the lady is delivered from a giant or a dragon. At Fürth in Bavaria a drama called the "Slaying of the Dragon" used to be acted every year about Midsummer, and here the victor delivers a maiden, as Sigurd delivers his valkyrie. She is present at the combat like Gudrun in the Norwegian ballad and in the tradition preserved in the prose of the *First Lay of Gudrun*. The ritual associations of the Fürth dragon are clearly seen in the fact that the onlookers carefully mopped up the (bullock's) blood with which the dragon is provided, believing that placed on their fields it would promote the growth of their crops[2]. The mediaeval English pageant of St George seems constantly to have included the rescuing of a lady from the dragon[3], and this form of the story is traced in the speech of St George in one of the English Easter plays:

> I followed a fair lady to a giant's gate,

in the attempt to free her

> A giant almost struck me dead,
> But by my valour I cut off his head.

---

[1] Cp. also the story of Ragnar Loðbrók in Saxo, IX. 302.
[2] Frazer, *Magic Art*, II. 163.
[3] Ordish, *Folklore*, IV. p. 152.

In the Lincolnshire Plow-boys' and Morris-dancers' Play the Fool fights a "Wild Worm"—evidently a Scandinavian dragon. The dragon is perhaps the most common of all beast-characters in folk-drama[1], and is especially prominent in the East of England—the Scandinavian districts. At Norwich, in the fifteenth century, the Guild of St George was responsible for the representation of the annual conflict. In the eighteenth century the Dragon was of basket-work, could move or spread its wings and distend or contract its head. But its antagonist is not always St George. At Rouen the *gargouille* is said to have been killed by St Romain. The dragon-slayer at Fürth is not called St George. Evidently the dragon is older than the Saint. The view which derived the folk-drama from the mediaeval miracle-plays has been ably refuted by Beatty[2], who points out that (1) "St George" himself is frequently slain and that (2) revivification is always a central incident in the play.

The influence of St George has however altered the plot, for where the hero is clearly identified with the Saint, as in the Norwich representation, propriety ultimately steps in to forbid the introduction of a female character.

Two poems preserved by Saxo contain a slaying as a condition precedent to a marriage, and may therefore be considered here. The use of disguise betrays their dramatic origin. Gram is betrothed to Signe, daughter of the King of the Finns, and learns that she is to be given in marriage to King Henry of Saxony. In disguise he appears at the wedding, and uttering verses boasting of his valour and reviling Signe[3] for "entangling, luring and bestaining" princes,

he cut Henry down while at the sacred board and amid the embraces of

---

[1] A dragon of painted canvas was one of the stock figures of the English mumming plays, although it is fast disappearing. In one play at least it is the only member of the caste which is not brought to life again. A man brought up in Lincolnshire and now (1915) at the war remembers the troublesome rehearsals necessary for taking the dragon's part.

[2] A. Beatty, *The St George or Mummers' Plays*, 1906, pp. 277 ff.

[3] "Now Signe, the daughter of Sumble, vilely spurns me, and endures vows not mine, cursing the ancient troth, and conceiving an ill-ordered love, commits a notable act of female lightness; for she entangles, lures and bestains princes, rebuffing above all others the lordly of birth; yet remaining firm to none, but ever wavering, and bringing to birth impulses doubtful and divided." Bk. I. p. 19.

his friends, carried off his bride from among the bridesmaids, felled most of the guests, and bore her off with him in his ship. Thus the bridal was turned into a funeral.

The hero of the other poems on this subject is Halfdan, who hears that his betrothed, Gyuritha, is to be married to Sivar, a Saxon. He arrives in time for the wedding and reproaches her in a "dark and ambiguous song" of the same tenor as Gram's. Here however Saxo gives Gyuritha's answer, pleading that she did not know where Halfdan was, and that she had yielded to pressure. "Before the maiden had finished her answer, Halfdan had already run his sword through the bridegroom. Not content with killing one man, he massacred most of the guests[1]." His disguise may be assumed from the circumstance that he is not recognised.

There can be little doubt that while lengthening the expression of each sentiment with his diffuse Latin, Saxo at the same time epitomized the dialogue, putting into one speech what was probably given in the original in a number of short utterances, interrupted by the replies of the other protagonists. Moreover Saxo does not give the whole poem, even if he knew it. It is probable that an actual love-scene followed the reunion of the bride and bridegroom, as in the Eddic poems. In the Sigurd trilogy, for instance, we pass from the dragon slaying to a love-scene, and this contains a significant little bit of ritual—the handing of the betrothal cup to Sigurd by his bride. This betrothal cup occurs in the two other poems of this class, *Skírnismál* and *Hyndluljóð*, but in *Sigrdrífumál* it is more ceremonial, being accompanied by a solemn invocation of two strophes. The prose says that these strophes are spoken by the valkyrie, but as Sigurd was to drink first it is probable that the first strophe, asking for victory, was originally assigned to him, and that the valkyrie uttered the second on receiving back the cup, asking for "hands of healing."

> Hail to thee, Day,   hail sons of Day!
>   Hail, Night and New Moon
> with eyes free from wrath   behold us here
>   and to us twain who sit here give victory.

---

[1] VII. 246. A story involving (somewhat unnecessarily) the disguise of the hero (Ole) and ending with his union with a bride destined for another, is given in VII. 253, and probably goes back to a poetic original.

Hail gods,   hail goddesses,
    hail Earth,   giver of manifold gifts,
wisdom in word and thought   bestow on us glorious twain
and hands of healing, while we live."

In the *Lay of Helgi Hundingsbane* Sigrún heaps a bridal bed before offering Helgi a cup. In the light of these instances the goblet of mead offered by Gerð to Skírnir (for Frey) by which she tacitly consents to be his, and that offered to Freyja by Óttarr, gain an increased significance. A bridal cup must have been an important ceremony at a wedding, as in local custom in Sweden[1]. Until recently it was still the custom in country districts in Sweden for the bride and bridegroom to drain a large bowl—the property of the parish—before entering the house on their return from church, as soon as they had ridden round the "bridal tree[2]." In Dalecarlia a large tree, called the "bridal ox," used to be brought into the house at weddings. It was "slaughtered" by having branches hewn off it, and the company drank the "ox-blood," represented by coffee and brandy[3]. There is thus an element of sacrifice about the bridal cup, but it is reserved for a Danish ballad to indicate its full significance. Ridder Stig drinks to his lady-love "saa Mark og Skov de blomstre derved"—"so that field and wood blossom thereat." The ceremonial bridal cup aimed not only at securing the prosperity of the bride and bridegroom but, if these were outstanding persons, of the whole country-side. Such a rite, then, would be an important feature of the ritual wedding. We may surmise that the representations on Runic stones and elsewhere of a female figure holding a horn are analogous in significance to the Norwegian gold plates representing the ritual wedding.

There is one other point worthy of note in *Sigrdrífumál.* The valkyrie is in a magic slumber till Sigurd rouses her, and as she

---

[1] And evidently in older times in Norway. Norwegian ecclesiastical ordinances of the twelfth century have to insist that a wedding is still legal, even though it be celebrated with nothing but whey. In Ydre härad, Östergötland, it was considered unlucky to have the banns called on an empty cask—i.e. before the ale was brewed. (Rääf, *Beskrifning öfv. Ydre härad,* Del. I., Linköping, 1856, p. 110).

[2] Hammerstedt, in *Maal og Minne,* 1911, p. 504. These bowls had names—Sven, Knatt (the Ball), and so forth. In Telemarken in Norway the bride used to drink a beaker before entering her new home. Helland, *Norges Land og Folk,* IX. p. 547.

[3] Hammerstedt, *loc. cit.* p. 492.

wears a helmet and byrnie he thinks, says the prose, that she is a man, and only discovers his mistake when he cleaves asunder her helmet. Then he has to split open her coat of mail before she wakes. There is a curious parallel to this scene in a little drama acted by French peasants at Briançon in Dauphiné, though here the parts of the sexes are reversed. The lads wrap a young fellow up in leaves: he is called "the king of the month of May." He lies down and pretends to be asleep. A girl comes and wakes him up and they repair together to the ale-house, where he takes off his outer covering of leaves. It is understood that they will marry within the year[1]. Frazer suggests the possibility that the pictorial representations of the forsaken and sleeping Ariadne, waked by Dionysus, have their source in some such little drama as this[2].

A number of stories in the late *Fornaldar Sögur* contain the *motif* of the maiden disguised as a warrior being subdued by the hero who strips her of her disguises[3]. One story in Saxo actually reproduces the scene in *Sigrdrífumál*: Alvilda is disguised as a viking, but her helmet is struck off and her opponent discovers that "here one should kiss and not strike[4]."

Several of Saxo's dialogic love-poems reveal their dramatic origin by the use of disguise. Regner, disguised, woos Svanhvita, the daughter of Hadding, who gives him a sword and plights her troth to him. The theme occurs again in the Hagbard and Signe poem, in which Hagbard is disguised as a woman. In two other poems it is the woman who is in some way disguised. The coy Syritha seems strangely transformed after her escape from the giant, when Otharus woos her[5], and again disguised in another fashion, as a bond-maid, when she finally yields to him[6].

Another poem is of rather a different type. It gives the speeches of Harthgrep, a giantess, to Hadding. She offers him her love, which he refuses on the score that he cannot mate with a giantess, but she assures him that she can and will change her shape, and he yields[7]. Some such scene must have occurred in

---

[1] Frazer, *Magic Art*, II. pp. 92 f.   [2] *Ib.* p. 138.
[3] These stories are discussed by B. Nerman, *Studier över Svärges hedna litteratur*, Upsala, 1913, pp. 110 ff.   Nerman regards them as specifically Swedish.
[4] Saxo, VII. 229.   [5] VII. 226.   [6] XVI. 227.
[7] I. 20–22.

one of the lost parts of the *Lay of Helgi Hjörvarðsson*, where the troll-woman woos Helgi, though here the ending is different, for he rejects her advances.

There are thus a considerable number of little wooing-scenes in dramatic form in Saxo. We may call them a contest or *agôn* ending in the union of the protagonists, and they are evidently the prototypes of the ritual weddings of modern Scandinavian custom. Such wooing-scenes are found again in the North of France in the twelfth century, and also in Italy. They became a literary type, which Jeanroy calls a "*chanson dramatique*," and Gaston Paris a "*chanson à personnages.*" At the end of these poems the poet boasts of the success of his wooing, but Gaston Paris maintains that this is not an original feature. He observes that in all cases there is a reference to the month of May, and regards them as a literary development from little popular scenes danced and acted at May festivals[1]. He points to the drama or dramatic poem composed by Adam de la Halle about 1200, and suggests that it may be merely the literary treatment of a popular game. Now it so happens that in the year 1392 we have a record of "people going out, *disguised*, in a game which is called Robin and Marion, such as is customarily performed every year, at the fair of Pentecost[2]."

Everything, then, suggests that these little dramas were evolved out of a spring festival. Since Saxo's poems are certainly as early as the records of the French ballets, it will hardly be suggested that the Northerners have borrowed the theme from France. In both cases the wooing-scene and its *dénouement* is surely simply a development from the ritual marriage of the spring festival. These Scandinavian wedding-plays correspond to the English *Ludi de Rege et Regina*, forbidden in the thirteenth century, and to the *Summer Lords* and *Ladies*, or *Lords* and *Ladies of Misrule*, and other "disguised persons" who show a tendency to dance and play unseemly parts in church or churchyard.

---

[1] Some of them are still so danced and acted, cp. V. Smith, *Romania*, VII. 62.

[2] H. Guy, *Essai sur...Adam de la Halle*, 1898, p. 187, quoted by Chambers.

CHAPTER XIV

THE FERTILITY DRAMA

WE must now turn to the poems in which the mating of the lovers involves tragic consequences. The plot combines what seem to be incongruous elements—a flyting, the slaying of a kinsman, and a love-scene, sometimes but not necessarily combined with a hint of resurrection. There is no mistaking the significance of these scenes. The flyting, the slaying, the love-scene are the integral parts of the most widespread drama in the world. It is acted to this day in Siberia[1] and in Thrace, and in our own villages. It represents the eternal contest of the Old and New Year, and has outlasted heathendom because the fulfilment of its aim is the age-long desire of the peasant. Its primary object is not commemorative but magical, and it is performed in order to induce the earth to bring forth abundantly.

In the extant poems, however, whether in the Edda or in Saxo, these ritual dramas have been "heroized." It is as heroic Saga that our poets treat them. Both the *Lay of Helgi Hjörvarðsson* and the *Lay of Helgi Hundingsbane* have been recast in a new metre by poets accustomed to the imported heroic lay; in all probability by Icelandic poets to whom the poems in their original state were awkwardly-told epics, not drama. Nevertheless we shall find in them, and in Saxo's poems of the same type, certain special characteristics, the characteristics of the Year-Drama, which we may define as follows:

(i) A slaying by the bridegroom. The slain man is a kinsman of either bride or bridegroom, usually a brother.

(ii) The implication that this slaying is in some way the bride's doing.

(iii) A flyting.

(iv) A love-scene.

---

[1] Czaplicka, *Aboriginal Siberia*, p. 298.

There may also be (v) hints of resurrection.

With regard to (ii) we must not overlook the fact that in all these Northern stories the woman is the central figure. She is not merely a prize acquired by the slaying of her natural guardian, as one might suppose from the Hamlet story and the kindred Greek stories. She is, as the old chant-metre strophe in the *Lay of Helgi Hundingsbane* darkly intimates, the very fountain-head of all the trouble: she stirs up the strife. Not for nothing does Sváva give Helgi a sword in the *Lay of Helgi Hjörvarðsson*, or Svanhvita give a sword to Regner in Saxo's poem. The freeing of the maiden and the wedding are the central points in the drama, and the English folk-customs, with their insistence on the May Queen, have kept the true perspective. We find it too in the May game of the Isle of Man, where the Queen of May delegates the fighting on her behalf to a captain.

Some years ago Professor Schück urged that the stories of pairs of brothers, Yngling kings, whose quarrels about a bride are narrated in *Ynglingatal*, are not historical, but must be explained as arising from a ritual drama akin to the May battle so widely acted in Sweden up to the sixteenth century. He traces the ritual back to a prehistoric cult of pairs of "alternating" twin gods[1], who succeed one another in possession of a mate[2]. Such a pair are no doubt the twin gods "Alcis" of whom Tacitus tells us that they are served by a priest dressed in women's garments, and worshipped by the (East Germanic) Lugian tribe of the Nahanavali. Since Professor Schück wrote, Professor Magnus Olsen has caused a similar pair of brothers, Ullin and Frey, to emerge from prehistoric times in Norway[3]. They, it appears, were followed by other pairs, Odin and Skaði, who shared a mate Njörð (Nerthus)[4], Odin and Mitothin, Odin and his brothers Vili and Vé, who succeed to his wife Frigg in Odin's absences, and so on.

i

In the *Lay of Helgi Hjörvarðsson* the original slaying was evidently fratricidal. Helgi is betrothed to Sváva. His younger

---

[1] "vekslingsguder."   [2] Schück, *Studier i Ynglingatal*, pp. 60 ff.
[3] M. Olsen, *op. cit.*
[4] It appears that Skaði was originally the male deity and Njörð the female.

brother Heðinn has been induced by an evil spell to swear that he will wed his brother's bride, and in his remorse he confesses this to Helgi, who says, in effect, that it does not matter, as he feels he is about to meet his death. Three days later he is mortally wounded by Álf, whose father he had killed. He sends for Sváva and there is a touching love-scene between them, in the course of which he persuades her to marry Heðinn[1], on condition that Heðinn kills Álf.

(i) The slaying within the family is burked. As Heðinn had sworn to wed his brother's bride, he must have contemplated killing his brother. But the poet, who could hardly face Sváva's marriage to Heðinn at the end, could not permit her to marry the slayer of her husband and a fratricide, and so allows Helgi to fall by the hand of another.

(ii) The implication that the slaying is in some way due to the woman is given in the prose statement that Helgi's valkyrie bride Sváva gave him a sword. It is moreover a woman who incites Heðinn to utter his oath.

(iii) Part of the flyting, in the original chant-metre, is between the hero Helgi and a giantess Hrímgerð.

(iv) Love-scene, str. 40–43.

(v) A hint of resurrection (and of Helgi's re-capture of his bride) is given in the prose statement at the end: "*It is said that Helgi and Sváva were reborn.*"

ii

The *Lay of Helgi Hjörvarðsson* contains a fragment of another poem dealing with a similar subject. Atli is befriended by an eagle to whom he vows a temple and worship. The prose tells us that Atli kills Franmarr and marries his daughter Álöf.

(i) The slaying is of the bride's father.

(ii) The few extant verses contain no trace of any implication that the slaying is due to the bride.

---

[1] It is usually said that Sváva refuses to marry Heðinn, but he evidently regards her words as a conditional consent. She says: "I *had* said that I would not embrace an unknown warrior" (Mælt hafða ek þat...). However natural the marriage may be from the ritual standpoint it was evidently difficult to treat it poetically, and in the ballads, where such a situation frequently occurs, we find the lady almost consistently refusing to marry the younger brother, though her dying lover frequently suggests it.

(iii) Practically the whole of the flyting is between Atli and Hrímgerð.

(iv) and (v) Any love-scene or hint of resurrection in this poem is irrevocably lost, since the poem only serves as an introduction to the poem about Helgi, and Atli plays no part after the flyting. The later part of the poem must have been lost.

iii. *The Lay of Helgi Hundingsbane*

(i) The slaying. At Sigrún's appeal Helgi slays Höðbrodd, who had been plighted to her by her father. This involves Helgi's fighting with and killing her father and one of her brothers. Nevertheless Sigrún marries Helgi. The brother whom he had spared, Dag, kills Helgi.

(ii) The one remaining chant-metre strophe makes Helgi declare Sigrún responsible for the fighting, as indeed she clearly is, according to the story. He says she has been a *Hild* to him. (Hild, in the Hjaðning story, was the cause of strife between Heðinn and Högni.)

(iii) Flyting between Guðmund (brother of Höðbrodd) and Sinfjötli, a companion of Helgi's. Helgi puts an end to it by reproving Sinfjötli for hurling abuse at his enemies. In the *First Lay* the flyting is much longer and the vituperation much coarser, and to judge by that in the *Lay of Helgi Hjörvarðsson*, which is in the original metre, this version is nearer to the original. It is probable that the *remanieur* of the *Second Lay* curtailed and bowdlerized the flyting scene.

(iv) There is a beautiful love-scene between Helgi's ghost and Sigrún, str. 43–49.

(v) The resurrection is within the compass of the poem, besides being further emphasized by the prose statement at the end:

" *Sigrún died young of sorrow and weariness. It was believed in old times that men were born again, but now that is called an old wives' tale. It is said that Helgi and Sigrún were born again: he was then called Helgi the Hadding warrior and she Kára Hálfdan's daughter, as is told in* Káruljóð, *and she was a valkyrie.*

The close adherence of this beautiful little play to the framework of the Year-Drama shows the strength of tradition. We even find in it, incongruously enough, the abusive verses which seem to have been an essential part of the ritual drama. Yet the poem is no crude magical mummery, but a piece of exquisite literature. Imaginative sympathy has transmuted the old story and altered its values, so that only the form of the Year-Drama remains: the spirit which infuses the poem is akin, in its dignity and restraint, to the spirit of Greek tragedy. The slain Helgi is not revived by the hocus-pocus of the folk-drama or the mummery of its predecessor, but by the bitter grief of his bride, which draws him back for a brief hour of rapture before death finally claims him for its own.

As the prose tradition connects this play with the lost *Káruljóð* we will next consider the story given in the legendary saga *Hrómundar Saga Greipssonar*, which is believed to reproduce a memory of the central scene of the poem.

iv

Hrómund, a warrior in the service of King Olaf, kills a Viking Hröngvið but allows Hröngvið's brother Helgi the Bold to live. Later on Helgi, now a warrior of the two Hadding kings, meets Hrómund in battle on the ice-covered Lake Venern. Helgi is accompanied by his concubine Lára (Kára) who flies above him in the form of a swan, chanting such magic incantations that no one can touch Helgi, who kills Hrómund's eight brothers. (Helgi accuses Hrómund of putting his faith in Svanhvít, King Olaf's sister, who has given Hrómund a shield, and urged him to the battle.) On preparing to attack Hrómund Helgi swings his sword aloft and accidentally cuts off the leg of the swan, whereupon Lára drops dead to the ground, and with her Helgi loses his luck and is killed by Hrómund, after inflicting a fearful wound on him. Svanhvít comes to the battlefield and heals Hrómund, who is placed in hiding with one Hagall. King Hadding hears he is there, and sends to look for him, but he is concealed, first under the cauldron and then as a maid. Finally King Olaf and Hrómund attack Hadding, and Hrómund kills him with a club, after which he marries Svanhvít[1].

---

[1] Certain episodes are evidently somewhat contaminated with those in *The Lay of Helgi Hundingsbane*, where the hero is concealed by Hagall and disguised as a bondmaid. It is probably impossible to disentangle all the threads.

In considering this story we must bear in mind the tendency of the legendary sagas to cut their heroes loose from all family ties. It is the episode, the adventure, which interests these late authors, not, as in the classical sagas, the human relationships and the tragedies arising out of them. So little do they care about such things that after the battle on the ice Hrómund is left lamenting not the loss of his eight brothers but that of his beloved sword. The saga says that Hrómund had a brother Helgi, and it is not impossible that the two brothers, serving different kings, were forced to fight against one another and that the Helgi Hrómund killed was his own brother. Such a hypothesis would explain Hrómund's extraordinary unwillingness to enter the battle. He says ill-luck will befall him, and skulks on shore until all his brothers have been killed.

The story is further complicated by the introduction of two brides, both possessing supernatural attributes (Svanhvít gives Hrómund a shield which will prevent him from being wounded and Hrómund is said to regard her as his tutelary genius[1]).

(i) The slayings, as we have them, are as follows : Hrómund kills Helgi's brother and finally Helgi himself. Helgi kills Hrómund's eight brothers (this is probably a very late addition to the story), Helgi kills his own bride.

The accidental slaying of the female character occurs occasionally in the English folk-plays. In a Yorkshire sword-dance the "Bessy" interferes while the dancers are making a hexagon of their swords, and is killed. In the Islip play, too, the hero kills the heroine, who is revived by the doctor[2]. The same theme occurs in some of the Swedish dramatic ballads[3].

(ii) The story ends with the marriage of Svanhvít to Hrómund.

(iii) No suggestion survives that Lára was responsible for the slaying, but it is expressly said that Hrómund was unwilling to accept the challenge and that Svanhvít induced him to do so.

(iv) There is no flyting in the saga, but it seems probable that this feature of the poem is preserved in Saxo. It has been

---

[1] Helgi says: "held ek fyrir satt þú truir á þá meyju."

[2] Chambers, *Medieval Stage*, I. 218.

[3] Lundell, in *Pauls Grundriss*, II. i. p. 1162.

recognised by scholars that the battle on the frozen surface of
Lake Venern, in Saxo, deals in the main with the same characters
as those of the *Saga of Hrómund Greipsson*, from a memory of
the lost poem. Saxo reproduces in Latin verse the flyting which
Erik, the victor in his story, exchanged with a supernatural being
immediately on his return from the battle[1].

(v) There is no intimation of rebirth or resurrection in the
story as we have it, unless Svanhvít's healing of the almost mortally wounded Hrómund may be taken as such an intimation.

v.   *Hjaðningamál*

We have perhaps one strophe of this poem[2], but it is told by
Saxo, and by the Norwegian skald Bragi, and by Snorri, and
through Snorri's prose we catch the gleam of a fine dramatic
poem[3]. The story was early known in England, but it originated
among the Teutonic tribes of the Baltic. Snorri's version is that
Heðinn carries off Hild, daughter of Högni, and Högni pursues
them and will not listen to any offer of terms from daughter or
son-in-law, but insists on battle. Their hosts fight all day, and
every night Hild rouses the dead, and at dawn the battle begins
anew. In Saxo the story is similar, but Heðinn and Högni are
"partners," and Heðinn and Hild are seized by a passionate love
at first sight. Högni suspects Heðinn of having defiled his daughter
before marriage, and fights him, but when he has wounded him,
spares him. "In the seventh year after these same men began
to fight on Heðinn's isle, and wounded each other so that they
died....They say that Hilda longed so ardently for her husband
that she is believed to have conjured up the spirits of the combatants by her spells in order to renew the war[4]."

Another version of the story is found in the late *Sörlaþáttr*.
In this, after Heðinn and Högni have fought they swear foster-
brotherhood, but by the evil counsels of Freyja Heðinn abducts
Hild and launches his ship over the body of her mother. Högni
pursues them and insists on fighting. Owing to Freyja's spells,
the dead are perpetually raised and continue the combat un-

---

[1] v. 139–140.   [2] See p. 79, *supra*.   [3] p. 78, *supra*.
                       [4] v. 158, 160 f.

ceasingly for "fourteen times twenty years, plus three," when one of King Olaf's men delivers them by "really" killing them all.

(i) Here the bridegroom slays either his own partner or foster-brother or the father of the bride, and in *Sörlaþáttr*, her mother[1]. It is generally recognised that the *Hjaðningar*—Heðinn and Högni—the counterparts of the Gothic Hazdingoi, are originally brothers, so the slaying was fratricidal.

(ii) There would be an opportunity for a love-scene between Hild and Heðinn's ghost, much like that between Sigrún and Helgi's ghost in the *Lay of Helgi Hundingsbane*, and Saxo's words, that Hilda longed so ardently for her husband, suggest a similar *motif*.

(iii) In the earliest recension of the story which we possess, the skaldic poem by Bragi, Hild is distinctly made responsible for the refusal of her father to make peace with Högni[2]. Snorri also attributes a kind of double-dealing to her. The late *Sörlaþáttr* believes that all the trouble was brought about by Freyja, who poses as a friend of Heðinn. We shall see later that this is equally significant.

(iv) No flyting is extant.

(v) In this story we have something very like the indiscriminate revival of all the slain which takes place in many folk-dramas.

Saxo says that Högni spared Heðinn on the occasion of their first fight, and that seven years after they began to fight again. The sparing of an antagonist, and his subsequent faithless attack on the man to whom he owes his life, also occurs in the *Lay of Helgi Hundingsbane*, where Helgi spares Dag, who finally kills him, and in the version of *Káruljóð* preserved in *Hrómundar Saga*, where Hrómund spares Helgi. It also occurs in the Hagbard story narrated by Saxo, which is of the same type as the tales we are dealing with. I cannot recall any other case of it in the stories of the North, so that its occurrence in these four drama-plots may be significant.

---

[1] The slaying of the mother by running the keel of the ship over her body while launching does not look like an invention of the late author of the *þáttr*.

[2] Bragi calls her "bǫls of fylda" "laden with evil fate" and accuses her of inciting the opponents while she pretended to wish for peace.

vi

Saxo has a dialogue-poem in which the bridegroom kills the bride's father, and the fact of the slayer's disguise reveals the dramatic provenance of the poem. Gram hears that Groa, daughter of the Swedish King Sigtrygg, is plighted to a giant. Gram repairs to Gothland disguised in goatskins ("being destined to emulate the powers of Hercules in resisting the attempts of monsters"). Meeting Groa he pretends that he is the brother of her betrothed, while his companion Bess vaunts his prowess. Finally "Gram cast off his disguises, and revealed his natural comeliness; and the damsel...was even incited to his embraces by the splendour of his beauty; nor did he fail to offer her the gifts of love[1]." Gram kills her father. The dialogue is between Groa and Bess, Gram and Groa, and in a closing monologue Bess vaunts the courage with which Gram killed Sigtrygg, Groa's father, with a gold-knobbed mace. The poem, which is corrupt and fragmentary, contains no mention of the slaying of the giant, and Groa alludes to a brother not mentioned in the prose: "Behold I will ride thence to see again the roof of my father which I know, that I may not rashly set eyes on the array of my brother who is coming. And I pray that your death-doom may tarry for you who abide." It looks as if in the poetical version the slain king was Groa's brother rather than her father.

The fragments of this poem are so short and so confused that it is no wonder we only find in it two of our five points.

(i) The bridegroom kills the father (brother) of the bride.

(ii) There is a love-scene between Gram and Groa.

We may note the similarity of the second poem dealing with Gram, in which, again disguised, he again snatches a king's daughter from her betrothed (and again probably kills her father, though this is not stated). Further, he is said to have been killed by Svipdag, who is apparently, in a sense, his brother-in-law, since the battle between them was due to Gram's desire to avenge the outrage on his sister and the attempt on his daughter's chastity. Svipdag in his turn was destroyed by Gram's son Hadding. Thus, like the three times re-incarnated Helgi, he is three times con-

---

[1] Saxo, I. 13–18.

cerned in slayings for the possession of a bride, and we may almost wonder whether in Denmark Gram was not a stock name for such heroes, as Helgi seems to have been in Norway.

vii

Another story given in verse by Saxo[1] must have been common property in Scandinavia in the ninth century, for it is alluded to in *Ynglingatal*. Hagbard, son of the kinglet Hamund, and two of his brothers, swore oaths of peace with the sons of Sigar after meeting them in battle. Hagbard then secretly wooed and won their sister Signe, whose wooer in public was a certain Hildigisl. Hildigisl bribes the blind counsellor of King Sigar to sow enmity between the sons of Sigar and the sons of Hamund, and when Hagbard is away the former slay his two brothers. Hagbard kills them, and penetrates in disguise to Signe's bower, where he is well received even after he tells Signe of the slaying of her brothers. She promises not to survive him if he is betrayed, and when this happens she sets fire to her palace so that Hagbard sees the flames just as he is about to be hanged. He utters a triumphant death-song, after flinging back at the queen, Signe's mother, a cup of wine she had offered him. Saxo tells us in the subsequent prose that Hagbard was avenged by his surviving brother. (i) Here we have the slaying of the bride's brothers by the bridegroom, and finally the death of the lovers, after (ii) a love-scene which Saxo gives in verse. (iii) Signe seems to be only indirectly responsible for the catastrophe. As in Saxo's other poems on this subject, the feature of disguise points to a dramatic origin.

But the dialogue-poems dealing with the theme of the Year-Drama do not nearly exhaust the stories dealing with the same plot. In Saxo we have the story of Feng, who kills his brother Horwendill and marries his wife, and is finally slain by Horwendill's son Amleth, who appears himself to have stood in marital relations with his mother. The resemblances of this story to Greek "Year-Drama" stories have been dealt with by a better pen than mine[2].

---

[1] Saxo, III. 87 ff.   [2] Gilbert Murray, *Hamlet and Orestes* (1914).

Saxo tells another story, of the strife between Balder and Hother for the hand of Nanna, in which we can trace fratricide, for in the Northern versions of the tale Hother and Balder are both sons of Odin[1].

In *Sögubrot af Fornkonungum*, one of the legendary sagas containing much old material, we are told how Helgi woos Auð, daughter of Ívarr King at Upsala, who however treacherously gives her in marriage to Helgi's brother Hrærek. Helgi, oddly enough, does the wooing. Afterwards Ívarr tells Hrærek that Helgi has secretly won Auð, and Hrærek kills Helgi and is himself killed by Ívarr.

In *Ynglingatal* there is the story of the two brothers Álf and Yngvi. According to Snorri Álf *sat at lǫndum*—stayed at Upsala and ruled over the kingdom, while Yngvi was a Viking. Yngvi returned, and through jealousy fanned by Bera, his wife, Álf slew him and was slain in his turn. The verses may be translated as follows:

"And he whom Álf, guardian of the temple-altar, slew, had to lie dead when the prince, from jealousy, reddened the sword in Yngvi's blood.

"It was not to be borne that Bera should egg the two brothers who slew each other to a fight in which for no good cause, for a strong desire for the woman, two brothers were the death of each other[2]."

Two points may be noted in these verses. (1) Álf is called *vörðr véstalls*, guardian of the temple-altar, and (2) the verb *sæfa* used of the two brothers slaying each other, has ritual associations, and is especially used in connection with sacrificial victims[3].

Álf and Yngvi were the sons of Alrek. It is surely no mere chance that according to *Ynglingatal*[4] Alrek and his brother Eirík

---

[1] Nerman (*Studier*, pp. 69 ff.) traces the names Balder and Höðr in the brothers Hæðcyn and Herebeald mentioned in *Beowulf* (Hæðcyn accidentally shoots Herebeald).

[2] *Yngl.*, ch. 21

Ok varð hinn	es Álfr of vá	Vasa þat bært	at Bera skyldi
vörðr véstalls	of veginn liggja	valsæfendr	vígs of hvetja
es döglingr	dreyrgan mæki	þás bræðr tveir	at bǫnum urðusk
ǫfundgjarn	á Yngva rauð.	óþurfendr	of afbrýði.

[3] Finnur Jónsson (*Hkr.* IV. 12) glosses it thus: "sæfa: at dræbe, slå i hjæl, særlig når der er tale om offerdyr."

[4] In Saxo (who ignores the relationship between Alrek and Eirík, though there is an allusion to it) Eirík first kills Alrek's son. v. 199.

also killed each other—with the bridles of their horses[1]. In the late *Gautreks Saga* Eirík survives Alrek, whom he kills. Schück considers that the May fights in Sweden reproduce the ritual play which lies behind the story of these brothers[2]. But if so, it lies much more clearly at the back of the poems in Saxo and the Helgi Lays.

Later in *Ynglingatal* we find a reference to a similar story, though it has been obscured by Snorri's misinterpretation of it in his prose. The verse runs:

> Önund's life was ended by stones[3] under the Mountains of the Sky (Himinfjǫll); and the too great burden of bitterness of the secretly begotten one took the enemy of the Esthonians unawares, and he who had furthered Högni's death was surrounded by stones (buried in a barrow)[4].

Professor Finnur Jónsson points out that the *Historia Norwegiae* says of Önund: *Sigwardus frater suus occidit [eum] in Himinheithi.* The "secretly begotten one" would thus be Sigvard, Önund's half-brother, and the allusion to Önund as the slayer of Högni suggests that Högni and Sigvard were closely related—in fact that Högni was probably Sigvard's father, his mother being also Önund's mother. As Sigvard was "secretly begotten" we must suppose that an intrigue similar to that of Hamlet's mother with Feng was the cause of Önund's slaying his step-father.

In the next chapter we observe that Ingjald, Önund's son, killed his wife's father[5].

In the more legendary part of *Ynglingatal* King Agni of Upsala kills Frosti, a Finnish king, and marries his daughter, who kills him at a feast[6]. Vanlandi is killed by his son Visburr,

---

[1] *Yngl.*, ch. 20.

[2] Schück, *Studier i Yngl.*, II. p. 59.

[3] *Lit.* "the sorrow of the sons of Jonák," alluding to the death of Sörli and Hamðir by stoning.

[4] *Hkr. Yngl.*, ch. 35.

Varð Önundr	Jónakrs bura	ok sá frǫmuðr
harmi heptr	und Himinfjǫllum	foldar beinum
of ofvæg	Eistra dolgi	Hǫgna hrørs
heipt hrísungs	at hendi Kom.	of horfinn vas.

[5] Ch. 36.

[6] A story of this kind is given in the Shetland ballad of Hiluge and Hildina, which is considered by scholars to be a rendering of the Heðinn and Högni story. Hiluge

his wife Drífa, daughter of the Finnish King Snær, being accessory to his death. Visburr in his turn is killed by his two sons. The names of the "Finnish" Kings—"Frost" and "Snow"—are, as Professor Schück points out, a strong indication that the stories originated in a ritual May battle for the possession of a bride, between antagonists representing respectively Summer and Winter.

Another story of a somewhat similar type occurs in Hrólfs Saga Kraka. Fróði kills Hálfdan and takes his wife, and is finally slain by Hálfdan's two sons. In Saxo these sons, significantly enough, go through a period of disguise as animals.

The similarity of plot of the Helgi Lays has of course been frequently commented on, and it is usually explained as due to contamination. The stories influenced one another, it is suggested, until they came to resemble one another very closely.

It is a somewhat strange circumstance, not redounding to the credit of the intelligence of the ancient Norwegians, that when there is so very little native heroic poetry extant, the outlines of the same plot should be presented to us not less than four times. It becomes much stranger when we note the constant repetition of the same theme in Saxo, and further observe its great popularity in ballads. The student of anthropology is forced to abandon the theory of contamination in face of such a number of variations on a common theme, and must look for the basis of the story in some oft-repeated piece of ritual. This piece of ritual is actually performed in our own days in the form of the May battle, and Professor Schück has already pointed out that the stories in *Ynglingatal* must go back to the memory of a heathen prototype of this battle. The plots of the Helgi Lays are hardly explicable save as originating in some similar ritual.

There yet remains one class of poem to be discussed—the flyting. *Hárbarðsljóð* and *Lokasenna* are the only complete poems of this type, and both deal with gods, but the Helgi Lays also contain flytings in which the human hero is one of the speakers, and similar flytings occur in Saxo. The flyting seems to have had

carries off Hildina after killing her lover. She sets fire to the house on her wedding night, and Hiluge perishes in the flames.

its convention, and a very strange one it is. It appears that the ceremonial flyting must be represented as taking place across water.
In *Hrímgerðarmál* one protagonist is on shore, the other in a ship,
and this is also the case with the flyting in the *Second Lay* and
with its imitation in the *First Lay*. The amenities of *Hárbarðsljóð*
are exchanged across a broad river. When all the gods participate
in a flyting they are gathered together in the hall of the sea-god,
presumably under the sea.

The setting of these poems might be regarded as a mere
coincidence, but for the strange confirmation it receives from
Saxo; confirmation all the more remarkable, as Saxo is evidently
unaware of any tradition in the matter.

The flyting between Fridleif and the giant (VI. 178) is thus
described. Fridleif, on shore, sees a captive youth in a boat
sailing past. The boy declares that the giant who holds him in
thrall would yield him up if challenged with sharp reviling.
Fridleif takes the hint, and is so successful that he is able to hew
a foot off the giant and to deliver his prisoner. Saxo does not
explain how Fridleif is able to attack the giant in the boat: the
setting of the scene is evidently a matter of indifference to him,
and he only mentions it because he finds it in his sources.

The sea is brought in equally strangely in the two other
flytings. The first is thus described:

> Then Erik went to the harbour...and the moment that he stepped out
> of the ship, tripped inadvertently, and came tumbling to the ground. He
> found in this slip a presage of a lucky issue and forecast better results from
> this mean beginning. When Grep heard of his coming, he hastened *down
> to the sea*, intending to assail with chosen and pointed words the man whom
> he had heard was better-spoken than all other men[1].

One would say that the flyting really took place between
Grep on shore and Erik in his ship, and that Saxo himself has
inserted the stock incident of the stumble.

Erik's next flyting follows immediately after he has successfully emerged from the battle on the ice-covered lake, for which
he had stipulated. Saxo says:

---

[1] It may be noted that the *nið* (the head of a horse as a mark of scorn) is in Saxo
placed on one side of a river as Erik approaches the further side; v. 135. This may
however be merely a natural precaution.

Then Erik went back in triumph to the king. So Gotwar, sorrowing at the destruction of her children...announced that it would please her to have a flyting with Erik.

Saxo, of course, does not imagine the scene of the battle to have anything to do with the subsequent "flyting," so slightly motivated, but the context is nevertheless significant. In the original source Gotwar may well have gone down to the sea-shore to await Erik's arrival.

There is another flyting in Danish tradition, preserved in the prose paraphrase of *Skjöldunga Saga*. Ívarr Widefathom is on his ship, and summons his fosterfather Hörð to interpret a dream. Odin assumes Hörð's form and answers the summons, but refuses to come on board. He rouses Ívarr to fury with his taunts, and Ívarr replies with vituperation. The scene ends with Ívarr's leaping into the water to attack Hörð, and we are told he was never seen again. So this flyting ends, like *Hrímgerðarmál*, with a sudden death.

The same tradition survives in the verse flytings of the legendary Icelandic sagas, though here, as in Saxo, the prose suggests that the author does not himself realise the existence of the convention. In the flyting between Ketill and the troll-woman Ketill apostrophises his antagonist:

> What demon is that
> which I see on the haunted[1] ness?

She retorts:

> Who is that pert-spoken one
> who has come to the skerry[2]?

In another late flyting of this type the hero, Grím, calls the troll-women "dwellers in the lava"—evidently the Icelandic conception. But his opponent answers:

> Here's my sister
>
> .   .   .   .
>
> come down to the sea[3].

The tradition has been stronger than the poet.

The sundering flood may be regarded as a mere device to

---

[1] *fornu.*   [2] *Ketilssaga hængs* ch. v.

[4] *Grímssaga loðinkinna,* ch. I. The troll-women are on the ship and Grím is on the shore.

keep the disputants from waging warfare with something mightier than words, but there can be no doubt that the flytings of the Edda conform to what must have been an ancient Scandinavian convention, presumably reflecting actual custom or ritual performance. Some ritual significance may perhaps be inferred from the fact that one of the two protagonists is almost invariably a supernatural being—Hrímgerð, Hörð (Odin), the giant whom Fridleif flytes, and the supernatural women in the legendary saga flytings. In Saxo Gotwar is a sorceress[1], and in view of Saxo's recklessness in divesting his characters of supernatural attributes we must not be too ready to decide that the three Greps are mortals[2]. The flyting in the *Second Lay* is much curtailed, but the *First Lay* appears to preserve a longer version, and we can hardly fail to note that certain of Sinfjötli's apostrophes can be more readily explained as actually addressed to a supernatural female being[3] than as attributing disgraceful feminine antecedents to the ostensible protagonist Guðmund, though no doubt this was a common form of insult.

The flyting is probably but another side of the May festival. Scoffs and gibes were part of the stock in trade of the Lords and Ladies of Misrule, the Summer Lords and Ladies, and other "disguised persons" who show a tendency to dance and to play unseemly parts in English church or churchyard in the Middle Ages. The ritual purpose of the flyting-scene appears to have been akin to that of the fight and the ritual marriage, and with the marriage and the mock slaying it is an integral part of Greek comedy, where it has been suggested that its real intention was to avert the evil which threatens the over-proud. Sir J. G. Frazer, however, regards such interchange of abuse and raillery as a crop-charm.

---

[1] v. 124.

[2] For the supernatural attributes of the other party in these flytings, Erik, cp. Schück, *Studier i Ynglingatal*, pp. 63 ff.

[3] 37^2 *skollvís kona*, 38^4 *svévís kona*, 38^1 *en skaeða!*

CHAPTER XV

CHARACTERS OF THE FERTILITY-DRAMA

Is there any doubt left in our minds as to the affinities of these poems, the stories of Helgi and Sigurd and their brides; heroic figures round which all the poetry of the North was woven? Do they indeed spring from the same soil as the grotesque mummeries performed to this day on English village-greens? We have seen that the scenes in the poems find their parallel in ritual or folk-drama. Akin to such representations is the flyting scene which mars the two extant Helgi lays, and which evidently formed part of the lost *Káruljóð*. Akin to them are the disguises so common in our poems and in Saxo's, which are similar in structure if not in style. It will be remembered that one of Saxo's disguised heroes is disguised in goatskins. It is surely more than an extraordinary coincidence that the Saga which reproduces the story of the lost *Káruljóð* observes, *à propos de rien*, that Helgi's adversary Hrómund put on a goat's beard before going into battle[1]. By this primitive trait the poetic and tragic tale of Hrómund and his love Kára is brought very near to Saxo's naïve poem on the mating of Groa and Gram, for Gram's disguise is equally motiveless. A hint of disguise remains, too, in the fourteenth century *Sörlaþáttr*, which reproduces the story of Heðinn and Hild of the lost poem *Hjaðningamál* and which states that Heðinn is a native of Africa. This must surely refer to a memory of his appearance with blackened face. A blackened face is of course a common form of disguise in folk-plays, and probably goes back to a beast-mask.

We have already read that the faces of the performers in the Swedish "sacrificial" play are blackened[2]. The goatskin disguise appears of course in the *Bukkevise* or Goat-song. This Swedish folk-play, with its disguise, its slaying, its resurrection

---

[1] *Hrómundar Saga*, ch. 2.   [2] *Supra* p. 126.

and its love-scene, may of course be entirely unconnected with the slaying, the disguise, the love-scene and the resurrection of the Helgi lays, just as Saxo's hero, who dons goatskins preparatory to slaying his rival, may be entirely unconnected with Hrómund in the lost Helgi lay, who puts on a goat's beard before battle: and these may both be entirely unconnected with the May-day contest with its skin-clad hero, and with the performance of the Goat-song with its disguise, its slaying, and its resurrection. But another instance of long-lived tradition will almost compel us to admit that the beautiful and tragic poems of Norway spring from the same root as the grotesque mumming of the peasants. In South Norwegian popular belief Sigmund or Sigurd rides the country-side at night in company with Guro Rysserova. Guro is of course Gudrun, and she is Sigurd's or Sigmund's bride even in the oldest story. But she is called Rysserova, —*horse-tail*, and this horse-tail is constantly alluded to as her chief characteristic[1]. In the Lincolnshire Plough Monday play one of the characters is a man dressed up as a woman, and called Bessy—the stock name for the female character. He wears a bullock's tail, and another character, Captain Cauf Tail, has a calf's tail[2]. The tail is supposed to be an emblem of fertility[3]. However this may be, the South Norwegian peasants have preserved the memory of a Sigurd and Gudrun play which is typologically centuries older than that presented in the Edda. Their Gudrun is nothing more than a stock figure of crude ritual drama, the beast disguise not wholly cast off. We do not know how long it is since the Norwegian peasants had an opportunity of seeing her in this guise. But her counterpart, the Bessy of the bullock's tail, must have appeared annually in England since the Scandinavian invasion.

We must consider Gudrun's status later, but it will be best to begin with the male actors. And first let us consider the names of Helgi and Heðinn. A Helgi is thrice wedded to a semi-divine being, and thrice he loses her. It is indeed possible that there were four Helgis. Tradition knows of a divine or semi-divine

---

[1] Cp. Helland, *Norges Land og Folk*, IX. p. 569; VIII. p. 419.

[2] Ordish, in *Folk-lore*, IV. p. 167.

[3] Cp. Dieterich, in *Arch. f. religionswiss.* 1908, p. 168.

woman, worshipped by the Earls of Hlaðir in Trondhjem under the name *þorgerðr Hölgabrúðr*, Thorgerð the bride of Hölgi. Hölgi is but an archaic form of the name Helgi. As Sváva and Sigrún and Kára might each be called the Bride of Helgi, is it not possible that this Thorgerð was also the Bride of Helgi in a ritual drama now wholly lost? Snorri says: " It is said that the king called Hölgi, after whom Hálogaland is named [this is an etymology after Snorri's own heart], was the father of Thorgerð Hölgabrúð: they were both worshipped, and the howe of Hölgi was heaped up with one layer of gold and silver,—that was the sacrificial offering,—and the next of earth and gravel[1]." Then he quotes a verse in which an Icelandic skald[2] uses the kenning " roof of Hölgi's howe " for gold.

It is difficult to believe that Thorgerð was not Helgi's bride rather than his daughter[3]. But in any case it looks as if the name Helgi were the traditional or stereotyped one for the chief character in the symbolic wooing. It is borne by four winners of supernatural brides. Oddly enough we find it again in the Shetland version of the Hjaðning story. Here the slayer of the Orkney earl and the final winner of the bride is called Hiluge[4]. Helgi, too, is the name of the slain brother suspected by Hrærek of having secretly won his bride, in the *Sögubrot*.

Was Heðinn perhaps an equally stereotyped name? It is Heðinn who wins the bride from Helgi in the *Lay of Helgi Hjörvarðsson*, and Heðinn who takes the bride from her father in the lost *Hjaðningamál*. The conjecture that Heðinn was a traditional name in the plays gains colour from another source. The name Heðinn is found compounded with -skjálf in a place-name in Sweden. Now Läffler[5] has shown that -skjölf, -skjálf, is always associated in compounds with a word connected with

---

[1] *Skáldskaparmál*, 42.   [2] Skúli þorsteinsson.

[3] Snorri may have translated *Hǫlgabrúðr* on the analogy of *Vanabrúðr*, a poetic title for Freyja. This title must refer to the tradition which makes Freyja the wife, as well as the sister, of Frey, one of the Vanir, and which is referred to in *Lokasenna*. Snorri however refuses to recognise that Frey and Freyja carried on what he tells us was the Vanir tradition in this respect, and he would therefore be driven to interpret *Vanabrúðr* as "daughter of Njörd" rather than bride of the other Vanir god, Frey.

[4] "Hilugi and Hildina," taken down in Shetland in 1774.

[5] *Arkiv för nord. filologi*, x. pp. 166 ff.

sacrifice[1]. If Heðinn is the traditional name for the winner of the bride, the latter part of the compound, suggesting holy ground, would be explained. Hidinskiælf in Uppland would be the holy ground where the sacred drama was enacted in which Heðinn won his bride. But there is more suggestive evidence than this. An Old Norse female name, lost in historical times, is *Hiþindís*. *Dís* is usually translated priestess, and is found in such compounds as Freydís, Thordís. But it can also mean any divine or semi-divine woman. If the divine Thorgerð was called *Hölgabrúðr*, Helgi's bride, would not *Hiþindís* mean Heðinn's divine bride?

What do the names mean? Helgi, older Hölgi, means "holy." This name is conferred on the hero of the *Lay of Helgi Hjör-varðsson* by his divine bride Sváva. Until he meets her he has been dumb, we are told, and had remained nameless. As a gift to go with the name she gives him a sword.

The very incongruity of the name Heðinn as a rival to "the holy one" is suggestive. It means "one clad in beast-skins"; and must go back to the earlier ritual prototype of our plays as directly as the epithet "horse-tail" for Gudrun in Telemarken folk-lore. Heðinn is like Gram, the wooer in goatskin disguise in Saxo's poem[2], and like Hrómund in the late version of the *Káruljóð* story, who puts on a goat's beard before going into battle. The Winter Lord, described by Olaus Magnus in the sixteenth century as clad in beast-skins, is his direct descendant[3].

Denmark appears to have had yet another stereotyped name for the hero who wins his bride by slaying her kinsmen or her bridegroom. We have already seen that Gram, like the three-times reincarnated Helgi, is three times concerned in slayings for the possession of a bride[4]. Gram means "adversary."

One of our Helgis appears to have been deified after death,

---

[1] Loaskjalf, sacrificial grove, Viskjaelf, vi for vé, sanctuary.

[2] We may also notice *Loðbrók*, "shaggy breeks," who dons this attire to win a bride. Cp. *infra*, p. 171.

[3] According to the suggestions of some scholars, the goatskin disguise in the Thracian play, and perhaps the whole connection of tragedy with the goat, is due to the fact that the drama had preserved the ancient costume of the peasant, composed of skins. This theory is inapplicable to our "skin-clad" heroes, for they are of royal race.

[4] p. 152, *supra*.

or at any rate buried with much store of gold. But we never hear of the Earls of Hlaðir worshipping him, though they continue to worship his bride Thorgerð into historical times. The superior divinity of the woman is thus as manifest in this case as in our plays, which make the bridegrooms mere mortal men, while the brides have supernatural attributes and are termed "valkyries" by Icelandic commentators. Besides the great goddesses, Frigg and Freyja and the like, "valkyries" were the only female divinities familiar to Icelandic mythologists. Perhaps they represented an older *dísir*, which seems to mean both "priestesses" and "female deities."

But to return to our Helgis. We are reminded of the kings or high-priests of Cybele at Pessinus, who were regularly called Attis. Frazer suggests that these were members of the royal family who enacted the part of the bridegroom of the goddess at the annual festival. Our "holy" and "shaggy" princes enact the part of the bridegroom to semi-divine women. Professor Ramsay holds that at the Phrygian ceremonies "the representative of the god was probably slain each year by a cruel death, just as the god himself died[1]." The combination of sanctity with a beast-disguise suggests that our heroes originally represented a divine being, not yet fully anthropomorphized. But this male deity was evidently not as important as his spouse; and it will be best to look first for female divinities who mate with a mortal man.

Professor Chadwick in his *Origin of the English Nation*[2] has brought together a good deal of evidence showing that the fertility goddesses Nerthus and Freyja were originally much more important than their male counterparts Njörð and Frey. *Freyr* means "lord," and he is called *Ingunarfreyr*, which would mean "lord or husband of Ingun." Ingun may well be a name of Freyja as Yngvi is a name of Frey. It looks rather as if Frey had once gained his position by standing in the same relation to Freyja as the Trondhjem Hölgi stands to his divinity Thorgerð[3]. We may note that Frey's grave-mound has gold and silver poured into it as "tribute," just as Hölgi's grave-mound is partly built with the sacrificial gold and silver.

---

[1] Frazer, *Adonis, Attis, Osiris*, p. 241.
[2] Ch. x.   [3] Cp. p. 253, *op. cit.*

We have already referred to the general opinion of scholars that potentates in Asia Minor represented a god in their own person, and that this god was usually the mortal lover of an immortal goddess. Chadwick has pointed out the significance of the fact that the name *Yngvi* was borne not only by the god Frey himself but by every member of the royal house of Upsala. " It may be inferred," he says, "that these princes were regarded not merely as descendants but actually as representatives of the god[1]." Thus every Upsala king would be regarded as representing Frey in his quality of Freyja's husband. A close analogy is found in Denmark for this association of the king and the goddess[2]. Skjöld, the eponymous ancestor of the Danish dynasty, is the husband of Gefjón, a fertility-goddess whose attribute is the plough. So in *Hyndluljóð* Freyja has Óttarr, the scion of a royal house, for a husband.

In Sweden, when the country suffered from famine, the disaster was attributed to the king, who was thus credited with the same powers as Frey. We may surmise that at such times the goddess was thought to be dissatisfied with her human bridegroom, and when this occurred he was sacrificed[3] and another of the royal house succeeded him. *Ynglingatal* tells us of a king who was sacrificed to stop a famine. If Professor Schück is right in his reading of another verse in that poem, Thjóðólf attributes the hanging of a king at a festival to a *dís*[4], a divine being, who was also the king's wife. Another king met his death at a *dísablót*, a sacrifice to such beings[5].

It looks as if the king's reign would normally terminate with his death at the hands of a member of his own family, who would succeed to the kingship and the espousals. Perhaps the story of

---

[1] Chadwick, *op. cit.* p. 252.

[2] *Sörlaþáttr* retains a memory of a similar association between Odin and Freyja. Odin, according to legend, was the first king at Upsala. *Grímnismál* 14 suggests the same, and so also the lampoon of Hjalti quoted in *Njálssaga*, coupling Freyja and Odin together. Cp. also *Skíðaríma*, which calls Freyja *Fjölnis víf*—wife of Odin.

[3] In Rome *ludi scenici* were performed in times of pestilence.

[4] Snorri translates *Loga dís* as "sister of Logi," who is not otherwise mentioned. Schück translates it "the goddess of the Lygir or Lugii."

[5] *Yngl.* ch. 29. Noreen, in *Uppsala studier tillegn. S. Bugge* (1893), considers that the verse indicates that the *dís* killed him.

Aun gives a hint as to the length of this term. This king sacrificed one of his sons every nine years, in order to secure long life for himself. Snorri regards his long life as a special favour of Odin in return for the nine lives, but the king's object would be automatically attained if he succeeded in delegating the fateful marriage with the goddess to these sons in succession. It is possible that a bridegroom "Helgi" indicates that some such substitution had been effected in certain dynasties, and that the goddess was thought to choose a member of the royal house to be her bridegroom[1]. If this be so, we can understand why Sváva gives Helgi his name and a sword in the *Lay of Helgi Hjörvarðsson*, and Svanhvita gives a sword to Regner in Saxo's poem[2]. It is to consecrate him out of all the royal family as her bridegroom elect, the slayer of his predecessor[3]. For the Swedish royal family, however, *Ynglingatal* testifies that a reigning sovereign was at least occasionally sacrificed, and the deaths of others often occur in suspicious circumstances[4].

---

[1] Cp. the method by which Skaði chooses her husband in Snorri's story (*Skáldskaparmál*, ch. 1.).

[2] In *Hrómundar Saga* Svanhvít gives Hrómund a shield.

[3] It is perhaps significant that *Hyndluljóð* says of Hrærek and his son Harald Hilditönn that they were men "marked with a sign for the gods." Hrærek killed his brother Helgi (p. 154, *supra*).

[4] It will be well to give Ynglingatal's accounts of the deaths of the first eighteen kings. Snorri put his own interpretation on the verses in his *Ynglingasaga*. Schück, (*Stud. i Ynglingatal*) suggests a different interpretation in some cases.

Yngl. ch. 11. Fjölnir, accidentally drowned in a vat at a *feast* in Denmark.
,, 12. Sveigdir disappears into a rock.
,, 13. Vanlandi, killed in his bed by *the agency of his wife and son*.
,, 14. Visburr, burnt in his house by his *sons, abetted by his wife*.
,, 15. Domaldi, sacrificed because there was a famine.
,, 16. Domarr, died of sickness.
,, 17. Dyggvi, died a natural death, says Snorri, but Schück reads the verse as indicating that he was carried off by a deity in the shape of a *horse*.
,, 18. Dag, killed by a hay-fork.
,, 19. Agni, *hanged by his torque at a feast by his wife, called Loga dís* (goddess of the Lugii?).
20. Alrek and Eirík—*brothers—killed one another with bridles*.
21. Álf and Yngvi—*brothers—quarrel about Álf's wife, and kill each other*.
,, 22. Hugleik, killed in battle.
,, 23. Eirík.
,, 24. Jörund, hanged by son of king Guðlaug whom he had slain.
,, 25. Aun—sacrifices his nine sons—dies of old age.

If the husbands of the goddess were particularly successful in causing prosperity they might readily take on the attributes of a deity and be worshipped in their own persons after death " for plenty," like the Norwegian kings Hölgi and Hálfdan the Black and Olaf Geirstaða-álf. Frey himself, as we have seen, finally usurped Freyja's position, and had a subordinate human wife, as Freyja had had a human husband.

Frey was regarded in later times as the ancestor of the royal house of Upsala. Hence Freyja must also have been held to be their ancestress, for she and Frey were originally regarded as husband and wife as well as brother and sister. Towards the Yngling dynasty she therefore occupies much the same position as Thorgerð Hölgabrúð occupies in respect of the Norwegian Earls of Hlaðir. The analogy seems very close, for it is implied in a passage in Olaf Tryggvason's Saga that Hákon, Earl of Hlaðir, was regarded as Thorgerð's husband. But who was Thorgerð, and who were Sigrún and Sváva and Kára and Hild, the " valkyries " or divine maidens of our plays?

It is possible that they were originally connected in the same way as Freyja with the royal houses from which they chose husbands. But their names render this supposition unlikely. Are they perhaps merely priestesses who personate the goddess in her marriages with members of the royal house? Such functionaries are common in the temples of goddesses of Fertility elsewhere[1]. Of these one would be chosen to represent the deity in the marriage with the king.

When the original significance of the ritual wedding was forgotten the priestess who represented the goddess would be apt to

---

Yngl. ch. 26. Egill—killed by a bull, says Snorri, but the verse according to Schück and Nerman says by a *boar*, sent as a punishment to Egill who has *burnt a temple.*

   ,,   27. Óttarr—killed in battle.

   ,,   29. Aðils—killed by a *dís* while riding round the temple. Cp. Noreen, *Uppsala Studier tillegn. Bugge,* p. 195.

[1] Cp. Frazer, *The Scapegoat*, pp. 288 f., referring to the sacrifice of women who personated the Maize-goddess. Also pp. 372 f., and *The Magic Art*, II. 135–6. We may note the story in Saxo, referring to a "King Fro" (Frey) of Sweden: IX. 301. Analogy shows us that children born of priestesses trace their descent to the goddess whom they serve.

appear in her own person and under her own name, though still with semi-divine attributes. Hence perhaps, Sváva and Sigrún and Kára and Hild. The tradition that Sigrún soon died of grief, and that Kára and Signe were killed at the same time as their lovers, suggests that perhaps the priestess impersonating the goddess was sometimes put to death after the slaying of the king.

Freyja's most famous possession was a torque called Brísingamen. A magnificent torque was also an heirloom of the royal family of Upsala, and according to Snorri it was doomed to be the death of the best man in the dynasty. In effect, a *dís* or goddess[1] hanged King Agni or Högni with it. It is therefore very suggestive that Bragi, and after him Snorri, should state that when Hild went with her false pleas for peace to her father, she offered him a torque. It is still more significant that the fourteenth-century story of Sörli, the Icelandic *Sörlaþáttr*, declares that the originator of all the quarrel between Heðinn and Högni was none other than the goddess Freyja[2]. The connection of the lost *Hjaðningamál* with a Freyja ritual is thus clearly indicated[3].

It is now time to consider what divine animal was personated

---

[1] Cp. p. 166, note 4.

[2] This is considered an original feature by Müllenhoff, *ZfdA*. xxx., 277 ff. But most scholars hold a contrary opinion; cp. Symons (Sijmons), *Kudrun*, p. xxiii.

[3] Here again the Brísing torque (i.e. its owner Freyja) is mixed up in a story of love and death. Saxo and Snorri tell a story of some interest in this connection. The legendary King Frode of Denmark is killed by a "sea-cow" in consequence of his punishing her son for stealing a gold torque (sometimes called bracelet).

The part played by Brísingamen in the Heðinn and Högni story reminds us of Heimdall. Heimdall seeks Brísingamen, meets his death, and is nine times reborn. This nine-fold rebirth has already reminded us of king Aun's nine sons, who, as we think, wedded in turn the goddess' representative. If, as seems probable, Heimdall is killed as a consequence of his Brísingamen adventure, his death could be laid at Freyja's door. We have already seen that a torque caused the death of a Swedish king, was the indirect cause of a Danish king's death and was in some way involved in the fate of Heðinn. Perhaps if we knew more of Heimdall we should find that he had relations with a fertility-goddess resembling those of Frey with Freyja. Perhaps he was related in this way to Gefjón. Loki says (*Lok.* 20) that this goddess was seduced by "the white lad" (*sveinn hinn hvíti*) who gave her a (neck) ornament (*sigli*). Heimdall is called the "Whitest of the Aesir" in *Thrym's Lay*. It is also worthy of note that in the late *Short Völuspá* it is said that his might was increased by (sacrificial) boar's blood (*sonardreyra*).

by "the holy one" or "the skin-clad one"—names for the successive bridegrooms of the goddess. Much of the evidence seems to point towards a boar. Frey's emblem is a boar: Freyja rides upon a boar, and one of her names is Sýr, sow. Even in the eighteenth century the boar and the sow together still watched over the prosperity of the old-fashioned Swedish village, where the *grannasten*, the centre of the little open playing space, used to bear two rounded stones. The larger was called *galten*, the boar, and the smaller *suggan*, the sow[1]. That these were long felt to have some protective function may be gathered from the names given to two particularly fine sixteenth-century cannon in Gripsholm Castle, the Boar and the Sow[2]. But we have much earlier evidence than this. A helmet called *Hildigöltr* or *Hildisvín*, "battle-boar," was, we are told, taken by the Upsala King Aðils from his opponent Áli, whom Beowulf makes his uncle and predecessor on the throne[3]. A ring called *Svíagríss*—the "sucking-pig of the Swedes"—was probably a religious emblem, and was an heirloom in the family. In the late *Hrólfs Saga Kraka* Hrólf and his men are attacked while at Upsala by a daemonic creature in the shape of a boar, sent against them by King Aðils, who sacrifices to it[4]. Snorri, on the basis of a misunderstood verse, tells us that one "Tunni" drives King Egill of Upsala out of his kingdom for eight years, when Egill kills him. Egill is finally killed by a boar[5]. "Tunni" is certainly the name of a boar, and Nerman regards the story as a memory of just such a divine boar as that which later defended Aðils[6]. In *Hyndluljóð* Freyja's bridegroom, Óttarr, is disguised as a boar. The prose of the *Lay of Helgi Hjörvarðsson* tells us that a live boar was led into the hall at Yule, and in modern Scandinavia the "Yule pig," a cake in the shape of a pig, is still consumed at Christmas.

So much for the evidence of folk-lore and tradition.

The evidence of archaeology is not only more conclusive but also far more striking. By a slow process of reasoning we have

---

[1] M. P. Nilsson, *Årets Folkliga Fester*, Stockholm, 1915, p. 313.
[2] Cp. Baedeker's *Norway and Sweden* (1885), p. 345.
[3] *Skáldskaparmál*, ch. 41 (44), *Hrolfs S.* 44.   [4] Ch. 42.
[5] Schück, *Studier*, shows that this king's name was really Óttarr (III. pp. 104 ff.).
[6] *Studier*, p. 195.

been driven to accept the hypothesis that the prototype of the mortal hero of the Scandinavian Eddic lays was a king or prince who established his right to a goddess bride by slaying his predecessor on the throne, and that on the solemn occasion of the battle he personated a god, and was accordingly disguised in the animal form sacred to the god. There is considerable *prima facie* evidence that this disguise was often that of a boar, anyhow in Sweden. Now archaeology steps in and seems to establish by ocular demonstration that early in the seventh century the leader of a procession of warriors all ready for battle did actually impersonate a boar[1]. Round the base of a helmet found in one of the very rich grave-mounds at Vendel in the Swedish Uppland are a series of plates each representing two helmeted warriors holding their spears in front of them. The warriors are facing the same way, they evidently represent some kind of procession. Most of their helmets are surmounted by a large figure of a boar. The leading figure of the series wears the same kind of helmet, but he is also clearly wearing a boar's mask, for an unmistakable tusk protrudes from his cheek, as a glance at fig. 1 of the Frontispiece will show. Here indeed we have *Hilditönn*, the Boar-Tusk King[2]. Evidence that disguise was sometimes more complete seems to be furnished by the combatants represented on plates found at Torslunda in Öland. The animal figure in fig. 2 is certainly intended to be a human being disguised—possibly as a boar. The left-hand figure in fig. 3 reminds us perhaps rather of Loðbrók, " shaggy breeks," than of Heðinn, the "shaggy one."

We are now perhaps in a position to appreciate the significance of Egill's being chased from his kingdom by a boar, overcoming it after eight years and ultimately being slain by a boar. And we begin to understand why Óttarr, Freyja's husband, can be disguised as a boar. Perhaps also we can understand why a sacred

---

[1] The extreme sanctity of the boar may be gauged from the fact that there have been about 80 finds of "boar's head" brooches, mostly from the island of Gotland. They are plentiful in the fifth and sixth centuries, but some earlier and many later examples are found.

[2] Nerman (*Svärges äldsta konungalängder*) regards Hilditönn as a king of the Götar. Hilditönn is of the family " marked with a sign for the gods" according to *Hyndluljóð*, str. 28.

boar is eaten at Yule. The boar, once the sacrificially consumed totem, became the divinity, and our records show the half-way stages of complete anthropomorphisation, if we may use such a word.

But apparently the animals symbolizing fertility may vary from district to district, or be variously pictured even in the same district. The horse, the goat, the ox, the calf, the cat, are all "corn-spirits" in the folk-lore of modern Europe—that is to say that they were all originally connected with a cult of fertility[1]. The cat is Freyja's animal as well as the pig; a white horse appears in North English mumming plays, and the bullock takes its place in Plough Monday ceremonies. We may also remember the reindeer disguise at Abbots Bromley[2]. There is some evidence that in pre-Viking times the horse was a sacred animal in Scandinavia; at any rate the Lapps took over a cult of this kind as early as 500 A.D. A theory has recently been put forward that the *dísir*, or minor goddesses of Scandinavia, were originally equine deities[3]. In connection with the verse on King Dyggvi, in *Ynglingatal*, which Schück reads as stating that this very early King of Upsala was carried off by a deity in the form of a horse[4], we may note the bracteate from the fifth century showing a helmeted warrior facing a horse reared up on its hind legs[5].

Several generations after Dyggvi we find the brothers Alrek and Eirík killing each other with bridles. It seems as if the Gudrun of Telemarken folk-lore, Guro rysserova[6]—Gudrun horse-tail—must be connected with the cult of the horse, and if so, as we said in another connection, must be centuries older than the Gudrun of heroic story.

---

[1] Is it not possible that the Norwegian and Danish stories of a dog-king imposed on a conquered tribe (*Hkr. Hák. góð.*, ch. 13; *Scr. Rer. Dan.* I. 151) may have originated in a memory of a dog-mask assumed by the king at certain festivals? A dog-headed female appears on one of the Scandinavian sculptured stones in the Isle of Man; cp. P. Kermode, *Manx Crosses*, 1907, pp. 187 f.

[2] See above, p. 133.

[3] L. Levander, *Sagotraditioner om...Aðils: Antiqv. Tidskr. f. Sverige*, XVIII. (1908), pp. 33 ff.

[4] *Stud. i Yngl.* II.

[5] Reproduced in *Sv. Fornminnesföreningens Tidskrift*, XI. (1902), p. 321.

[6] See above, p. 161.

There is a good deal of evidence, too, that the goat was at one time[1], or in some places, the animal connected with fertility and personated by the hero. We have Saxo's story of Gram, the "Adversary," disguised in goatskins; and we have seen Hrómund, the hero of the lost *Káruljóð*, put on a goat's beard before going into battle. For modern times we have the *Bukkevise*, the Goat-song[2]. In modern Telemarken folk-lore Sigurd and Gudrun and their ghostly following are mounted on swine and goats.

It is possible that we have archaeological evidence for the connection of the goat with such a ritual as we have been discussing in the bracteates representing an animal figure with horns and a goat's beard surmounted by a human head[3].

Salin points out that the immense popularity of this subject on bracteates can only be explained on the hypothesis that it represented a religious theme known to all the North[4].

In the last paragraph of his essay, "Helmets and Swords in *Beowulf*," Dr Knut Stjerna said:

Thus we have conclusive evidence that certain parts of the Helgi poetry (the Helgi Lays) deal with events of the period about A.D. 600, i.e. centuries earlier than one is disposed to think on philological grounds[5].

---

[1] It appears that in the seventeenth century it became difficult to secure goats heads for the *Bukkevise* representation, because a prohibition had been issued against goat-keeping. The result was that the goat was metamorphosed into a kind of devil, and the representation went on until it was checked on the ground of impiety (Troels Lund, *Danmarks og Norges Hist.* (1885), I. Bog. VII. p. 89). It is conceivable that the goat itself is the result of a similar substitution.

[2] See p. 125, above. This goat-song itself contains what is possibly an indication of its connection with a deity of fertility. All versions make the father and son describe the building of a boat. Now Tacitus says that the Suevi worship a goddess "Isis" (i.e. a fertility goddess) and that her symbol is a light galley. Frey, a god of fertility, has a magic boat made for him by the dwarves. For this point cp. Chadwick, *Origin of the English Nation*, pp. 239 f., 249.

[3] B. Salin, De nordiska guldbrakteaterna, *Antiqv. Tidskr.* XIV. pp. 49 f. Salin's Type 4 are of the kind indicated above.

[4] *Ib.* p. 90. It would seem that the boar must first have been the sacrificially consumed totem, later the divinity. Perhaps we can trace the earlier totemic stage for the goat in Gregory the Great's story of the Langobardi dancing in a circle round the head of a she-goat which they had sacrificed to the devil (*Scr. Rer. Langob.*; ed. Waitz, p. 524).

[5] The traces of a bird cult in *The Lay of Helgi Hjörvarðsson*, and the part played by the birds in *Fáfnismál*, point in the same direction. Bird figures are extremely

The evidence Stjerna gave was the similarity between the descriptions of weapons in the poems and the actual finds of the sixth century—i.e. it was archaeological evidence. Starting from a wholly different point, and pursuing a wholly different route, we have been led to the same conclusion—that if we wish to illustrate the Helgi Lays in their original form we must go back to the helmet-plates of the sixth century.

We have traced the successors of our mortal heroes and divine heroines down to the present Lords of the May, the Winter Lords and May Queens of last century, and we have traced them up to pre-Viking times. Can we see any trace of them in still earlier times? Probably the earliest prototypes of our " Holy ones " go back to that pair of twin gods called " holy " (Alcis, Gothic *alhs*) mentioned by Tacitus[1], who were served by a priest in women's clothing, and stand in some close relation to the other pairs of " alternating " twin gods who succeed each other in the favour of a divine bride, and whose cults have been traced in the place-names of southern Norway by Professor Olsen.

The story of Odin, whose wife is taken during his absence by his brothers, seems to be the link between the form of the story in which the bride's brother is killed, and the probably earlier form, of which we have traces in the *Lay of Helgi Hjörvarðsson*, in which brother kills brother, a form of the ritual slaying to which the "alternating" twin gods testify. The transference of the slaying from bridegroom's brother to bride's brother would be all the easier, because Frey and Freyja, Njörð and his bride, were regarded as brothers and sisters, as well as husbands and wives[2]. We may note that Frey slew his bride's brother, and that Iðunn, a divinity of the same type as Freyja, has mated with her brother's slayer.

It is difficult for us to decide at what stage the chant-metre

---

common on sixth century helmet plates. What appears to be part of a bird figure, cut in white bone, was found in "Odin's howe" at Old Upsala (Nat. Hist. Museum in Stockholm, Room III., case 172). Brooches in the form of a bird are common in Sweden in the seventh century.

[1] Tacitus, *Germania*, ch. 43.

[2] Probably this tradition preserves a memory of Ptolemaic marriages (brother and sister) in the Upsala dynasty.

prototypes of our Helgi Lays stand in the development from the tragic earnest of the ritual slaying to the mumming of the May battles. There can be little doubt that they had made the great step between drama and dramatic ritual, in that the representation of the slaying had long been merely make-believe.

So the plain historical tale of how one Helgi Hjörvarðsson loved and died, of how Helgi Hundingsbane had the misfortune to kill his wife's brother, how one Heðinn fought with his bride's father, was spared by him and seven years later fought again, of how another Heðinn won his brother's bride—these stories slip from our hands as we try to grasp them. They are not history but literature, literature working on memories of a drama which was not commemorative, but magical.

Yet we must not underrate the *rôle* of history in the Helgi Lays. Saxo connects our Helgi Hundingsbane with the son of a Danish king who must have lived in the latter part of the fifth century. He says of him that he conquered Hunding and took Jutland from the Saxons. Now a couple of episodes treating of the feud with Hunding open the Second Lay as we have it, and the prose tells us that Helgi afterwards slew Hunding. All this has no connection with the plot of the poem, and is not even alluded to afterwards, except in a late passage which seems to mirror an historical occurrence.

Beside such broken fragments of history we must set the folk-tale element in the Helgi Lays. One might almost fancy that the strange and beautiful names in the poems—the Land of Love, the Hills of Slumber, the Fells of Flame[1], the Shimmering Grove—were meant as a hint that we should not too greatly sorrow over the unhappy fates of the lovers, for they had no real existence, but are symbols of something greater and more mysterious than human love or death. But the scene with the otter and the pike in the Sigurd trilogy, and the meeting between Heðinn and the troll-woman in the play of Helgi Hjörvarðsson —these seem to have their source in mumming which we are not in a position to trace to ritual. Like the scene which shows

---

[1] Schück however regards this term (Logafjöll) as a piece of fossilized poetic diction originally referring to a tribe, the Lugii of Tacitus.

Helgi Hundingsbane in the disguise of a bondwoman, they both afford opportunities for the favourite dramatic device of disguise.

But these folk-lore scenes, divorced from any ritual with which we are acquainted, are few and are only treated with a light touch. It remains true that the main scenes in the dramatic poems are closely moulded on ritual drama.

CHAPTER XVI

ACTORS AND AUTHORS. THE CHORUS. THE SCENE

i. *Actors and Authors.*

SINCE most of the dramatic poems of the Edda show stylistic peculiarities usually associated with a tradition of improvisation, the actors and authors of the primitive drama cannot have been very clearly differentiated[1]. This fact increases our chances of finding some kind of answer to the hitherto unsolved problem of the authorship of the poems, for if we can come upon any traces of the actors we may be fairly sure that we are also on the track of the authors.

There seems however to be one set of personages in the plays to whom we can deny all claim to part authorship. These are the effigies of the gods. Any reader of the dramatic poems must be struck by the curious immobility of such gods as are not playing the chief *rôle* in any given poem, and by their tendency to send messengers instead of moving themselves. In *Skírnismál* Njörð and Skaði sit still and send Skírnir to ask Frey what ails him: Frey despatches Skírnir to seek Gerð. Now scholars tend to regard Skírnir as Frey himself. Possibly the motive for introducing both the god and his double in the play was simply dramatic convenience: the *rôle* of Gerð's seeker was too active for an effigy and was delegated to a human being. In the poem on Gná's journey Gná performs the same service for Frigg that Skírnir performs for Frey. In *Lokasenna* all the great gods, except Thor, sit still. In the lost poem on Balder's death only Hother and Loki move—or rather—and this may be significant—Loki moves

---

[1] Improvisation of the speeches by the actors is of course common in primitive drama. The dialogue is still improvised in the modern Swedish plays (see *supra*, p. 124). In sixteenth century Germany and Austria the Meistersinger were the actors as well as often dramatic authors (Schweitzer, *Étude sur...Hans Sachs*, Paris, 1887, p. 351). In the Roman drama the dialogue was left to the *mimi* or actors, and even in the Japanese drama the play is composed by the actors sitting in committee (cp. Art. "Drama," in *Encycl. of Religion and Ethics*, IV. pp. 905 and 895).

Hother's arm. The other gods do not even stir when Balder falls, and in the funeral scene Thor is the only god who does more than "stand by." In the *Lay of Thrym* there is a similar concourse of gods who may only have "assisted," in the French sense, at dressing up Thor. Earlier in the poem a certain immobility on Freyja's part forces itself on our attention: Thor and Loki go to ask her for her feather coat, and then again to bid her put on bridal garments. In the lost poem on Heimdall's death we have already surmised the use of an effigy.

But we cannot jump to the conclusion that all gods were invariably represented by effigies. Some of the minor deities in *Lokasenna*—Viðarr and Sif—give Loki mead, and Loki himself, who seems to act as a kind of messenger to the other gods, can hardly have been represented by an effigy in *Reginsmál* or the poem on the death of Balder. In most of the poems Thor is very active and must, one would assume, have been personated by a human actor. The story of Gunnarr helming, who fought and overcame an image of the god Frey, deprived him of his insignia and impersonated him, can hardly be explained except by a tradition of impersonation of deities by human actors.

One feature of the poems points very distinctly to this double representation of deities—sometimes by human actors and sometimes by effigies. There is no tendency to avoid placing a number of stationary gods on the scene at once and letting them all speak. *Lokasenna*, the *Lay of Thrym*, and the lost poem on Balder's death show no tendency to limit the number of such personages. But the more one examines the technique of the dramatic poems, the more one is inclined to suspect that both in the mythological poems and in the Fertility-drama not more than three human actors played speaking parts on the stage at the same time. It is significant that this limitation of characters does not hold good in the Nibelungen poems on borrowed subjects, poems for which we cannot postulate a dramatic origin. In the *First Lay of Gudrun* we have a conversation in which six women take part. In the *Atli Lay* four men are present—Knéfröð, Gunnarr, Högni and Högni's son. That the rule does not apply, in the dramatic poems, to the deities who are merely present but who do not move about on the scene is fairly strong presumptive evidence that these were represented on occasion by effigies. We have already seen that an effigy of markedly heathen associations called "Bovi" played a part in a dramatic game in Denmark in the thirteenth century, and a straw puppet is used in a Swedish traditional game with dramatic dialogue[1]. About the eighth century the ceremony of the expulsion of Winter was commonly performed in Western Europe by the destruction of a lay figure[2]. Evidence for the use of effigies in the dramatic poems of the Edda is furnished by Snorri's account of the lost *Hrungnismál*, where a giant of clay is fashioned by the giants. Very probably this figure represented Hrungnir himself, Thor's antagonist, in the actual drama, and only became an accessory after the dramatic tradition was lost. This Mökkrkálfi, we are told, had a mare's heart put into him. We may remember the wooden effigy called Thorgarð, furnished with a human heart cut out of a man killed for the purpose, sent by Earl Hákon to Iceland to kill his enemy Thorleif[3], and the two "wooden men" placed in Frey's grave-mound, and afterwards called Frey and worshipped[4].

There are several references in later tradition to effigies of gods which "talked" and acted. Saxo knows of a statue of Odin, covered with bracelets, stripped by Frigg's orders. Odin "mounted the statue upon a pedestal, which by the marvellous skill of his arts he made to speak when a mortal touched it[5]." An image of Thorgerð Hölgabrúð, the divine protectress of the Earls of Hlaðir, walks and speaks[6]. The Norwegian king Olaf Tryggvason is re-

---

[1] See above, pp. 123 f.   [2] Art, "Drama," § 8, in *Encycl. Brit.*

[3] *Flat.* I. 213.

[4] *Ib.* I. 403. If these were supposed to have been vitalized in the same way as the effigy Thorgarð, the cutting out of Högni's heart, in the northern version of the Nibelungen story, may have had a sacrificial significance.

[5] Saxo, I. 25. G. Schütte, "Gudedræbning i nordisk Ritus," in *Samlaren*, 1915, pp. 21 ff., thinks that this story, that of the two "wooden men" referred to above, and the story of Gunnarr helming, all go back to a rite in which the new representative of the god destroys the old one—involving the destruction of an effigy. He connects the stories of the preservation of Froði's corpse for three years, and the concealment of Frey's death for the same period, with a custom of using the flayed skin, with an effigy or living person inside it, as representative of the dead god. This theory receives some confirmation from the story in *Bósa Saga*, where flayed skins of dead men are used to disguise the two visitors to the wedding.

[6] *Flat.* I. 213.

ported to have encountered a statue of Thor which could not only speak and walk, but could even wrestle with him[1]. Gunnarr helming, too, has to wrestle with an image of Frey.

It would be idle to speculate further on this subject, but we may call attention in passing to the little wooden figure[2] discovered in 1917 by excavation in the neighbourhood of the ancient Danish sanctuary at Saltofte, in Sjælland. It is just such an effigy as might have appeared in the dramatic representations: a seated figure about eighteen inches high, with its hands in its lap, and evidently originally affixed to a stand or pedestal. The huge torque round the neck of the figure dates it as between the fifth and eighth centuries. The view that it is the effigy of a deity is borne out by its general resemblance to the description of little wooden figures which were objects of veneration in Southern Norway until the eighteenth century. Their direct descent from heathen idols seems to follow from the fact that one of them is said to have been regularly rubbed with fat up to 1777 or later[3]. According to *Frithiófs Saga* this treatment was accorded to the images of the gods.

Whether the gods were represented in effigy or not we know at least that in what we may call the heroic drama the actors were real human beings. As we trace this drama back into primitive ritual they merge into more tragic figures. They are still actors, it is true, for they personate gods or giants, but their acts are no mere make-believe, and in the ritual which gave birth to the drama

---

[1] *F.M.S.* I.; *O. Tr. S.* 150.

[2] Figured in H. V. Clausen, *Fra Holbæk Amt*, Copenhagen, 1918, p. 371.

[3] Visted, *Vor gamle Bondekultur*, Christiania (n. d.), pp. 18 f. Cp. Nicolaysen, *Norske Fornlevninger*, pp. 227 f., and Helland, *Norges Land of Folk*, VIII. pp. 408 f. The offerings of ale and the rubbing with fat show that even if the figures were actually effigies of Saints they can only have been the successors of heathen idols. The description of them, with their metal eyes and flat heads, does not suggest Saints' effigies.

The use of effigies in drama is by no means uncommon. Drama in which the parts are taken by puppets exists in Russia, Persia, and in the Far East. In Japan the marionettes of the *Nō* plays are supposed to have developed from idols. In the Javanese *wayang purwa* or shadow-play, the *dalang*, the play director, moves the puppets and recites the parts, making nice distinctions between the voices of the various personages. In Mexico the singer raises and sets down again the "feather-sticks" which represent the various divinities. All sorts of devices exist for indicating change of scenery.

their deaths were no stage effects. *Ynglingatal* preserves enough memories of the past to show us that once the chief male actors were responsible to their people for the fruitfulness of the earth. They were the king and his slayer, the king-to-be, and the cause of their strife is the goddess who is the third character in the drama. Later the name Helgi, conferred on the slayer, and certain intimations in the extant poems that the hero in the drama was chosen for his fate by his divine bride, suggest that the dual functions of the priest-king had been separated, and that another member of the royal family represented the king in his relations with his divinity. Is there any other trace of such priest-kings in the North?

In an illuminating essay the late Professor Olrik suggested that the *goði*, the secular priest of the period immediately preceding the introduction of Christianity, had been preceded by a priest-king, a *þulr*, "thul," who in course of time suffered much the same fate as the Roman *rex*; that is to say that his functions became more and more specialized, and in the North a warrior-king, a *konungr*, usurped his place as supreme ruler[1]. He reaches this conclusion partly on the evidence of the ninth century Danish Runic inscription, set up to a *thul* at Salhaugar, "Temple Howes," with sacred symbols carved on it[2], partly on the Scandinavian traditions of kings sitting on hills or grave-mounds, which he finds to be typical of sacred or "magiform" kings, and partly on the references to the *thul* in *Beowulf* and in the Eddic poems. This evidence we still have to discuss, but we may pause to note that working on totally different lines we have been led to form a hypothesis identical with that postulated by such a scholar as Professor Olrik—namely the existence of a special class of royal princes whose main duty it was to maintain good relations with

[1] "At sidde på höj," in *Danske Studier*, 1909, pp. 1 ff.

[2] At Snoldelæv, in Sjælland. "The stone of Gunnwald, son of Hróald, thul at Salhaugar" (Wimmer, *Danske Runemindesmærker*, II. pp. 338 ff.). It appears that the stone was actually set up *inside* the smaller of two adjacent grave-mounds It must have been sacred since the Bronze Age, for on it are traced a wheel-cross and a saucer-shaped depression, characteristic for that period. At a later time two more sacred symbols were added, three horns interlaced, and a swastika. Prof. Wimmer regards the swastika as a symbol of Odin, and deduces that Gunnwald, or Hróald, was a priest of that god. The horn, on the other hand, is a symbol of Frey.

the divine protectors of their dynasty and country. The dramatic poems of the Edda have however enabled us to proceed a step further, and to detect how these "men marked with a sign for the gods," as *Hyndluljóð* says, originally owed their sanctity to their union with the divine protectress of their race, and how each fell a victim to some member of his family who became in turn the mate of the divine bride. In later times, no doubt, the slaying was only simulated, but the ritual drama was none the less holy, and the services of the "slayer" and "slain" none the less vital to the community.

Olrik associated the priest-king with the word *þulr*. Let us see whether this term fitly describes our author-actors.

In the Danish Runic inscription, as we have seen, the word is usually taken to mean "priest," or, as Professor Wimmer suggests, "speaker of religion[1]."

In the early Anglo-Saxon poem *Widsith* the name of a king ruling over the tribe of the Rondings[2] is given as *þyle*, "Thul."

In *Beowulf*, a *þyle*, Unferð, occupies a seat of honour at the Danish king's feet, and enjoys a position of such independence that he can insult the king's honoured guest without reproof—save from the guest[3]. He possesses what is apparently the best sword among the Danes—"one among the foremost of ancient heirlooms"—which he lends to Beowulf for the fight against Grendel's mother, and finally gives him as a parting present[4]. This *þyle* is evidently expected to fight Grendel's mother himself, and loses his "renown for valour" because he does not do so[5]. Nevertheless he is highly honoured among the Danes, a circumstance all the stranger because besides lack of courage he has been guilty of the crime which in every other case excites the horror of *Beowulf's* author above all others—the crime of fratricide. Thrice in the course of the poem the author takes occasion to express his loathing of this crime—twice in passages about Cain[6], and once in the pathetic passage describing the grief of King Hrethel

---

[1] *Loc. cit.* "geistlig taler, Odins præst."

[2] *Widsith*, l. 24, Þeodric weold Froncum, Þyle Rondingum.

[3] ll. 499 ff.   [4] ll. 1455 ff.

[5] ll. 1469 ff. Like Reginn, who is called a thul in *Fáfnismál*, he incites another (by giving him his sword) to do what he should have done himself.

[6] ll. 107 ff., 1262 ff.

when one of his sons, Hæthcyn, accidentally slew the other, Herebeald: "an attack beyond compensation, sorely sinful, sickening to the heart[1]." Hæthcyn, it seems, was ultimately hanged, or hanged himself. Yet Unferð lives in honour among the Danes, and "all of them trusted in his spirit, that he had great courage, though he might not have been honourable with his kinsfolk in the play of swords[2]."

The later meaning of *þyle, þulr,* as we have it in the Anglo-Saxon glosses and in the Eddic poems, seems to have been "speaker," "utterer of (solemn) words." In the glosses we find "*þylas:* oratores"; "rhetorica : *þelcræft.*" In *Hávamál* Odin, or someone impersonating him, opens his speech with the words:

(str. 111.) Mál's at þylja   þular stóli á
It is time to speak on the (or my?) *thul's* seat.

Later in the same section of the poem Odin says:

(134) At hárum þul   hlege þú aldregi
Laugh thou never at hoary thul.

In *Vafthrúðnismál* the giant Vafthrúðnir uses the word of himself : "we shall see which of us knows the more, the guest (Odin) or the ancient *thul*[3]." In *Fáfnismál* the birds apply the term to Reginn, advising Sigurd to send "the hoary thul" to Hel and shorten him by a head. These are the only passages in which the word occurs, but the compound *fimbulþulr,* "chief *thul*" or "mighty *thul,*" occurs twice in *Hávamál,* where it is usually thought to be a term for Odin. In each case this *fimbulþulr* is said to have inscribed magic runes or staves[4].

Because the speaker in *Hávamál* announces himself to be a traveller, the word has usually been taken to mean "wandering singer," but Sijmons points out that it really means no more than "speaker[5]." When the giant Vafthrúðnir speaks of himself as a "thul" he cannot mean that he is a wandering singer, or indeed a singer at all. He may be referring to himself as one who "speaks" his part, i.e. an actor, or the word may have the secondary sense sometimes attributed to it in the passage in *Fáfnismál,* "chatterer,"

---

[1] ll. 2346 ff. Clark Hall's translation.   [2] ll. 1167 ff.
[3] Str. 9.   [4] Str. 78, 142.
[5] *Einleitung,* p. clxix, " Als den ursprünglichen wortbegriff werden wir 'sprecher' anzunehmen haben."

though this term might more fitly be applied to Fáfnir than to Reginn. The injunction in *Hávamál* not to laugh at the hoary *thul* might be paralleled by the plea for indulgence made by any actor in folk-drama, more especially when, as in this case, he is taking the *rôle* of a god—Odin. Odin appears to be regarded as the *thul par excellence*, if the term *fimbulþulr*, "chief *thul*" or "mighty *thul*," is rightly attributed to him.

The phrase in *Hávamál*, "It is time to chant on the thul's seat," is sometimes regarded as implying that all *thulir* invariably sat on thrones or chairs to deliver their wisdom. But we are in search of a meaning for *thul* which will satisfy us in all cases where the word is used, and to suppose that Reginn habitually sat on a special seat and disbursed wisdom is ridiculous. Yet it is unjustifiable to regard the reference to the *thul* as an interpolation in *Fáfnismál*. Let us look at the context in *Hávamál*. The expression occurs in the first strophe of the section called *Loddfáfnismál*. The most reasonable view of this poem is that recently urged by Sijmons[1], that the speaker and author is a "spielmann," a wandering minstrel who makes his appeal to his audience by roguishly impersonating Odin, taking his audience into his confidence in the second strophe. Certainly the extant verses fit such a hypothesis admirably. In the course of his solemnly uttered exhortation to regard discretion as the better part of valour, he repeatedly urges the audience not to laugh at him.

The Eddic evidence thus elucidates three points. At the time of the composition of *Hávamál*, *Vafthrúðnismál*, and *Fáfnismál* (1) *thul* seems to have meant "speaker," "he who utters (solemn) words." (2) A *thul* is usually thought of as advanced in years. (3) Odin is the chief of *thulir*.

In later Icelandic and Orkney skaldic verse the word is used in the sense of "skald," poet.

We can now descry the following more or less chronological series of ideas associated with the *þulr* or *þyle*. 1. Name of king. 2. Priest. 3. Speaker in dialogue-poems. 4. Poet. The only *thul* of whose career we have any knowledge is regarded as a fratricide—a fratricide who apparently remains unpunished and full of honour though the crime of which he is guilty is one which aroused the

---

[1] *Einleitung*, pp. cccliii ff.

greatest horror among the half-Christian Anglo-Saxons for whom the poem was composed. In this point, Reginn, who is called a *thul* in *Fáfnismál*, resembles the *thul* in *Beowulf*, since he too may be regarded as a fratricide.

The sequence of ideas—king's name—priest—fratricide— speaker in dialogue-poems—poet, corresponds with strange exacti- tude to the evolution we have traced from the alternating twin gods, the "holy ones" of Tacitus, the "holy" and "shaggy" royal brothers of our poems, who succeed each other in the possession of a divine bride, sink to the mere actors in an unfashionable drama, and end, like the Ancient Minstrel, as wandering singers from an earlier day, the storehouses of forgotten verse of which their predecessors had been the authors as well as the actors[1].

In course of time it would become natural for the *thul*, who stood in specially intimate relations with the divine world, to be regarded as the repository of ancient traditions, the instructor of the people in all kinds of divine lore. Only by the priestly pre- occupations and traditions of the *thul* can we account for the mythographic *longueurs* which hamper the action in so many of the poems—most of all, be it noted, in the extremely archaic Sigurd trilogy. In the Helgi Lays the later *remanieur* has probably purged the verse of much irrelevant matter.

Odin is the *fimbul-thul*, and his history affords a curious parallel to that of the human *thul*. *Lokasenna* tells us that his wife Frigg[2] had granted her favours to his brothers Vili and Vé, and in *Yng- lingasaga* Snorri states that on one occasion, when Odin had been so long away that he was no longer expected to return, his brothers Vili and Vé divided his inheritance and shared his wife, but that soon after Odin returned and took his wife. (" Vé " has the same significance as "Helgi"—the "holy one.") This story and Saxo's tales of Ollerus and Mit-Othin, who supersede Odin, Ollerus for

---

[1] Possibly we see the last traces of our two actor-authors in the two poets who sing duets before their lord in *Widsith* (103 ff.). There is a reference to a similar duet at Attila's court in Priscus (K. Muller, *Fragmenta Hist. Graec.* IV. p. 92). It is pre- sumed that Attila was following Gothic custom (Chadwick, *Heroic Age*, p. 84).

[2] *Ynglingatal* also tells us that he mated with Skaði, whom he shared with the fertility-god Njörð (*Yngl.* ch. 8). Originally Njörð (Nerthus) was the fertility-goddess, and Skaði her husband; cp. Bing, "Ull," in *Maal og Minne*, 1916; Schück, *Studier*, II. 163 ff.

a term of ten years, are generally considered by scholars as an indication that Odin was originally regarded as one of a pair of "alternating" twin gods, who succeed each other in the possession of a divine bride[1]. In *Hávamál, Hárbarðsljóð*, and *Reginsmál* he has become the typical *thul* of later times, the disburser of ancient formulas or the teller of old unedifying tales, and like the human *thul* he has shared the fate of all prophets of an earlier day, and come to be regarded as necessarily old.

With the gradual loss of prestige suffered by female divinities in the Viking Age the third performer, the goddess, once the most important, would lose her importance and tend only to appear in the semi-ritual May-drama. Whether her *rôle* was originally taken by a man, a woman or an effigy is difficult for us to determine, but we may note that the Alcis twin gods of Tacitus are served by a priest in woman's clothing.

ii. *The Chorus.*

Scandinavian and Anglo-Saxon sources have vouchsafed us a glimpse of the chief actors and authors of Eddic drama, which is presumably but a branch of an early Teutonic dramatic ritual intended to ensure fertility to the soil. But when we look at the folk-plays which are undoubtedly the lineal descendants of this early Teutonic ritual, we find that besides the chief actors—the hero, the fool, and the Bessy or female character—there is invariably an indefinite number of other minor actors, whose *rôle* is usually limited to singing, dancing or sword-play, almost invariably in a beast disguise. It seems probable, then, that the Eddic drama, too, had some sort of chorus in animal disguise, and that this chorus sang or made music and probably danced in a ring round the chief performers as in the later dramatic games so widespread in Scandinavia. We can perhaps trace some memory of this chorus in the motley crowd of animals which are present at Balder's funeral, together with frost-giants and mountain-giants. Where Thor kicks a dwarf into the fire we are reminded of the Swedish game described by Olaus Magnus. It is the practice, he says, for young men to dance in a ring round huge bonfires kindled outside the palaces of kings or princes, and when the ring breaks the last is dashed into the fire. He soon jumps out again, however, is placed on a high seat, and is "sconced" as a punishment for injuring the king's fire[1]. We have already noted how the sudden and universal lamentation described by the same author resembles the lamentations raised for Balder in an earlier part of the lost poem[2].

It is generally held that the ring-dance of Scandinavia came from France with the ballad which accompanies it, but a glance at our sources will show that the ring-dance is first found among the East Germanic tribes, and must therefore, in all probability, have been practised in Scandinavia long before it reached France. Thus Priscus tells how in the year 446 Gothic maidens received Attila by dancing in a ring and singing in their native tongue[3]. Gregory the Great, writing of the year 579, describes the Lango-bardians dancing in a circle round the head of a she-goat which they had sacrificed to the devil[4]. And it will hardly be suggested that the ring-dance described by the Danish monk in the thirteenth century, where the dance circles round two women and a straw effigy who is adjured to speak, is of the courtly kind introduced from France[5]. Dancing round an uprooted tree, or tree-trunk, must have been common in Scandinavia as early as the Viking Age, since the Lapps borrowed the custom at that period[6]. But the nearest approach to a chorus accompanying the Eddic drama is probably to be found in the account of Constantine Porphyro-genitus, in the ceremonial book of the Byzantine Court compiled by him in the first half of the tenth century. As parts of this work go back to the sixth century it is impossible to decide at present whether the Christmas custom described by him, and entitled τὸ γοτθικόν, is performed by Goths (who did not serve at the Byzan-tine Court after the time of Justinian) or by Varangians—Scan-dinavians[7]. In any case the chief players seem to be members of an East Germanic tribe, and the points of resemblance with the dramatic ring-dances of Scandinavia are worth noting, for what-

---

[1] Olaus Magnus, III. Bk. xv. ch. 27, pp. 154 ff.
[2] *Supra*, p. 130.   [3] Priscus, ed. Bonn, p. 188.
[4] *Scr. Rer. Langob.*, ed. Waitz, p. 524. Cp. p. 173, note 3, *supra*.
[5] P. 123, *supra*.
[6] Hammerstedt, in *Maal og Minne*, 1911, p. 514.
[7] Codinus (*Offic.* p. 90, note 2), describing a similar game, calls the players βάραγγοι.

ever else this game is, it can hardly be held to be French.   It is
played on the ninth day of Yule.

There appear to be two parties, the Blue and the Green, each
side with a leader, and each side has two or more "Goths" wearing masks of various animals, and clad in reindeer-skins or fur
pelisses in such a way that the hairy or shaggy side is turned out-
wards.   In his left hand each carries a shield, and a staff in the
right hand.   The two groups stand facing each other, and at the
word of command run up to near the Emperor's table beating
their shields with their staves, and crying "Tul! Tul!"   They
then form two circles, one within the other, and in this formation
seem to dance thrice round the table of the Emperor: they then
retire, while "those who out of the two groups represent the Goths
recite aloud the so-called Gothic chant, the instrument players[1]
giving the time."   The chant is a Greek alphabetical poem in
quatrains.   These are very corrupt, but appear to contain congratu-
lations and good wishes to the Emperor.   The groups repeat the
quatrains, and at intervals, on the signal of the leaders, who cry
"*Ampaato*," the "Goths" form a circle enclosing the two leaders,
striking their shields with their staves, and saying "Tul! Tul!"
Finally, the Goths again beating their shields and repeating again
and again "Tul! Tul!" go out at a run, the Blue on the left side
and the Green on the right[2].

It is obvious that the game or play has been modified to suit
the requirements and manners of the Byzantine Court, but it may
well be that the repetition by the masked chorus of the quatrains
of the leaders, the dance in a double circle, and in a circle enclosing
the two leaders, can give us some idea of the part played by the
chorus in ancient Scandinavian ritual drama[3].   A number of unknown words, once thought to be Gothic, in the verses sung, are
now suspected of being musical directions which have become
incorporated in the text, but there remain "Ampaato" and "Tul,"

---

[1] The instrument is called τρυγητικόν.   Kraus thinks it is a stringed instrument.

[2] Reiske, *Corp. scr. hist. Byz.* I. p. 4, gives a Latin translation on which the above
is based.   Cp. C. Kraus, "Das gotische Weihnachtsspiel," in Paul and Braune's
Beiträge, XX. (1895), pp. 224–257.

[3] In Germany the *Knechte Ruperts* wander about in beasts' skins, from Jan. 25 to
Dec. 6, and, as Kraus says, innumerable passages attest similar practices in the Middle
Ages.

which are generally regarded as of Gothic origin, though no agreement has been reached as to their meaning.

iii. *The Scene.*

The question as to where the performances took place is answered by the pertinacity with which the mediaeval "Lords" and "Ladies" and "Queens of the May" and other disguised persons insist on dancing and playing unseemly parts in the church and churchyard[1], often during the services. There are frequent notices of such practices in France, but the custom appears to have been most difficult to root out in England, where "disguised persons," "Lords and Ladies," hobby horses and the like interrupt divine service even after the Reformation[2].

Since the common people so obstinately connected these rites with religious centres, we must suppose that in heathen times, too, they were acted in temples or in sacred places. The extant poems of the Edda seem to allot their scenes fairly equally to halls, which we may take to mean temples, or to places where there are grave-mounds. In *Thrym's Lay* the giant is seated on a grave-

---

[1] In 1240 Walter de Chanteloup, Bishop of Worcester, lays stress on the aggravation of the *ludi inhonestae* (*de Rege et Regina*) by their performance in churchyards and in other holy places. In the thirteenth-century *Ancren Riwle* the anchoresses are forbidden to look on at a *ludus* in the churchyard (Chambers, I. p. 91). The threat of excommunication pronounced in the seventh century *Judicium Clementis*, c. 20, against anyone who "ad ecclesiam veniens...aut saltat aut cantat orationes amatorias," seems to be directed against Anglo-Saxons or Frisians (cp. Chambers, I. p. 161).

[2] After the Reformation May-games were forbidden in churchyards, but in 1576 Bishop Grindal enquires whether any "lords and ladies of misrule, or summer lords and ladies, or any disguised persons"...have been suffered "to come irreverently into the church or churchyard and there to dance, or play any unseemly parts with scoffs, jests, wanton gestures, or ribald talk, namely in the time of common prayer." (Quoted by Chambers, *Mediaeval Stage*, I. 181.) Ph. Stubbs, *Anatomy of Abuses*, quoted by Tisdel ("The Mystery Plays," *Journ. of Eng. and Germ. Phil.* v. 1903—5, p. 330), says of England: "Then have they their Hobby-horses, dragons and other antiques,...then marche these heathen company towards the church and churchyard, their pipers piping, their drummers thundering, their stumps dancing, their bels iygling,...their hobbie horses and other monsters skirmishing amongst the route, and in this sorte they go to the Church (I say) and into the Church (though the Minister be at praier or preaching). Then after this, about the Church they goe againe and again, and so forth into the churchyard, where they have commonly their sommerhaules, their bowers, arbors and banqueting houses set up." We may remember that Gregory the Great speaks of arbours outside the churches where the newly-converted might feast on oxen, as they had been accustomed to sacrificing them "to demons."

mound when Loki approaches: in *Skírnismál* a shepherd occupies a similar position on the approach of Skírnir; in the *Lay of Helgi Hjörvarðsson* the hero himself, still nameless, is sitting on a grave-mound when the valkyrie Sváva first accosts him. In the *Second Lay of Helgi Hundingsbane* the grave-mound forms the central scene of the drama.

Many stories show that a grave-mound was the regular seat of prehistoric Scandinavian kings, and it cannot surprise us that Helgi Hjörvarðsson should be seated on one. Thrym may have been following royal precedent. But since the shepherd, too, sits on a grave-mound, the natural explanation is that the grave-mound was actually there, on or beside the scene, and was the most convenient spot to place a character who was to be "discovered seated." This suggestion receives confirmation from the statement of Saxo, already quoted, that performances of a panto-mimic character were performed at Upsala at the time of the sacrifices. A scholion to the history of the See of Hamburg by Adam of Bremen, written about 1075, says that the temple at Upsala is situated in a hollow and is surrounded like a theatre by "montes[1]." The three remaining "montes" or knolls at old Upsala are grave-mounds.

Have we here an indication that the ancient Scandinavian drama originated after all in dramatic games celebrating heroic ancestors? One group of the poems, the Helgi Lays and their like, do of course celebrate the royal dead, and even represent the manner of their life and death. Moreover Frey, or some similar god, was considered an ancestor of the Upsala dynasty, and in so far as our Helgis and Heðinns represented him, the plays may be said to have had affinities with ancestor-worship. On the other hand it has been made abundantly clear that the original *object* of the celebrations cannot have been the placating of royal ancestors, except in a very secondary sense. The play was originally a public ritual. Royal ancestors had indeed performed the same ritual in order to secure the same ends, nevertheless the performance did not aim at representing their acts: it was not commemorative but magical. Thus the grave-mounds in our plays cannot be taken as an indication that the plays originated in ancestor-worship.

---

[1] Adam of Bremen, IV. Sch. 135.

But they do suggest that the ritual drama may have been performed at the spot where earlier royal protagonists were buried, or perhaps where the god whom they represented was thought to be buried. The Fertility-drama was acted at Upsala in the neighbourhood of a temple and of grave-mounds. These grave-mounds contain antiquities from about the beginning of the sixth century. The statement of *Ynglingatal* that the kings, Aun, Egill and Aðils were buried at Upsala agrees so well with the archaeological evidence furnished by excavation that Professor Montelius is inclined to regard the three mounds as the places of interment of these three kings[1]. It is worth while to recall what we know of their history. Aun sacrificed nine sons, one every tenth year, to secure long life for himself; Egill was killed by a boar, Aðils was killed by a fall from his horse in the temple of the *dis*—female divinity. The suggestion of sacrificial deaths could hardly be clearer. From the absence of weapons in these graves Professor Montelius regards the kings of Upsala as temple-kings, and thinks that the warrior kings probably lived at Vendel, at a considerable distance from Upsala. If cumulative evidence is of any value, we must admit that the evidence in favour of the ritual sacrifice of priest-kings at Upsala is very considerable. We may further note that the name Salhaugar, the residence of the ninth century *thul*, or priest-king, in Sjælland, implies the presence both of a temple and of grave-mounds. At Lejre in Sjælland the report of a nine-yearly sacrifice[2] makes us suspect the existence of a Fertility-ritual somewhat similar to that at Upsala. Here there are two grave-mounds, the popular names of which, as recorded in the seventeenth century[3], suggest that the gods Frey and Ull were believed to be buried there[4]. The researches of Professor Magnus Olsen have shown that these gods were once a pair of alternating twin gods, their cult closely associated with that of female divinities.

---

[1] *Nordisk Tidskrift*, 1918, pp. 213 ff.

[2] *Thietmar's Chronicle*, I. 9. Prof. Chadwick is inclined to connect this sacrifice with the cult of Nerthus—a fertility goddess (*Origin of the Eng. Nation*, p. 267).

[3] Ole Worm gives these names as Hyldehøy and Frijshøy.

[4] Bing, *Maal og Minne*, 1916, pp. 107 ff.

CHAPTER XVII

THE BEGINNINGS OF TRAGEDY. THE GREEK ANALOGY

ARISTOTLE said that Greek Tragedy emerged from a stage in which the plots were slight or trivial, and the style ludicrous. Certain scholars have contested the truth of his statement, and of late years there has been a tendency to seek the origin of Greek Tragedy in ritual laments on slain heroes or slain gods. But whatever is true of Greek Tragedy, Aristotle's words are certainly true of the beginnings of Northern Tragedy. The plots of the mythological poems, the plot of the Sigurd trilogy, might fitly be described as slight or trivial, and the style is altogether lacking in sustained dignity, though it has a naïve charm of its own.

Scenes of a trivial kind did no doubt occur in the Helgi plays. Aristotle would certainly have condemned the bond-maid and the troll-woman and the flyting scenes as trivial and ludicrous, and he would probably have been right. It is all the more astonishing when in these same poems we suddenly find ourselves in a world of unmarred beauty and pathos, of lofty and sympathetic imagination. If once we accept the narrow limits of our plays we must admit that the latter part of the *Lay of Helgi Hundingsbane* could hardly be better done. Of course some of the warmth and colour of the scene between the lovers is due to the later *remanieur*, trained in skaldic devices. But the one old chant-metre strophe[1] which survives makes us feel that the stark simplicity of the older poem was probably more truly tragic than the embroidery of the Lay as we have it, beautiful though that embroidery often is.

---

[1] Sigrún weeps when she hears of the death of her loved ones at Helgi's hands. *Helgi said*: "Take comfort, Sigrún. A battle-maiden hast thou been to us, and kings must yield to Fate." *Sigrún said*: "Fain were I that some should live who now are dead, and yet I would clasp thee in my arms."

So much of the *Lay of Helgi Hjörvarðsson* has been lost, or badly mangled by the *remanieur*[1], that it is not such a good specimen of the tragic manner as the *Second Lay of Helgi Hundingsbane*. But the gleam of a fine poem transfigures Snorri's prose account of *Hjaðningamál*, and its evidence is all the more important, since his source was probably a passage of the old chant-metre original, or a very faithful reminiscence of its lilt and its alliteration. There is a haunting sense of Fate about Högni's answer to his son-in-law, who pleads for peace at the last moment. "Too late hast thou spoken, if thou wouldest have peace, for lo! I have unsheathed Dáinsleif, which the dwarves made: it must be a man's death every time it is bared, and never does it fail in its stroke, nor ever the wound heal that is struck therewith."

Why is it that these poems can utter the authentic note of tragedy? What is it that has fired the imagination of their authors so that out of symbolic figures in a ritual drama they make human beings swayed by passion, torn between one love and another; human beings so passionately felt to be the play-things of an indifferent Fate?

It has been claimed that Greek tragedy owed its pervading atmosphere to ritual lamentations—lamentations on dead heroes or dead gods. There is a trace of the influence of such lamentations in the Balder poem. But something more than grief, whether real or simulated, has gone to the making of Northern tragedy. The springs of tragedy are laid bare to us in these Helgi lays, and we can see that they arise directly out of what we may still call the Fertility-drama, in which the slain king is kinsman of the slayer.

In the folk-drama, where the symbolism of the plays is clearly apparent to the audience, this feature occasions no distress, rouses no questionings. So in Saxo's poems, and very often in the ballads, the heroine accepts the inevitable with philosophic indifference. She is little more than a symbol as she plays her appointed part. But in a more enlightened society, when once the symbolic significance had faded, the play was regarded as

---

[1] As for instance in the scene between Heðinn and his brother Helgi. Str. 34-35.

commemorative, and the characters, now historical persons, took on human passions. Ancient tradition made the women follow their father's slayer, soon himself to be slain, or else it turned the sword of brother on brother. Hence the moral conflict and the sense of fate which are of the very essence of tragedy. Yet a dim memory among the audience and actors that their forefathers had seen a significance behind the pain, that there was some purpose in the woe, made it a tradition that the stormy scenes, the slayings and the griefs, should end on a peaceful note. The close of the *Lay of Helgi Hundingsbane* has, as Professor Ker says, been "carried beyond the tragic stress," and a note of exultation is uttered in that dim grave-chamber:

For me let none chant wailing dirges, though wounds show on my breast. For now is a bride housed in the grave-chamber, a royal maiden, with me a ghost.

No theory of lamentation for gods or heroes will explain these beginnings of tragedy in the North. The moral conflict, the family feud, the love-scene and the hint of re-birth—these are the tragic formulas with which we have to deal, and they are inexplicable except as springing from the soil of the ritual marriage and the ritual slaying.

The ways of literature are strange. The primitive belief of early folk that fertility could be secured by keeping their goddess supplied with husbands from the royal family—this was the root from which tragedy was to flower. But we must not imagine that these ritual dramas, with their grotesque beast-disguises, the crude realism of their symbolism, and their scurrilous interludes, had themselves attained the lofty tragic atmosphere. Aristotle spoke more truly than he knew when he said that tragedy had emerged from a stage in which the plots were slight or trivial and the style ludicrous. The dramatic poems preserved by Saxo have the structure of the Fertility-drama, but they are not tragic. The ritual is too close behind them. The grotesque or animal disguises of the characters are typical of their attitude: they are not merely non-heroic, they are non-human. If the Helgi Lays developed from such poems as these we are justified in asking what chance disengaged the essential tragedy of their theme and made it a subject for high poetry. Perhaps a literary analogy

P. 13

may illuminate this stage in the development of a barbarian literature. Aeschylus acknowledges his debt to the "banquets of Homer," and it is generally agreed that the epic raised and ennobled Greek tragedy. It seems more than probable that heroic Saga or heroic lays purged and quickened the drama of the North. *Beowulf* shows that the heroic spirit was abroad in Sweden and Denmark from the sixth century onwards, and Norway could hardly remain unaffected by it, even though the foreign minstrel with his professional poetry passed her by. It is probable, however, that this influence had not been long exerted on the prototypes of our Helgi Lays. For heroic Saga has barely entered into its full inheritance in this early Northern tragedy.

In considering these first groping steps of the tragic Muse in the North, it is impossible not to think of that tragic drama which suffered no untimely death, but was allowed to develop to its full stature. Many will consider that the Northern drama mainly justifies its existence if it can throw light on the development of Greek tragedy, of which the beginnings are hidden from us. If Greek tragic plots show, as they do show, the same features of unhappy divisions and bride-snatchings within the family, the Northern analogy makes it difficult not to accept the view of those who would trace the origin of Greek tragedy to a ritual Year-drama.

But in the North this ritual points back, not to dances celebrating a vegetation-spirit or Eniautos-daimon, nor to Dionysiac revelries, but, ultimately, to totemism—that is to say to the relations between certain dynasties and the totem of their clans or groups. As Reinach says, the sacrifice of a man disguised as an animal is preceded by the sacrifice of the animal itself[1]. The sacrifice of the Yule boar must have originated earlier than the slaying of the prince dressed up to represent him ; just as the idea of the Sow divinity must be earlier than the idea of the goddess Freyja with the sow as her emblem and title.

The evolution of the ritual drama in Greece may of course have been quite different. But there is another point which bears very directly on Greek tragedy. Northern drama shows the Fertility-ritual almost in the act of developing from magical into

---

[1] S. Reinach, *Cultes, Mythes et Religions*, ch. 1.

commemorative drama without any assistance from race fusion or conscious transference of cults, such as has been postulated to explain Greek tragedy[1]. The poems preserved by Saxo, with their very thin historical veneer, the Helgi Lays, and the evidence of folk-drama suggest that the grim dramatic ritual of the sixth century, crudely magical in intent, had divided into two streams, perhaps by the eighth century. One was on the way to becoming folk-drama, though still performed with a consciously magical aim, while the other, under aristocratic influence, had become purely commemorative and historical—literary, in fact. Northern tragedy can also show how dramatic performances may be closely associated with the tombs of heroes[2], and ultimately perhaps be performed in honour of them, and yet originate in something very different from propitiation of the dead.

If we consider only the extant plays we might well hold that their plots are so stereotyped by ritual formulas that a great drama could never have arisen from them. But it behoves us to remember that many tales which we know only in outline were probably treated dramatically—notably the story of Amlodi or Hamlet. And we can trace indications, even in extant plays, that drama was beginning to claim its right to dispose of its characters as it willed, even while it still clung to the stock figures of ritual. This is especially apparent in the difficult matter of allowing the heroine to survive her lover and to marry again, an ending which almost all the ballads found frankly unbearable. The *Lay of Helgi Hjörvarðsson* hedges. Sváva is undoubtedly going to marry Heðinn, but the poet will not say so directly. Evidently the time was not far off at which Northern tragedy would have flung off the trammels of the ritual drama and asserted its right to shape its own plots.

In another point the literary instinct of the poet has been

---

[1] Leaf, *Homer and History* (1913), ch. VII.

[2] Of those heroes who had fallen in the sacrificial drama and whose tombs were in the sacred place (see pp. 189 f.). In Greek drama the connection of Achaean heroes with their tombs appears to be a difficulty. In the North the difficulty is rather to know how heroes came to be dissociated from their tombs : e.g. how the Norwegian *Second Lay* comes to celebrate a Danish hero. Such a play must either have become entirely divorced from the Fertility-drama, or else it must be accounted for by some tribal migration.

victorious over the ritual tradition. For the play, as Professor Jevons says of the Mummer's play, " the combat was essential, and the revival was a dramatic difficulty: for the rite the revival was the one thing essential." Tradition dies hard, and even in the Greek tragedies it appears that there are traces of the resurrection of the hero. Our Northern poets seem usually to have ignored the resurrection[1], but the tradition remains in the prose.

We have said very little of the actual structure of the Helgi plays. It would only be a waste of words to do so. To compare small things with great, let us imagine that only a few scenes had survived from the Orestes-plays of Aeschylus and Euripides: that some later collector, himself unacquainted with drama, combined these fragments and connected them with prose arguments, inserting also a scrap of an epic lay. That at some time lyric poets had re-cast the finest scenes into a fashionable metre: one marring the simplicity of the heroine's grief with sophisticated metaphor, and another, a better poet, studding the love-scene with jewelled phrases. The history of the extant *Second Lay of Helgi Hundingsbane* can hardly be less complex than that: it may well be more so. Obviously it would be futile to attempt to judge of the poem as if it were an organic whole.

The *Lay of Helgi Hjörvarðsson* is in one point even more composite, for a play with different characters has been welded into it by the collector. Atli, Iðmund's son, an earl or king[2], promises to worship a bird, is foiled once in his courtship, kills the father of his bride and takes her. At some point in the play he has a flyting contest with the giantess Hrímgerð. Atli's history is like that of other heroes of a Fertility-drama, and evidently once formed a play by itself. It has been awkwardly combined with the Helgi plays, probably on account of references to Hjörvarð and Sigrlinn[3], who are regarded as Helgi's parents. If this part

---

[1] Except in the case of Helgi Hundingsbane's return as a ghost—a poetic treatment of the resurrection *motif*.

[2] He appears to be able to promise the bird anything in the king's establishment, str. 2. The prose however calls him an earl.

[3] The references in the verse to Hjörvarð and Sigrlinn suggest that Hjörvarð and Atli were brothers or kinsmen, who both wooed the same bride. The bird seems to act somewhat the same *rôle* as that of the troll-woman in Hhu. II.

is removed the story of Helgi is represented very directly, though with many gaps.

It would obviously be unfair to judge of the dramatic structure of the poems as they now stand. But there are two points about them which were probably characteristic of them even at their best. They show a lack of proportion in the amount of space they allot to scenes of minor emotional importance, and they are too short. Both these faults are probably due to the traditions of the ritual drama, and they are both more visible in the *Lay of Helgi Hjörvarðsson* than in the *Second Lay of Helgi Hundingsbane.* In the former—or rather perhaps we should say in the Atli drama —the flyting with Hrímgerð was probably as long as any other scene in the play, even when it was intact. It is of course quite out of place if we regard the drama as literary, and must be accepted as one of the ritual survivals which poets would later have curtailed or rejected. In the *Second Lay* the corresponding scene is much reduced and very much less flagrant in tone. But then it has been remodelled.

The other point is more serious. The poems are too short to accommodate the action. Their length was probably determined by the brief show of the Year-drama, and the framework is not spacious enough for real tragedy. There is a sense of haste in all the action, and though this has a certain effectiveness, suggesting the hurrying footsteps of doom, the brevity of the whole thing prevents the characters from developing themselves.

It is interesting to compare the drama of Hans Sachs, which developed from the traditional carnival-play, representing a single episode. So long as Hans Sachs has to deal with drama of this type he moves at ease: he can draw his characters in his own way, and he is an adept at heightening dramatic tension. A good critic has observed that his *Farend schuler mit dem teuffel pannen* shows a knowledge of the technique and the resources of dramatic art far beyond that possessed by Molière in his earlier farces[1]. But where Hans Sachs attempts historical drama, a Sigfrid or a Griselda play, his traditional technique fails him. The limits suitable for the Carnival-play are all too narrow for serious drama, and his idea of dramatic unity deserts him. He gives a series of scenes in chronological order, as he has learnt them from the

---

[1] Ch. Schweitzer, *Étude sur la vie et les œuvres de Hans Sachs* (1887), pp. 303 f.

chronicler, and in order to include everything he barely gives his characters time to declare their intentions—far less to comment on the situation. He is admirable as an author of dramatic episodes, and quite deplorable as a historical dramatist.

The remnants of Eddic heroic plays are on an infinitely higher level than those of Hans Sachs. For one thing they are not founded on narrative but on earlier dramatic originals. They have plots, and the action shapes the characters. Where Hans Sachs merely mirrors events, they paint passions. And even though they cannot always subordinate their material, they are always aware that "the end is the most important thing." Perhaps this would finally have led them to expand their limits. In the last scene of the *Second Lay*, from the moment where the maid meets Helgi riding to his grave-mound, there is no undue compression; and we feel that if the poets had always composed on this scale they would have achieved magnificent things.

We have laid stress on the indications that Northern tragedy was about to break through the rigid traditions of ritual drama, for they justify us in maintaining that the poems promise more than they actually attain. From the purely literary standpoint these beginnings of tragedy must be valued for this promise. But their actual importance transcends their literary merit, whether actual or potential, for they, and they alone, can illuminate the origin and the earlier stages of some of the greatest literature in the world. True tragedy is as rare as drama is common. Its appearance in modern literature is due to the influence, direct or indirect, of Greek drama. " Tragedy," it has been said, " is the exceptional phenomenon that calls for some special explanation. There seems to be no parallel to its independent growth in Greece, and this fact makes the problem of its origin there particularly difficult to solve."

Our Northern Helgi plays, however rudimentary, however shattered, do afford another instance of Tragedy as an independent growth. There can be little doubt that this growth, though independent, springs from the same seed as Attic tragedy. The Fertility-drama bequeathed to both a plot which contained in germ the moral conflict, the sense of Destiny and the religious background—the essential characteristics of Greek and Northern tragedy.

CHAPTER XVIII

CONCLUSION

It has been said that in any half-won sphere of knowledge that hypothesis must hold the field which correlates the largest number of known facts. The theory of the origin of the older Eddic poems in religious drama does correlate a number of facts which else appear meaningless and unrelated. In the Eddic collection, otherwise an inexplicable jumble, we can recognise the essential unity of the older poems on native subjects, with their special metre, their dialogic or monologic form, bearing traces of improvisation by one or more speakers, their stage directions, their stock scenes, their taste for disguised or theriomorphic characters, and their fixed traditional plots. The association of the poems with heathen religious drama explains the disappearance of this form of literature after the close of heathendom. Further, our theory of the genesis of the heroic poems has been seen to have a vital relation with what we are beginning to know of prehistoric religion and ritual in Scandinavia, and the light thrown by the heroic poems themselves on these discoveries illumines to some extent the evolution and decay of an ancient Scandinavian priesthood.

But our hypothesis must not only serve to cast a ray of light into the obscure places of history and religion in prehistoric Scandinavia. If it is correct it should shed light forwards as well as backwards, on the beginnings of mediaeval literature—and not only in Scandinavia, for the existence of folk-drama in the rest of Teutonic Europe points to the existence of religious drama there also. We will begin by considering the influence of heathen drama on non-dramatic mediaeval literature, and first on the ballad.

i. *The Ballad.*

Professor Ker says somewhere that "it is very difficult to understand how the imported French ballad could become so entirely and wholly popular in Scandinavia." The mystery is solved if we show good grounds for believing that the fashionable French rhymed verse was merely superimposed on an indigenous dramatic song-dance[1], the main feature of which, the ring[2] enclosing two singers, and sometimes an effigy as well, had been characteristic of Scandinavian and East Germanic religious ritual for centuries[3].

Since children are the most faithful transmitters of traditional action we must regard the immense number of ballads dramatically acted by them in Sweden and Denmark as indicating that the prototype of the song-dance in Scandinavia was eminently dramatic. The strophic form of all ancient Scandinavian verse is generally held to point to a choric origin, and Professor Chadwick has so far anticipated the results of our researches that he has suggested that the primitive choric type of poetry may very well have been the only one used in Norway before the beginning of the Viking Age[4]. If then the ballad in Scandinavia is markedly more dramatic than its supposed French prototype, and if at the same time there is reason to assume the existence of choric song in Scandinavia in the earliest times, it would in any case seem rash to attribute the most flourishing type of popular choral dance entirely to French influence, though of course no one would dispute that its metrical form is of French origin. The earliest form of the ballad in France seems to have been a little wooing-dance acted as a sort of May-game and originating in the ritual wedding[5]. There are great numbers of such wooing-dances in Sweden and Denmark, and the presence of several dialogue-songs of this type in Saxo[6], coupled with disguise, make it highly improbable that they were borrowed from France[7].

---

[1] This view has already been put forward by Léon Pineau, *Le Romancéro Scandinave*, Paris, 1906.

[2] Sometimes a double row. In the "Gothic game" at Constantinople the double row alternates with the ring, p. 187, *supra*.

[3] P. 186, *supra*.   [4] *Heroic Age*, p. 100.

[5] Gaston Paris, *Mélanges de litt. française*, 1912, pp. 570 ff.; J. Bédier, "Les plus anciens danses françaises," *Revue des Deux Mondes* (1906), XXXI. pp. 398 ff.

[6] Saxo's sources are considered to have been of the ballad and folk-tale order; Chadwick, *Heroic Age*, p. 113; Olrik, *Kilderne til Sakses Oldhistorie*, pp. 18 ff. If his poems are founded on ballads they form strong evidence in favour of the originally purely dramatic nature of the ballad, since they are all (with the exception of one skaldic verse) purely dialogic.

[7] France is too often made the birthplace of some custom or literary form on the sole ground that it is first or most often mentioned there—a circumstance amply

In the wooing-dances of which country, France or Scandinavia, did the Scandinavian ballad originate?

We do not know much about the French wooing-dance, and still less about the ritual wedding in France. But from the Edda and from Saxo we do know a good deal about the Fertility-drama, the ritual wedding and the wooing-dialogue in Scandinavia, and their characteristically Scandinavian features re-occur in the Scandinavian ballads dealing with the same themes.

The fact that the plots and characters of several important groups of Scandinavian and English[1] ballads are identical with the plots and characters of certain Eddic poems[2] has been discounted by scholars on the ground that the stories were common property in the North, and naturally supplied material for the new *genre*. But it is important to notice that just this group of ballads, with the slaying within the family or the recognition-scene, also contains other features of the Eddic poems of these types. The most significant is the ceremonial bridal cup, which occurs, as we have seen, in *Hyndluljóð*, in *Skírnismál*, in *Sigrdrí-fumál*—all poems of the ritual wedding type—and in the *Second Lay*. Not only is it a frequent feature of ballads with recognition- or family-feud plots[3], but both Danish and English ballads remember its significance as the actual bridal or betrothal ceremony[4]. This is shown by the last words of Lord Ingram,

---

accounted for by the vastly greater proportion of early extant records in France. The real *rôle* of France is not that of creator of popular customs or types of literature, but of refiner of them. The Franks took with them to Gaul the common Teutonic patrimony of dramatic dances, such as we catch sight of in the story of Bovi, purged them of their heathen associations, made literature out of them, and so made them acceptable to the upper classes of society in other Teutonic countries, thus giving them a new lease of life.

[1] Certain groups of English ballads so closely resemble the Scandinavian that it is often thought that the Scandinavians borrowed directly from England. But since the main home of English ballads is Scandinavian Britain, it seems more likely that the resemblance originates in the ritual songs and dances which preceded the ballad in both countries.

[2] The plots and characters they reproduce are those of the ancient dramas, not of the later Eddic poems.

[3] In all the versions of *Hind Horn* the lady offers her disguised lover a cup. So also in *Old Robin of Portingale*. The old hag whom King Henry has promised to wed insists on a drink at his hands, and only then does she reveal herself as a fair lady.

[4] See p. 141, *supra*.

who is stabbed by his brother, Chiel Wyat, for the sake of his
bride:

> Wae mat worth ye, Gill Viett
> An ill died mat ye die
> *For I had the cup in my hand*
> *To hae drunken her o'er to thee.*

A Danish ballad even remembers the significance of the ritual:
Ridder Stig drinks to his lady-love "so that field and wood blossom
thereat."

.Saxo tells us that bells figured in the erotic pantomime at
Upsala, and his statement is corroborated by modern wedding
customs in Scandinavia, as well as by a sculptured stone at Hab-
lingbo in Gotland, depicting what appears to be a bell in con-
junction with a female figure offering a cup to a mounted man.
In the Danish wooing game *Den rige Hr. Randsbjærg* the wooer
wears bells, and we can hardly fail to connect with this tradition
the curious references to selling the bride for a bell or bells[1], found
in a group of Scandinavian ballads with what we may call a Helgi
Lay plot.

In the *Second Lay* Sigrún heaps a bed for Helgi. This action
is performed in a Swedish wooing-game, in which a girl goes into
the ring and collects twigs to make the bed[2]. The *motif* occurs
in English ballads of the Fertility-drama or ritual wedding type[3].

If we look at Eddic dramatic poems of other types we can
hardly fail to admit that the Eddic *Song of the Quern* and the
modern Swedish mimetic game "The Handmill" must go back
to a common dramatic source. That such mimetic songs did exist
in ancient Scandinavia is shown in an interesting passage in
Njáls Saga, where a man sees valkyries weaving a deadly woof,
with human heads for weights and spears for shuttles, while they

---

[1] *Ribold og Guldborg, Veneros, Hildebrand och Hille.*

[2] Arwidsson, III. p. 229. A knight approaches her and offers her his love, which
she refuses until he flings open his coat and reveals himself as her own true love. Cp.
Saxo's poem where Gram flings aside his disguise and reveals himself in his natural
comeliness to Groa: "nor did he fail to offer her the gifts of love." The recognition-
scene is as common in the ballad as in Saxo's wooing-scenes.

[3] In several of the *Guldborg och Ribold* group: Child, I. pp. 89 ff., in many versions of *Earl Brand* (*ib.* p. 97), *King Henry.*

sing a chant referring to their actions[1]. A song-game like this, "Weaving Wadmal," is actually recorded in Sweden. Children act the part of shuttles and thread their way in and out of their elders.

How are these memories compatible with the hypothesis that the ballad was imported into Scandinavia by the court, and for long remained the amusement of the aristocracy alone? French metre, French manners, must merely have rendered fashionable the age-long pastime of the common folk.

ii. *The Epic and the Saga.*

Scandinavian scholars have recently been driven to postulate the existence of historical ballads on native subjects as early as the seventh century, in order to account for the preservation of traditions. In the ring-dances of the Gotlanders to celebrate the discomfiture of the Danish king Valdemar we see how easily such dramatic chants and dances, once freed of their ritual associations, could lend themselves to the representation of events.

Recent researches have shown that ballads, sung and danced by the peasants, preserved for centuries the memories of Siegfried and Roland which finally furnished the sources of the French and German mediaeval epics[2].

The Anglo-Saxon epic *Beowulf* has probably a different history, and appears to be founded on court minstrelsy[3] rather

---

[1] *Darraðarljóð*, a semi-Eddic poem, apparently of the eleventh century, preserved in *Njálssaga*, ch. CLVII.

[2] Schück, *Den nya teorien om uppkomsten af Chansons de geste,* Upsala, 1914, pp. 28 f. Certain peculiarities of ballad technique have been traced in the French *chansons de geste.* M. K. Pope, *Modern Language Review*, articles in vols. VIII.—X. No doubt, as Schück points out, the example of the Latin epics must have had an influence on the composition of such poems as the *Chanson de Roland*, but Miss Pope shows that the first epic poems can hardly have been translations from Latin poems, since they show traces of ballad technique. The evolution of a May game (ritual wedding) into ballads, and of ballads into a miniature epic, can be traced very clearly in the development of the May game Robin and Marion (originally mere variants of the traditional Lord and Lady). The sequence is worthy of more attention than it has yet received from students of early literary forms and corresponds suggestively with the emergence of the more or less epic *Sjurðar Kvæði* from the Faroese ballad.

[3] Possibly of Frisian origin; cp. Chadwick, *Heroic Age*, pp. 89 f. It is interesting to note that though *Beowulf* has full epic spaciousness, it yet has certain characteristics

than on ballads. Its connection with ritual drama is however much more direct, for the actual exploits of Beowulf, his fights with water-monsters[1] and with a dragon, are of the type which is represented dramatically all over Eastern England, Scotland, in Normandy, and, as the Sigurd trilogy testifies, in Scandinavia. We may note in passing that the dramatic tone of Anglo-Saxon poems has frequently been remarked on[2].

In Iceland the May Day game, the ritual wedding, and the wooing-scene seem hardly to have survived the settlement, partly no doubt because the settlers were mainly of a travelled and enlightened class, and partly because these rural observances are connected with agriculture, which could not be an important branch of activity in Iceland.

It may be significant that it is in Iceland, where the danced and sung ballad was only introduced late[3], that the epic poem never came to perfection. We can see clearly that the poets of the Icelandic Eddic Lays failed to attain the epic style through too blind an adherence to the traditions of the dramatic poem, and that they had no other model to help them. The older poems had needed no narrative to indicate the action of the characters or the sequence of episodes, for these things had been clear to the spectators. Icelandic Eddic poets had therefore no examples of the art of passing from one episode to another save the abrupt transitions

---

showing affinity with the Icelandic Eddic Lays, which are directly founded on dramatic poems. As ten Brink observed, English epic has a difficulty in progressing from one episode to another; like the Icelandic Eddic poems, it finds monologues the easiest way of narrating events, and like them it generally has too few speakers, whose speeches tend to be unduly long. It contains 38 speeches as against about 300 in the *Nibelungenlied* (so Schwartzkopff, *Rede and Redescene in der d. Erzählung* 1909).

[1] Ordish, *Folk Lore*, IV. p. 152, points out that the pageant of St George in the fourteenth and fifteenth centuries, and the representations of a Christian knight rescuing the King of Egypt's daughter from the dragon invariably took place by a well or water-conduit.

[2] Cp. Chambers, I. p. 80, and the works there cited. Chambers observes that "English literature indeed had had from Anglo-Saxon days a natural affinity for the dialogue form." Wülcker's denial of drama to the Anglo-Saxons (*Grundriss*, p. 386) is based on grounds since shown to be mistaken.

[3] For the late introduction of the ballad cp. Kålund, Arkiv f. n. Fil, XIX. (1907), *Stud. over Crymogæa*, pp. 228 ff. Similarly in the Faroes the ballad-dance seems to have been introduced late, at the period when it became fashionable in Scandinavia.

of skaldic poetry. Hence their narrative verse approximates in brevity to the skaldic, and does not match the spacious style of the speeches. The narrative links being too weak to bear the story, they chose the simpler method offered them by dramatic tradition and allowed their characters to narrate the past or the future[1], so making the speeches still more out of proportion to the narrative parts. The few "mixed" Nibelungen poems extant (narrative-plus-speech) give an impression that the poets were struggling against an adverse medium, and they are certainly most at ease when they abandon narrative and fall back on the well-trodden path of dialogue and monologue. However this form was now meaningless, and the finest of the Nibelungen poems are those which do attempt narrative. But they are not epic—not because they are too short, for some of them are as long as the *Battle of Maldon*, which certainly deserves the name of epic, but because a form of verse which consists mainly of lengthy conversations or soliloquies cannot be called epic.

That nothing was wanting but poetic technique—a tradition of verse to fit the style—is demonstrated by the creation of the new prose form. Here Icelandic authors were hampered by no fossilized tradition, and out of the stories current in the countryside they fashioned the Saga, the true Icelandic counterpart of the epic. The Sagas are new, but evidently the art of telling short stories rests on a long tradition, and it is interesting to observe that most of the peculiarities which differentiate the Saga from other story-telling can be best explained on the assumption of a dramatic tradition. Not that the Saga is constructed like drama: far from it. But the attitude of the author is emphatically the attitude of the looker-on at a dramatic performance[2]. He describes his characters, but only by their words and deeds as they move before him—and us. We also are onlookers at a drama, and he knows no more than we do. Never does he enter into the

---

[1] It is interesting to note that Hans Sachs adopts this method of telling his stories in his historical drama; cp. Schweitzer, *Étude sur...Hans Sachs*, 1887, p. 326.

[2] Professor Ker, after discussing the pathetic passages in *Beowulf*, goes on to say: "In the Sagas the sense of the vanity of all human wishes is expressed in a different way: the lament is turned into dramatic action; the author's sympathy is not shown in direct effusions, but in his rendering of the drama (*Epic and Romance*, p. 216).

mind of his character and tell us what he finds there. And if the
hero is engaged in a fight, we do not see it from his point of view,
but as we might see a scene in a play. Sometimes, as in the great
scene of Kjartan's slaying in *Laxdæla Saga*, an onlooker is placed
on the scene and we see the action through his eyes.

Then there is the extraordinary directness of the narrative.
The authors are, as Professor Ker points out, careful of the order
of perception: they see the events happening one after another,
as if upon a stage, and never misplace a scene[1].

The dramatic discipline shows itself also in less technical ways.
These authors realise that " the end is the most important thing."
Wherever the story allows of it the Sagas work up to an inevitable
catastrophe with the same skill as is shown in the *Second Lay*,
and (to a less degree) in all the poems where the god's antagonist
meets his death. Drama too focusses interest upon character, for
the actor can make of the plot what he will. The glory and the
marvel of the Saga is the interest in character, coupled with the
restraint which lets the personages reveal themselves and makes
the reader, like the author, an onlooker.

It is curious that the technique and the traditions which
stultified the Icelandic Eddic poetry, the direct descendant of the
dramatic poems, should have had such decisive influence in
making the Sagas what they are. But there can be no doubt
that the theory of the dramatic origin of the Edda poems explains, so far as literature can ever be explained, the technique
of the Sagas, one of the greatest literary achievements of the
Middle Ages.

iii. *Folk-drama and Church-drama.*

We have shrunk from any definite localization or dating of
the dramatic poems of the Edda in their present form. Many of
the imperfections and omissions of this book must be supple-
mented by research into local customs, local nomenclature, local
lore of every kind, before any definite conclusions can be reached
on these points. Such knowledge as we possess points to a South

[1] Cp. *Epic and Romance*, p. 274.

Norwegian origin[1], and to a complete cessation of drama of the Eddic type at, if not before, the introduction of Christianity[2].

It seems that at Lejre and Salhaugar in Sjælland, at Upsala in Sweden, and possibly at the old Skíringssal in South Norway the Fertility-drama was presented in ancient sanctuaries consecrated by the tombs of kings or gods. There is some reason for believing that it was the central rite of a religious confederacy. This drama was apparently performed only once every nine years, by actors of royal birth, and there was a tradition of an actual slaying. Such stately drama as this was bound by immemorial tradition to one locality. The sanctuary, the goddess, the priest-king[3] could not migrate with the members of the confederate tribes. There is therefore no trace of what we may call literary drama, or of such highly developed tragic drama, outside Southern Scandinavia, where Teutonic peoples had been settled for several thousand years. Drama of this kind develops in the home country, epic among migrating peoples, whether they migrate to France or England or Germany—or to Ionia, for the analogy with Greek drama holds good here too.

But if they could not take the stately developed ritual of a great confederacy with them, the peoples who migrated from the shores of the Baltic could and did take with them the idea that the fertility of the soil depended on the ritual dance, the ritual wedding and the sacrifice, even though the victim was only slain for appearance' sake, and resurrection followed immediately. And that the drama remained real drama, and not a mere mummery or a game, is vouched for by the effect it had on the Christian Church after the Teutonic peoples had been in contact with it. Chambers says that the degenerate stage of the Roman

---

[1] Very definitely as regards the Sigurd trilogy (p. 49, *supra*) and for *Hyndluljóð* (p. 58, *supra*), Professor Magnus Olsen's researches point to South Norway, Oplandene, for the Fertility-drama, *Hedenske Minder*, caps. 12 and 13. Olrik observes that there are more ballads in the small districts of Sætersdal and Telemarken than in all the rest of Norway.

[2] The absence of the *thul* in Norway in the period immediately preceding Christianity may have some connection with the decay of drama.

[3] As a matter of fact the priest-king did survive migration among the Franks. But the migrations of the Franks did not last long and affected their customs very little.

Empire had ceased to exist owing to the indifference of the barbarians and the hostility of the Church. Yet wherever these
barbarians were received into the Church what he elsewhere calls
the "irrepressible mediaeval tendency to mimesis" forces the
Church to admit acting at her very altars, often by her own
priests. The Teutonic converts were no doubt indifferent to
secular drama, but they were evidently obstinately attached to
religious drama. We may quote the words used by Ordish in
one of his valuable articles on Folk-drama:

> When we are told, that the origin of the English drama was the miracle
> or mystery-plays, which were organized by the priests and monks of religious
> houses, we, who seek for causes, ask: *Why* did the Church organize these
> dramatic representations[1]?

His answer to the question appears to be that there were
heathen performances which it was desired to supplant, but this
explanation is hardly sufficient. If policy had been the only or the
ruling motive for introducing drama into the Church services, we
should find dramatic performances encouraged by the ecclesiastical authorities. As a matter of fact, until they become a source
of revenue, they are sometimes tolerated locally but are prohibited
by the central authority[2]. Was not the real cause of the inclusion
of drama in the liturgy the fact that to the mass of converts of
the Teutonic peoples religion was so intimately connected with
dramatic representations that the Teutonic priest sought drama
in the Christian liturgy and introduced it where he could, in
response to an overwhelming demand, which he himself probably
shared to some extent[3]? The places where religious drama first
crops up—England[4], North France and Germany—sufficiently
indicate its connection with the Teutonic peoples. And it flourishes

---

[1] *Folk Lore*, II. p. 317.

[2] A decretal of Innocent III, in 1210, forbade *ludi theatrales* in churches (Gayley,
Representative English Comedies, 1903, p. xix).

[3] Policy was also a motive, but to a less degree. There were no doubt plenty of
priests who thought what a Wyclifite sermon says: "it is lesse yvels that thei have
theyre recreaceon by playinge of myraclis than bi pleyinge of other japis" (Chambers, I.
p. 84).

[4] Religious drama in England was known in the Anglo-Saxon period; cp. Gayley,
Representative English Comedies (1903), p. xiii. See also following page; and
O. Waterhouse, *Non-cycle Mystery Plays* (E.E.T.S.), 1909, p. x.

particularly in regions where a Scandinavian invasion follows upon an earlier Teutonic immigration—North France and the East and North-East of England.

The religious character of the mediaeval folk-play is often overlooked, though the evidence for it is overwhelming. The determination with which the people continued to regard the church or churchyard as the only place to act their May Day game, with its bride and bridegroom, camouflaged under many respectable names, its scurrilous flytings, its bells and its beast-disguises—this defiance of the authority of the Church can only mean one thing: that there was still a religious, a ritual significance in the ancient popular drama, and that the people obstinately believed that their welfare depended on its performance at a sacred spot and at a sacred time. In whatever other form religion was presented to them, they must have this too.

The religious origin of the heathen drama will scarcely be questioned. But the heathen origin of the ecclesiastical drama practically follows from that premise. There is a very significant passage in the thirteenth-century continuation of the eleventh-century *History of St John of Beverley, Archbishop of York*[1] (writing of about the year 1220):

> It happened one summer[2] in the churchyard of St John's Church, on the north side, that there was a representation *as usual* by masked performers (*larvatorum*) of the Lord's Ascension in words and acting.

There are two features of this play which go directly back to heathen religious performances: it was acted on the *north* side of the church, and by masked players. The north side of the churchyard is intimately associated in popular belief with heathenism, and in the masked actors we can hardly fail to see the tradition of the heathen drama.

The history of the St George's play is equally significant. It used to be thought that this performance began by being a miracle play and was degraded into a popular observance with or without St George. It has recently been shown that the exact opposite is

---

[1] Quoted by A. F. Leach, *Some English Plays and Players*, p. 206.
[2] Church dramas were frequently acted at Midsummer—a heathen festival. Chambers, I. p. 177.

the truth. To whitewash a primitive play of the Slaying of the Dragon the name of St George was tacked on to the slayer[1].

The heathen folk-plays did of course eventually give rise to a purely secular drama. In England this development seems to have begun early. The *strifs* or *estrifs* are taunting disputations between two characters, on the lines of the flytings between Summer and Winter, and they are remarkable because the interlocutors are not mere abstractions, but species of birds and animals[2]. The explanation of such poems as these is surely that they are derived, and gain their vitality, from the exchange of repartee between Winter and Summer in the May Day game[3].

Thus the ritual drama of the Teutonic peoples survived in two forms. It forced itself into the Christian Church and took for its subjects the whole wealth of the Bible, but it could never shake itself free from its popular origin, and though it could present an epic tale in dramatic form[4] its most vital ingredient always lay in the *planctus*, the lament, and in its comic scenes: the scenes which were most intimately connected with the folk-play and drew fresh life from it.

It has often been pointed out how much the Elizabethan

---

[1] Beatty, *The St George or Mummers Plays*, 1906. Similarly in Germany there are striking resemblances between the Passion Plays and the Fastnachtsspiele, showing that one must have borrowed from the other. The significance, as Creizenach pointed out, lies in the fact that the Fastnachtsspiele are derived from popular customs (Tisdel, "The Mystery Plays," *Journ. of Eng. and Germ. Phil.* (1903–5), pp. 323–40).

[2] Of the best known of these *estrifs* Professor Ker says that "the early English poet has discovered for himself a form which generally requires ages of training and study before it can succeed." Though it is a disputation, yet "it is a true comedy, not only is the writer impartial, but he keeps the debate alive, he shows how the contending parties feel the strokes and hide their pain, and do their best to face it out with their adversary" (*Mediaeval English Literature*, p. 53).

[3] In Germany the *Sommergewinn*, the flyting between Summer and Winter, and the Kämpfgespräch, which arises out of it, early became a literary *genre*, but the Fastnachtsspiel, and the Nuremberg Schembart, well described by a recent French writer as a *Komos*, both arising out of the folk-drama, carry on the secular dramatic tradition until the sixteenth century, when Hans Sachs profits by the accumulated dramatic experience to write extraordinarily good comedies. But his historical plays are extraordinarily bad, for want of a tradition.

[4] Especially in England. We know nothing of the Scandinavian Church drama, though we hear of it in Sweden before 1400. But in Scandinavia the associations of drama were probably too obviously heathen to be early tolerated in the Church. The heathen drama survives mainly in the folk-plays and ballads.

dramatists owe to the Church drama, and an essay recently published has broken fresh ground in demonstrating Shakespeare's
indebtedness to the folk-drama[1]. But we must not forget that
Church drama and folk-drama are but the two streams into which
the ancient Teutonic ritual drama divided on encountering the
mediaeval Church. They meet again in Elizabethan times, and
through them there passed into the Shakespearean drama "a
wealth of tradition and sentiment elsewhere intercepted by changes
of language, religion and education[2]."

The literature of a whole race is hard to kill. The ritual drama
of the early Teutonic peoples is banned by a hundred ecclesiastical ordinances: in Scandinavia it has to abandon its ritual
associations, and so hardly succeeds in forcing itself into the
Church, but its songs and dances are revivified by the French
ballade—itself a branch of the same tree—and it crops out in-
cessantly in dramatic customs among the people. In Germany
popular drama survives in the Schembart and Fastnachtsspiel
and blooms again in the comedies of Hans Sachs, only to wither
afterwards. But its twin-brother, the mystery, flourishes to-day
at Oberammergau. In France it blossomed into many forms,
though none of them were long-lived. In England the common
Teutonic stock of ritual drama was reinforced by the influx of Scandinavian customs. The influence of the folk-play and the Church
drama converged at an auspicious moment, and the ancient
tradition took hold on a surer immortality in Shakespeare. In
England, in fact, the heathen drama has shown itself as tenacious
of life as the heroes whom it commemorates, who fall but to fight
again. When *Hamlet* is acted in Scandinavia may we not fancy
that the ghost of the ancient ritual returns to the region to which
it once spelt life itself, as Helgi Hundingsbane, after a double
dissolution, revisits the scene of his love; a figure none the less

---

[1] Spens, *An Essay on Shakespeare's relation to Tradition*, Oxford, 1916.

[2] Tucker Brooke, *The Tudor Drama*, 1912, p. 37. The whole passage is as follows:
"When we come to estimate the sources whence the Elizabethan drama derives the
particular vigor and depth which it possesses above all the literary forms of the time,
who shall say just how potent was the fact that the drama alone could boast, through
the guild plays, an uninterrupted descent from English literature of the Middle Ages?
Through them passed into the drama a wealth of tradition and sentiment elsewhere
intercepted by changes of language religion, and education."

significant for being but a broken ghost. Like the armies of Heðinn and Högni the ancient drama is raised out of the stocks and stones of heathenism, the flotsam and jetsam of the folk-play, to an apotheosis which in its universal appeal to humanity will survive even Ragnarök.

INDEX

The figures in clarendon type indicate the page where the general tenor of a poem is discussed.

www.ingramcontent.com/pod-product-compliance
Ingram Content Group UK Ltd.
Pitfield, Milton Keynes, MK11 3LW, UK
UKHW042153280225
455719UK00001B/322